DEAD
WOMEN
WALKING

DEAD WOMEN WALKING

Jennifer Su

MONARCH
BOOKS

Oxford, UK & Grand Rapids, Michigan

Sevenoaks, UK
www.omf.org.uk

First published in the UK in 2007 by Monarch Books
(a publishing imprint of Lion Hudson plc)
and OMF International.

Monarch Books:
Mayfield House, 256 Banbury Road, Oxford OX2 7DH.
Tel: +44 (0)1865 302750 Fax: +44 (0)1865 302757
monarch@lionhudson.com www.lionhudson.com

OMF International:
Station Approach, Borough Green, Sevenoaks, Kent TN15 8BG.
Tel: +44 (0)1732 887299
omf@omf.org.uk www.omf.org.uk

ISBN: 978-1-85424-805-3 (UK)
ISBN: 978-0-8254-6158-3 (USA)

Distributed by:
UK: Marston Book Services Ltd, PO Box 269, Abingdon, Oxon OX14 4YN;
USA: Kregel Publications, PO Box 2607, Grand Rapids, Michigan 49501

Unless otherwise stated, Scripture quotations are taken from
the Holy Bible, New International Version, © 1973, 1978, 1984
by the International Bible Society. Used by permission of
Hodder & Stoughton Ltd. All rights reserved.

The text paper used in this book has been made from wood
independently certified as having come from sustainable forests.

British Library Cataloguing Data
A catalogue record for this book is available
from the British Library.

Printed and bound in Great Britain by
Cox & Wyman Ltd, Reading.

OMF International works in most East Asian countries, and among East Asian peoples around the world. It was founded by James Hudson Taylor in 1865 as the China Inland Mission. Our purpose is to glorify God through the urgent evangelisation of East Asia's billions.

In line with this, OMF Publishing seeks to motivate and equip Christians to make disciples of all peoples.

Publications include:

- stories and biographies showing God at work in East Asia
- the biblical basis of mission and mission issues
- the growth and development of the church in Asia
- studies of Asian culture and religion

Books, booklets, articles and free downloads can be found on our website at www.omf.org

See the next page for addresses of English-speaking OMF centres.

English-speaking OMF centres

Australia: PO Box 849, Epping, NSW 1710
Tel: 02 9868 4777 email: au@omf.net www.au.omf.org

Canada: 5155 Spectrum Way, Building 21, Mississauga, ONT
L4W 5A. Toll free: 1 888 657 8010 email: omfcanada@omf.ca
www.ca.omf.org

Hong Kong: PO Box 70505, Kowloon Central PO, Hong Kong
Tel: 852 2398 1823 email: hk@omf.net www.omf.org.hk

Malaysia: 3A Jalan Nipah, off Jalan Ampang, 55000, Kuala
Lumpur. Tel: 603 4257 4263 email: my@omf.net
www.my.omf.org

New Zealand: PO Box 10159, Dominion Road, Balmoral,
Auckland, 1030. Tel: 09 630 5778 email: omfnz@omf.net
www.nz.omf.org

Philippines: QCCPO Box 1997–1159, 1100 Quezon City, M.M.
Tel: 632 951 0782 email: ph-hc@omf.net www.omf.org

Singapore: 2 Cluny Road, Singapore 259570. Tel: 65 6475 4592
email: sno@omf.net www.sg.omf.org

UK: Station Approach, Borough Green, Sevenoaks, Kent TN15
8BG. Tel: 01732 887299 email: omf@omf.org.uk
www.omf.org.uk

USA: 10 West Dry Creek Circle, Littleton, CO 80120-4413
Toll free: 1 800 422 5330   email: omfus@omf.org
www.us.omf.org

Taiwan: PO Box 6-145, Chungho, 235, Taiwan. Tel: 229 489
442 email: taiwaninfo@omf.net www.omf.org/taiwan

OMF International Headquarters: 2 Cluny Road, Singapore
259570. Tel: 65 6319 4550   email: ihq@omf.net
www.omf.org

To my mother,
whose love and sacrifice
have brought me to where I am.

Taiwan

Taipei

Taichung
Changhua
Ming-jian
▲ Ali Mountain
Chiayi
Tainan
Taitung
Kaohsiung
Green Island

50 miles
50 km

Contents

Acknowledgments

I'd like to thank Elisabeth Weinmann, Ling Hu, Yufen Wang and Mei Chen for allowing me to tell your stories, and for your patience and understanding as I peppered you with seemingly irrelevant questions.

Thanks also to: A-fang Tan, Lillian Tsai, Kai Lin, Bao Lin, Peijen Zhang and Matai Zhang, for allowing me to interview you; Mom, for diving into this project with me; Thomas McIntyre, for your love; Keziah Wasserfall, Martin and Angela Symonds and Pin Hoon, for your additional translation help; Rebecca Brooker, for guiding me through my first book; David Ullstrom, for your vision; Alex Kotlowitz and Ann Hagedorn for inspiring me and training me well; and Mary Jeanne Buttrey, Jeremy Quek, Ken and Lillian Huang, Phil and Irene Nicholson, Beth Bowyer, the Taipei Shopworkers Centre, my prayer team – especially Dr Arnold Chan and family – and OMF Taiwan, for your tremendous support.

Above all, thanks be to God – the real Author of these stories.

Author's Note

I know that many of you may find some of the stories contained in this book difficult to believe; Western education teaches us to automatically question demon possession, spiritual warfare and the supernatural – especially when an occurrence cannot be confirmed by empirical evidence. But Eastern society operates very differently. In fact, missionaries have found that most Taiwanese people, especially those belonging to the less-educated working class, unfalteringly believe in an active spirit world.

That being said, I've tried my best to retell these life histories just as their main characters have described them. I've refrained from including any personal judgments about the causes of their behaviour and experiences – especially those of a more 'unusual' nature. I hope that you too will refrain from making personal judgments about the men and women you are about to meet just because you may not wholly agree with their theology.

I deeply admire the people in this book – and not just because of what they've been through and how they've allowed the Lord to transform them. Over the past two years, I've had opportunities to travel with and minister alongside them. I also had the special privilege of living with Mei Chen for six months, and during this time I found her to possess a Christ-like integrity that is all too rare in the church today. The main characters in the book are among the most consistent, dedicated, self-sacrificing Christians I've ever met. When I'm around them I find it easy to forget that they've actually gone through every-thing that you are about to read.

On a practical note, I've used pseudonyms for all the characters in this book, except for missionaries and pas-tors, in order to protect their identities. Also, I have gener-ally followed the Wade-Giles romanization system for place-names and Hanyu Pinyin for Chinese phrases.

I hope that the stories in this book will break your heart – as they have mine – for one of the most overlooked, spir-itually hungry nations in the world.

Jennifer Su

Prologue

Isla Formosa – Beautiful Island, Bountiful Spirits

The idols speak deceit, diviners see visions that lie; they
tell dreams that are false, they give comfort in vain.
Therefore the people wander like sheep oppressed for
lack of a shepherd.

Zechariah 10:2

The dark-skinned woman gazed at the steep,
cypress-covered mountain ridge, illuminated by the morning sun. It was a view that should have taken her breath
away. Indeed, despite the crispness of the mountain air, she
started to tremble, gasping for breath.

Mei Chen had come to this place thinking that she
would finally be safe. She had fled the bustling, cosmopolitan capital city of Taipei and had ridden in a taxi
overnight for eight hours so that she could return to her
childhood home in Ali Mountain. Yet as the taxi wound
through the twists and turns of the mountain road, she
could not escape from the voices:

'You'd better listen to us, or we're going to kill you!'

Even the familiarity of her family's wooden cabin couldn't
protect her from their grip.

'I need to go now,' Mei announced, after only a few hours at home.

'Why do you need to leave?' her mother protested. 'You're so pale. You look like a dead person.'

'I don't know,' Mei replied as she walked away. Her steps quickened, though she did not know where she was going. She only knew that she had to get away from them.

A steep, seemingly insurmountable mountain slope loomed in front of her. She started to crawl like a spider on her hands and feet. Even though she wore slippers, she had no trouble scaling the nearly vertical surface. Adrenaline pumped through her thin, gaunt frame so that she didn't feel an ounce of fatigue.

Then came the pain. It was as if her skin was being punctured by a thousand needles. She searched desperately for a flat spot where she could sit down. Then she started to meditate, as she had done so many times before in the temples.

'Why don't you all leave me alone?' she cried silently.

But of course they would not. After all, her father had been chosen by the spirits to be the shaman of their aboriginal tribe – and it appeared that, despite Mei's fashionable exterior, altered by urban life, she had been chosen to be next. If she mastered the power, she would have the ability to cast spells and ask the spirits to heal – or hurt – others.

But ever since the spirits had come, her life had become a living hell.

Mei had already endured thirty years of misery. Her stunning beauty and rebellious nature had brought to her doorstep what seemed to be every vice known to mankind. But nothing, absolutely nothing, could compare to what she had experienced in the past two years.

Even now, in the deep reaches of this lush, serene mountain, the evil spirits refused to leave her alone.

'We should kill you!' they taunted. 'You should die!'

Overcome by thirst, Mei bent down to drink some water from a small mountain stream.

'Poison!' the spirits cackled. 'You can't drink that!'

Excruciating pain poured through her body.

'We're a legion armed with lasers, and we can torment you,' the spirits continued. 'Our lasers will cut you to the bone!'

She flailed around wildly, attempting to face her tormenters. She saw nothing. She staggered about until sunset.

'Father!' she cried out instinctively, though she knew that her father was miles away. Now that the mountain was cloaked in darkness, shadows began to accompany the taunting voices.

'We're a legion! We want to study your body with our lasers. You have a special and strange ability to damage us, so we want to do some research on you. If you don't listen to us, we'll hurt or kill you!'

When Mei tried to run away, the spirits used spinning brown blades to cut her body and carve out her innards. She wanted to fight back.

'You're so evil! I cannot listen to you, because good can never become evil, and evil can never become good!'

She ran and ran until she saw dim lights lining a distant road. Full of hope, she ran to what she thought was a house. As soon as her hand touched the door, the house disappeared into a field of weeds. She saw another road in the distance, but this one was lined with corpses, their long, mangled hair trailing in the dirt. Shadowy spirits circled around the bodies.

She ran and ran, oblivious to the rocks that struck her, the frosty wind that penetrated her T-shirt and shorts.

'We should kill you! You should die! We should kill you!

You should die!' She felt as if she was running around in circles. Then, came a command.

'Return to Taipei,' the spirits said.

'How can I do that?' she protested. 'I'm so tired and so thirsty. I need something to drink.'

'OK, we'll go get you some water,' they promised. Sure enough, she heard the sound of running water in the distance. Hope filled her heart as the shadows came to her with such speed that they looked as if they were flying. Then, they spilled the water onto the ground.

'You've tricked me!' Mei cried out.

'We'll go get more,' they lied. But then something else appeared – a glowing white cup.

'This is living water,' a soothing voice whispered. Mei wanted desperately to take hold of it.

'If you drink that water, you're going to die,' other, louder voices threatened. At the very mention of death, she started to tremble in fear. The cup disappeared.

In the darkness, a set of glowing footprints appeared on the ground. Then the whisper.

'Follow the footprints, and you'll go back to where your people are.' The footprints started to move forward. But before she could follow, a louder voice interrupted.

'Don't go that way! Go this way. There's water over here.' She heard the rush of a stream and dashed towards it. She reached down but scooped up a handful of dirt. She continued to run.

'We should kill you! You should die! We should kill you! You should die!'

Could it be – a boat? In the middle of the mountains?

'Sit in the boat and relax,' a voice sneered. Weary from hours of running, she tried to climb in – but couldn't. She grew hot with frustration.

'We should kill you!' the voices scoffed. 'Why won't you die? You must have something special.'

'You're so evil!' she shouted back, darting around haphazardly. 'I have to tell the world about you! The whole world!'

'Oh, don't do that. We won't hurt you any more.'

'You're a bunch of liars! I have to tell the whole world ...' She stopped in her tracks. Something had caught her feet, though she felt no pain. Then she watched in horror as a shadow pierced her foot with a red-hot wire and tied her down. She felt all remaining strength seep from her body. Resigned, she crumbled to the ground and waited.

As dim rays of light began to peek above the horizon, Mei squinted her eyes to face her captor. Instead she saw her feet were caught in a web of thorny vines. She loosened her feet from their grip and stood up. The she saw it.

Directly in front of her was a 1,000-foot drop. She cautiously peered down at the raging river below. Her eyes wide with terror, she realized: If it weren't for the vines, she would have surely plunged to her death.

The legion of shadows had disappeared. The spirits now took the form of two male figures – tiny and brown, like diabolic gingerbread men.

'We are here to help you. Come back to Taipei,' they insisted.

Again came a whisper. 'You will meet a person,' it said. 'You should believe in whatever religion that person tells you to believe.'

Mei didn't know what to believe any more. She did know that there was no way to escape from these voices, no words that would repel them. The little men followed her closely as she ran and ran. Hopeless tears streamed down her face.

'You're all liars. LIARS!' she thought. 'Father, save me! Mother!' Despite her ongoing bitterness toward her parents she felt like they were the only people who could save her now.

Another sound caught her attention. The sound of chirping doves. She turned her head to find the source of the comforting sound, but couldn't find it. Then she saw him.

Standing there was a boy, around seventeen or eighteen years old, who happened to be on a hunting venture in this part of the forest. She stared at him. He stared at her. They stared at each other as if they had come from two entirely different worlds.

'You are ... really pale,' he said. From her wild, harried expression, it was hard for him to tell whether she would attack or embrace him.

'A lot of people are looking for you,' he continued. Mei's eyes darted around, as if she was being cornered by an invisible army of assailants. His face filled with concern.

'I'm a Christian. You really need to believe in Christianity.' Still no reply.

'Well ... OK, then. Just come with me.'

Mei Chen had finally found someone who could lead her home. But even then, all she could think about were the spirits.

Part 1

Childhood Among Spirits

They say to wood, 'You are my father,'
and to stone, 'You gave me birth.'   Jeremiah 2:27a

Chapter 1

The legends said that long ago a flood covered the earth, and that the rising waters trapped a group of people on a mountain peak. While people around the world perished, these people managed to survive. That was how the unbreakable and resilient Tso tribe came to be.

Many moons later, in the Western year of 1964, seven-year-old Mei Chen still felt trapped on Ali Mountain. She was not proud of being a Tso. She hated it. She also hated her family's leaky wooden cabin, which reeked of mildew, smoke and decades of sorrow. As she rubbed her calloused palms together over a wispy fire, she wished that she could be like three of her siblings, who had been sent away to live somewhere else. Instead, she was among the unfortunate nine who remained.

After school, Mei and her six-year-old brother had hiked for an hour with their feet wrapped in pieces of cloth to protect them from the mountain snow. Such was their daily journey home. Mei's feet felt little pain because they were already covered with toughened scars from when, at the age of three, she had accidentally stepped on smouldering embers that her older brothers had been playing with. Even though her body shook from the chill, she did not utter a word of complaint. She and her brother had to save every ounce of energy for all the work that had to be done.

While their mother worked and their father hunted in another part of the woods, the two children embarked, hand in hand, on a quest for firewood. Mei heaved an axe at a tree trunk while her brother hacked at another with a scythe. Then the two siblings wrapped the logs together and hoisted the wood onto their backs. After returning home, Mei started a fire and boiled a pot of water, which she would use to wash clothes, prepare baths and cook dinner. She wished she could boil some fruit this evening. Or some rice. But aside from their usual fare of sweet potatoes, there was nothing left to cook.

A faint tune crackled in the distance as a neighbour turned on her old, rusty radio. Mei loved music. Since her family could not yet afford such a luxurious appliance, she wanted nothing more than to stand in the doorway and listen to the song. Instead, she struggled to fix her eyes on the sweet potatoes that hissed over the fire. If she left now, she would risk burning them, which would mean no dinner for the Chens. Her stomach grumbled as a reminder that she could not afford the risk.

*   *   *

Everyone in the Tso tribe knew about the spiritual powers of the Chens. In every generation of the Chen family, one person had been chosen by the spirits to serve as a shaman – an intermediary between the spirits and the entire tribe. They were bestowed with occult powers that could help them heal the sick, drive away or call together the spirits, predict the future and more. Both Mei's father and great aunt had been granted this privilege.

Mei never actually saw her father heal anyone. In fact, she couldn't even remember hearing stories of successful healings. Sometimes she saw him leave the house to visit someone in need. Other times, she was allowed to accompany him on these visits, though she was never allowed into the room where he would cast his spells.

'These things need to be done very carefully,' he would say to her. 'If you're around, my god could hurt you.'

Interestingly, Mr Chen's role as the tribe's shaman didn't prevent him from practising Taiwanese folk religion, which had been brought to the island by early settlers from China's Fujian and Guangdong provinces.[1] As simple shrines erected by these immigrants blossomed into mega-temples, idol worship became an integral part of Taiwanese culture, even in the most remote aboriginal villages.

Mei, however, wasn't particularly interested in temples or burning incense sticks for the gods. She was most intrigued by the magical powers her father and great aunt seemed to possess and the cloud of secrecy that shrouded her father's work.

In the meantime, Mei had a secret of her own.

It started when she was eight years old. At the time, her entire family slept like sardines in one bed. Mei had always felt uncomfortable about this arrangement, though she did not know why.

'Should I feel afraid of my father?' she thought. 'I don't think so.' In fact, Mei thought that her father was a kind man. He never beat his wife. He drank less frequently than Mei's uncle, who would eventually die from the habit. He was unlike Mei's philandering grandfathers – she had heard that one had several affairs and the other had two or three other wives. As Mei lay in bed, trying to fall asleep, she simply could not pinpoint the reason for her revulsion.

One night, Mei was at home alone. Her oldest brother, then twenty, suddenly appeared at the door. He walked brazenly towards her and pinned her down. As he tried to take advantage of her, she started to scream. He hit her. She fought back. Using muscles toned from a lifetime of heavy lifting, she managed to escape his grip and flee.

From then on, Mei lived in state of constant fear. Whenever she was alone, her brother would try to overcome her. She desperately wanted help, but the one thing that she feared more than her brother was telling her parents about the situation.

'They already have enough problems of their own,' she thought woefully. Her mother, busy enough from working and taking care of the children, suffered from an asthmatic cough that made her frequently irritable. If Mei told her mother about her predicament, surely she would evoke the woman's menacing temper. Terrified, Mei tried her best to be an obedient, quiet child. But sometimes she still couldn't escape her mother's wrath.

One time, the screaming woman grabbed Mei by the hair and dragged her outside into the rain. She yanked hard, causing Mei's feet to slip. This made her mother even angrier. Mei's scalp burned with pain. Tears mixed with the rain that streamed down her round face.

During another outbreak of fury, her mother decided to lock Mei in the family outhouse. As the door slammed shut, Mei started to tremble and weep hysterically. Overwhelmed by the stench of human excrement, she gasped for breath. She was profoundly afraid of the dark.

A few hours later, her father set her free.

Most often, her father would intervene before the worst had come. Despite Mei's underlying suspicions about him, she adored his mild, tender manner and loved the feeling of running away from her mother into his arms.

Her second-oldest brother, however, did not receive such gracious interference. The mere sight of her mother bringing out a wooden club would make Mei's stomach churn. After tying her brother's hands behind his back, her mother and father took turns beating him with the club for more than thirty minutes. Once they were satisfied, they simply turned and left his limp body on the ground. Mei snuck over, untied him and held him in her arms.

'How could they treat you this way?' she said as they

wept together. She knew that the Japanese, who had occupied Taiwan from 1894 to 1945, had taught her parents to be strict – but this was just too much. In an effort to mitigate the pain, she gave her brother the only thing she had to offer. A sweet potato.

In time, Mei's heart became like a rock hardened by the weight of compounding debris. She developed two personalities: alone, she was full of quiet rage and resentment; but when accompanied by people, she appeared to be a normal, carefree child.

Mei and her siblings liked to play in a nearby stream, teeming with fish. Since its banks could be precariously slick, their uncle had come along with several of his children. As Mei splashed around, she could feel the strain of daily life seeping out of her body. As her sinewy limbs moved nimbly in the water, she momentarily forgot about the sexual attempts of her brother and the unquenchable temper of her mother. She loved being with her sisters, younger brother and cousin. As their afternoon of swimming came to an end, they tried to forget about the housework that lay ahead by cherishing the fact that they could do it together.

* * *

A throng of children ran to the general store to get a front-row view of the spectacle. They would come to remember 1964 as the year when a television came to their village.

Purchased by the store's proud owner, it was the first television that Mei had ever seen. For the first time, Mei saw what the world was like outside of Ali Mountain. She couldn't take her eyes off the beautiful clothes that the actors and actresses so casually flaunted. She was stunned. And overwhelmingly envious.

'Why are we so poor?' she complained to herself. 'Why

was I born into such a poor family? Why do I have to be an aborigine? Why is my life so bitter?'

The television had given Mei eyes to see the rapid changes that were taking place in her country outside the confines of Ali Mountain. In the decade before she was born, the country had undergone dramatic political upheaval. In 1945, Japan relinquished official control of Taiwan, and the Chinese Nationalist leader Chiang Kai-shek, who had fled to Taiwan after being defeated by the Communists, began to exert authority over the island. He brought along two million Kuomingtang[2] supporters. All the Taiwanese who had adopted Japanese names ten years earlier now resumed using their original Chinese names.[3] The government was reorganized. During the first eight months of Kuomingtang rule, the inflation rate sky-rocketed to 350 per cent.[4] As in most periods of governmental transition, the air was thick with tension.

On 28 February 1947, a seemingly nondescript occurrence sparked an island-wide outbreak of chaos that would be memorialized in years to come. It started when six government agents in Taipei came upon a woman selling illegal cigarettes. As expected, they confiscated her goods and cash. But they did not stop there. As she fell to her knees and begged them to return her things, an agent beat her until she lost consciousness – all in front of a horrified crowd. An enraged mob pursued the agents and cornered one of them near a movie theatre. The agent fired into the crowd and killed a man. After the agents found refuge in a nearby police station, the mob surrounded the building and demanded that the agents be turned over to them. In the process, a government truck was tipped over and set on fire.

The following morning, the incident appeared on the front page of the New Life News. Riots sprang up throughout the city. Some people attempted to invade the new government's headquarters in Taipei and were met with gunshots.

Others broke into the China Broadcasting Corporation building and broadcast a call for a mass uprising against Nationalist rule. Over the next few months, the Nationalists embarked on a forceful man-hunt for insurgents. People suspected of being involved with Taiwanese independence movements – from scholars to blue-collar workers – were arrested or executed. Some simply 'disappeared'.

When the political heat caused by the government's transition started to cool down, Taiwan's economy took an unexpected turn. It started to industrialize at unprecedented speed. In the 1940s, 75 per cent of all Taiwanese worked on farms, and many of them were tenants.[5] But twenty years later, as Mei chopped wood for heat, Taiwan was transforming into a mobile, modern society. As her father hunted for food, factories had started to spring up throughout the island. The air now smelled of change, and Mei caught a whiff of it as she stood wide-eyed in front of the television. She couldn't stop thinking about the clothes. What she saw was so different from the hand-me-downs she was given to wear.

'Mummy, can you make me beautiful clothes?' she asked one day. When her mother eventually made her a dress out of an old blanket, Mei's heart fluttered. 'It's beautiful,' she thought.

'Mummy, can you make me beautiful clothes?' she asked on another occasion. 'A skirt like you made for my older sister?' This time, her mother responded with a languid cough.

'I'm too tired and too busy. Besides, you don't behave,' she said. Mei had no sympathy.

'You don't love me!' she pouted inwardly.

For the next three or four hours, she refused to move, her face plastered with a frown. Her mother had rejected her. Her home life was a mess. And, worst of all, she would never be as well dressed as the beautiful women on television.

Ling Hu

Four years later, Ling Hu pranced about in her custom-fit-ted, Western-style dress after a long day of moving boxes and furniture. The ten-year-old couldn't wait for the party to begin. She dashed to the kitchen and flung open her family's new refrigerator, which stood as high as her mother. Pushing aside the fruits and vegetables that would be used to prepare that evening's house-warming feast, she grabbed a dripping, cold can of He-Song cola, compliments of her uncle, a soft-drink distributor. She took a gulp and ran out to the balcony to see if she could spot her father's black motorbike. Careful not to let any cola drip onto her new white dress, she plopped onto the sofa.

By now her relatives and family friends had finished moving everything into the new apartment above the Taiwan Tobacco and Wine Monopoly office, a state–private joint enterprise that offered generous salaries to its employees, including Mr Hu.

Moving had been a fairly simple task, for the company had already outfitted their apartment with an assortment of modern furniture – aluminium beds, a four-legged black-and-white television and, of course, the refrigerator. Most of the other furniture had been transported by taxi from the Hu's previous residence in Panchiao, a suburb of Taiwan's capital city, Taipei.

The first and most important taxi trip had started early that morning, before the city's noisy, crowded awakening. Ling, along with her younger brother and sister, dressed up for the momentous occasion. A round basket was prepared for three intricately carved tabletop idols: Tudi Gong[6], the lord of the land, bore a perpetually mild grin and a flowing, black beard. He could have been taken for a great uncle if he were not known as one of the oldest and most widely worshipped deities in Taiwan. Then there was Guan Gong, a sword-toting Chinese general who had been deified into a red-faced Taoist[7] god of prosperity and protection. Finally, there was Mazu, the goddess of the sea, who wore an ornate, beaded headpiece and a gold-coloured robe covered in delicate designs.

Although the Taiwanese worship a wide variety of gods outside of the home, they usually choose a few as their household gods. The Hu family had a particular affinity for these three, and felt that their auspicious selection had kept them prosperous throughout the years.

And now it was time to move their gods, ever-so-carefully into their new home. In order to assure peace in their new home, the gods' well-being was critical, they reasoned. They placed the idols, along with pineapples and other fruit, into the basket. Then Mrs Hu bowed to them.

'We're moving to a new home now,' she told them reverently. Ling was deeply moved.

When the gods, escorted by the entire Hu family, arrived at their new home in Chungho, they were placed on an altar affixed to a wall in the living-room. The Hu family ancestral tablet, containing the names and birth/death dates of Ling's ancestors, was also placed on the altar. Offerings of vegetables and rice were presented to the gods. Mrs Hu started a fire inside an uncovered metal barrel on the floor, and each family member sat behind it. They started tossing in stacks of yellow paper known as 'joss money' – the currency of spirits and ghosts[8]. After Ling gave her offering, she put her hands together in prayer and bowed. She loved starting the day in this way.

Even on a normal day, Ling loved to watch her mother burn sticks of incense for the gods and her *zu-xian*, her family's ancestors. Every morning and evening, Mrs Hu lit a small bundle of sticks, turned towards the gods and held the sticks upright in front of her face. She methodically shook the sticks and bowed, again and again. Ling knew every movement by heart. She dreamed that some day she would have the full-time job of managing a home, raising children, and making daily offerings to the gods.

Now, as Ling sat on the couch, sipping her soda, she began to daydream about a second session of worship that would take place that evening. Then they would honour Diji Zhu, the god in charge of protecting their home.

'I'll pray, "Please bless us in our new home,"' Ling thought. So deep was her desire to connect with the gods that she couldn't help but smile.

* * *

This was Ling's second move since she started elementary school, but she wasn't complaining. After all, each move was an indication of her father's professional success. Each new home came with new amenities.

Her father had been a high achiever at a young age. A top student, he had the opportunity to study in Japan during the Japanese occupation, when most Taiwanese had little access to education beyond primary school. In 1937, while more than 500,000 children attended primary school, only 4,117 were educated further.[9] Ling's mother was also considered a woman of privilege. She, too, was well educated – extremely rare for girls at the time. She also had a wealthy father who owned a bank and a movie theatre, which meant free movie tickets for all his progeny. After his wife died young, he hired a wet nurse for each one of his many children.

At that time, daughters were not considered part of their parents' households after marriage. Many parents neglected daughters, who would ultimately be 'given away' to their future husbands. To make matters worse, many women suffered hideously under the hands of their mothers-in-law. To avoid this situation, Ling's maternal grandfather employed a common tactic: he arranged a marriage between his daughter and her wet nurse's son, and then sent his daughter away to be raised by her new 'foster mother'. This way, the woman would treat the girl like her own daughter from an early age.

Mrs Hu was also fortunate in that she was able to maintain a successful career. Although Taiwanese women of the past were almost always relegated to the home, 36 per cent had other jobs by 1961.[10] In addition to raising her children, Mrs Hu also worked in the clothing industry. She eventually ran her own business, selling custom-tailored, Western-style clothes. Her mother-in-law, who was very fond of her, moved in to help with child-care. Mrs Hu considered this an honour, for her mother-in-law could have chosen to live with any of her six sons.

Due to all these successes, Ling's family seemed to constantly move from place to place – first from Tucheng, a rural farming village, to a rental apartment in Panchiao when she was six years old. Although the geographical distance between the two places was not great, it was as if Ling had entered another world: cars instead of carts, concrete buildings instead of farmland. Then they moved to Chungho, and now Panchiao. No matter where they lived, Ling's mental map always included the nearest temples. Twenty years earlier, a well-known Buddhist leader[11] had been warned that if the Buddhist Association of the Republic of China did not become more proactive in reaching the general public, then Christianity would take over Taiwan.[12] The increasing extravagance of Taiwan's temples proved that this prophecy went unfulfilled. With their sweeping, ornately decorated roofs, the temples were immediately recognized as the most important structures of any Taiwanese community.[13] Not only were they palaces that housed Buddhist and Taoist deities, but they were also architectural masterpieces.

Tradition dictated that wealthy families like the Hus had been granted divine favour, and should therefore show their gratitude through temple offerings.[14] The temples were reaping the benefits of Taiwan's increase in affluence.

As long as Ling could remember, she visited temples on her own and sought temple fortune-tellers for advice. She also encouraged her mother and siblings to worship at various temples. She had the natural ability to proselytize.

Among the Hu's three household gods, Tudi Gong received offerings most often. Twice a month, most businesses across the island would feed him by placing raw fish, pork or chicken, incense and joss money on tables in front of their store-fronts. But this was nothing compared to the fanfare awarded to Mazu, goddess of the sea.

Mazu was reportedly born in 960 CE off the coast of China's Fujian Province. Legends about her life vary dramatically. According to one, a Taoist priest educated her in mystical arts when she was a teenager. One day, while in a trance, she was able to save her father from drowning – a respectably filial act. Even after her death at the age of twenty-eight, Mazu purportedly continued to save imperilled fishermen. Through these good deeds, she became revered as a goddess. Some considered her to be the patron goddess of Taiwan.

On the twenty-third day of the third lunar month, Mazu's birthday was celebrated across the island as a national holiday. Ling generally enjoyed school, but on this day the minutes seemed to creep by as she waited anxiously for her last class to end. The school day was cut short for the holiday.

As soon as school was dismissed, Ling rushed home to help her grandmother prepare for the festivities. Together, they carried offerings of fruit, fresh flowers, raw chicken and fish to their doorstep and waited expectantly for the procession to begin. As the rhythm of pounding drums and the twang of traditional Chinese instruments crescendoed, Ling craned her neck to catch sight of the procession coming down the street. Temple representatives had cast lots before the event to determine their position in the procession – at one time, the rear end was desirable because of its ritualistic superiority, but later the front would be considered advantageous because sometimes those in the back would not finish marching until the next morning.[15] Musicians, including some of Ling's uncles, clanged cymbals and pounded drums fervently. Dancers performed martial-arts routines that required as much as three months of rehearsal. Then two men dressed as Mazu's guardians, 'Thousand League Eyes' and 'Favouring Wind Ears', would appear.

At last came Mazu, the 'Queen of Heaven', emblazoned with a golden gown that glistened in the afternoon sun. She sat enthroned on a wooden chair with two poles on either side. Four men proudly carried the poles, bouncing them up and down. Mazu's statue appeared to dance.

As the jubilant goddess passed by, many of Ling's neighbours ran into the middle of the street and bowed down. Others lay on the ground, letting the statue of Mazu pass over them – another act of protection and blessing. Ling couldn't help but feel entranced by the overwhelmingly festive aura of the day. She hoped with all of her heart that the feeling would never end.

During Ling's childhood, rural mothers in Taiwan tended to use aggression in discipline, while upper-class women tended to use affection.[16] Ling's situation was a typical example of the latter. Her father was a warm, dependable man who worked hard to provide for his family. Ling adored him. Sociable and generous, he often invited colleagues over to his house for dinner.

Ling had inherited her father's talkative nature. Though their home often bustled with guests, she most looked forward to Sunday evening dinners with her paternal extended family. Her father saw himself as the glue that held his siblings together, and he often welcomed them to his house for birthdays, weddings, and virtually any other reason for celebration. Ling's mother had a larger family with eleven brothers and sisters, so getting them together proved to be more difficult. Nonetheless, Mrs Hu and her sisters tried to meet together at least once a month.

Sometimes, Mr Hu organized extended family outings. If, for some reason, a family wasn't able to pay for travel or activity costs, Mr Hu would cover the difference himself.

At one family reunion, Ling overheard a conversation between her father and uncle. Unlike her father, the uncle had struggled in school. Eventually he started a company that manufactured cement. He did well because the improving economy had brought about a construction boom that was transforming Taiwan's landscape.

'I think my daughter should help me in my business instead of going to school,' he said to Mr Hu. 'She's mute anyway and wouldn't do well.'

'Don't do that,' Mr Hu admonished. 'She should at least have the opportunity to get an education.'

'But I just don't think it would be worth it,' the uncle insisted. This fuelled a debate that ended with a generous solution: The daughter could live with Ling's family and help take care of Ling's younger brother. In return, the family would pay for her school tuition when she felt ready to start. As the most financially well-off brother of the family, Mr Hu had assisted his brothers many times in the past, financially and otherwise.

Mr Hu's generosity even extended outside of the family. Occasionally, he would help neighbours or friends pay for their children's school fees. He would often remind Ling and her siblings, 'If you have the means to give, then give. Don't just think about yourself.' The admonitions were rarely accompanied by lessons on money management. His wallet provided a flow of cash that never ended and never ceased to fulfil his family's every need.

For Ling, even the concept of hunger had never crossed her mind. Neither had the concept of Christianity.

Yufen Wang

Seven-year-old Yufen Wang knew what was coming and wanted to run away. It was 1958, the year of Ling Hu's birth. Although the two girls would grow up on the same island, their worlds could not have been more different.

Yufen could hear her mother scrambling around the kitchen, looking for something – anything decent – to cook for that day's feast. On any other day, her mother would have been able to make do with whatever odds and ends she could scavenge, but this day was different. It was the thirteenth day of the first lunar month, the birthday of Tian Gong[17], the main god of her village. It would have been shameful to honour him with the same meagre fare that she typically served her husband and nine children.

Yufen had never before been called upon to perform the unspeakably humiliating task that lay ahead. At first, her mother had gone out by herself. After growing weary of the jeers and whispers, she began to dispatch her children instead. Yufen had always managed to look busy in years past. This time, perhaps she could pretend to read by looking at the pictures in her brothers' books. Or perhaps she could preoccupy herself with one of her few toys – a doll she had made out of chopsticks and a worn piece of cloth.

'Yu! Come here!' It was too late. Yufen's mother had called. Her turn had come.

As Yufen carried the pot out of the house, she tried not to think of how, after all the food was prepared and ritualistically offered to the god, she and her siblings would enviously watch her father's friends and relatives consume the food. She tried not to think of how, on a day when the Wang family table would be graced with steamed fish and home-raised chicken, the children would just watch everything disappear bit by bit. She tried not to think of how – on a day when she should have been happy about having so many guests at her house – she would be grieved. For by the end of the night, she would be lucky to get a few left-over scraps. Mr Wang had saved money for a whole month so that he could impress others and gain 'face'[18] through this meal. For the next few days, his own family would recover from the heavy cost by eating little.

But Yufen couldn't possibly think of these things now. Trembling, she knocked on the door. As the neighbour's wife peered out, what might have been a cordial glance quickly turned to disdain as she laid her eyes upon the empty pot in Yufen's tiny hands.

'Please,' Yufen whispered, trying to hide from her voice the sound of her pride being viciously snuffed out. 'Let us borrow something to eat.'

*   *   *

The seventh of nine children, Yufen was trained at an early age to be grateful for what little her family could afford – basic daily necessities and three meals a day. Sometimes even the latter was uncertain, and Yufen learned to enjoy every meal as if the next one might not come. She knew that for others in Ming-jian, a small town accessible only by dirt roads and footpaths, having three meals a day was a luxury.

Like many lower-class men who did not work in the

factories, Mr Wang single-handedly owned and ran a small shop. His sold Chinese herbal medicine that often came in the form of medicated cloth bandages.

Mr Wang's income allowed his family to live in a house with cement and dirt floors and walls made of cinder-block. A decade earlier, mud houses were common residences in towns like Ming-jian. Since they provided little protection against the typhoons and earthquakes that so frequently ravaged the island, the switch to cement was much welcomed.

To reduce the ugliness of their surroundings, the Wang children would try to adorn the grey cinder-blocks with colourful pieces of paper they collected. But nothing improved their surroundings quite like Mr Wang's hand-scripted calligraphy. Since his Japanese teachers didn't teach him how to write Chinese characters, he learned how to do this on his own. Knowing that his children were plagued with a sense of helplessness because of their constant lack of money, he tried his best to infuse them with positive thinking through his writings.

Mostly, Mr Wang copied down traditional moral sayings emphasizing Confucian[19] values that dated back to their ancestors' days in Mainland China. These sayings often referred to Taoism's 'Eight Cardinal Virtues' – filial piety, brotherly love, loyalty/honesty, truthfulness/trustfulness, propriety, righteousness, integrity/purity and shameful-ness – and 'Four Ethical Principles' – propriety, righteous-ness, integrity/purity, and shamefulness.[20] Mr Wang's calligraphy also stressed his personal mantra, which was more of a faraway wish than an employable piece of advice: 'Whatever you do, depend on yourself. Don't lower your head, and don't ask others for help.'

In person, Mr Wang was a man of few words. Yufen knew that her father loved his ever-expanding family because he worked hard to provide for them. Yet she felt a strange mix of emotions when around him – fear, as well as a sense of awkwardness that came both from his reticence and his age; he was old enough to be her grandfather. Mr Wang met Yufen's material needs but not her emotional ones, which was not an atypical situation for Taiwanese working-class families. Years later, Yufen would say, 'Everything my father taught us about life was communicated through calligraphy.'

Yufen felt closer to her mother, partly because Mrs Wang could be talkative, especially when aunts or relatives came over. The visits provided much-needed respite from the daily duties and rituals.

Like Mrs Hu, Mrs Wang was responsible for household matters like religious practice. One way she demonstrated her devotion was by following a Buddhist form of vegetarianism for fifty years – abstaining from meat before 11 a.m. Every morning she would light incense sticks in front of their family altar, which held an ancestral tablet and a wood-block figurine of the long-bearded Tudi Gong. In proportion to the family's financial standing, their altar was similar to but simpler than that of the Hus. On the first and fifteenth of every month, fruit and sometimes meat were ritualistically placed on the altar. Similar rituals were conducted on the anniversary of a relative's death. Yufen preferred worshipping the ghosts of her deceased ancestors because the offerings could be eaten afterwards; since they were family after all, the ancestors would understand.

From Yufen's point of view, worshipping the gods was more frustrating. At times, she felt it was plain inconvenient. After days of prepararing for certain idol feasts, everyone in the family would nearly collapse out of exhaustion.

'If this is supposed to bring peace, then why aren't we getting anything from it?' she began to ask herself. 'What's the point?'

Indeed, despite the time, energy and money the Wangs had spent on their gods, they had not received much in return. Even the luxury of enjoying a fried egg was reserved for those suffering from a stomach ache.

For the Wang family, life was as stable as walking across a pit on a bamboo cane. One day, school was affordable. The next day, it was not. One day, all the children could eat their fill. The next day, they would go hungry.

While Mei's object of envy was clothing, Yufen's was the sight of a classmate's lollipop. Even then, she tried to obscure her covetous feelings with other thoughts. She already felt insecure. Wanting the impossible would only exacerbate the pain. She felt trapped in a dark pit of futility. If she pretended that the whole world was suffering the same, then her existence might just be tolerable. Escape was unthinkable.

The one thing she did wish she could escape from was her daily walk to school. Although only the wealthiest kids in town could afford to take the public bus to school, she would still stare at the passing buses in envy, wishing for at least one chance to avoid the thirty-minute walk ahead of her. Shoes would have been nice. A bicycle would have been even better, but her family only had one of those, and it was reserved for her father.

One day in the second grade, Yufen decided that she didn't want to go to school. As she struggled to get out of the bed that she shared with her two younger siblings, she caught a draught of the wintry, early morning air and decided she was not going anywhere. Not today. Unlike Mei, her bare feet couldn't stand the cold.

'It's COLD. I don't want to go! I don't want to!' she started to whine. One of her older brothers sensed her apprehension and shot her a menacing look. He stormed outside and returned a few minutes later.

'I don't want – ' Yufen's fussy display of rebellion was interrupted as she caught sight of the object in her brother's hand – a bamboo cane. Before the availability of running water, Yufen's brothers used bamboo poles to carry buckets of water from the local well back home. Yufen, who was too young for such duties in those days, had no right to complain now.

Resigned, she ate her breakfast and packed her books. As she started walking to school, she glanced over her shoulder. Sure enough, her brother was right behind her, ready to beat her if she turned back. A few minutes later, she looked again. He was still there. By then, she knew there was no way home. The last thing she wanted was a beating from brother number three.

Sometimes, Yufen did enjoy walking. As she walked between her home and her father's shop, for example, she would pass a beautiful Presbyterian church.

The Presbyterians had a long-standing legacy in Taiwan. They first came from England in the mid-nineteenth century when Taiwan was still known in the West as the Isla Formosa, which means 'Beautiful Island'. The names of several of these missionaries would be remembered for posterity: Dr James L. Maxwell, who, despite being accused of murdering Taiwanese children and hiding their bodies under his bed, managed to baptize his first eight converts in the southern part of the island on 12 August 1866; and Revd George Mackay, a Canadian Presbyterian, who started work in the northern part of the island.

Formosa's first Protestant missionaries arrived with the Dutch in 1624. Early churches were often assaulted by mobs because of local anti-missionary sentiment. For more than 200 years, missionaries were more successful among aboriginal peoples than among locals of Han Chinese origin.[21] Captain Bax, a naval officer, wrote in 1875:

'Christianity is spreading more rapidly among the Peohoans [a tribal group] than Chinese, on account of their character being simpler, and their having no great attachment to the Buddhist form of worship, which has only become known to them since their conquest by the Chinese.'[22]

In the 100 years following Captain Bax's observation, Buddhism and Taoism had tightened their grip on Taiwanese hearts. Christian churches were still few and far between. If it weren't for the aesthetic appeal of the Presbyterian church in Ming-jian, Yufen probably wouldn't have noticed it at all.

Her initial interactions with the church began at the age of five, when she was not yet old enough to go to school. Every day she would walk to her father's shop to hear him talk with his customers and friends. She particularly loved listening to him telling them stories, even though many years later she would not be able to remember a single one. Sometimes on Sundays, she sneaked into the church on the way to the store. She was captivated by the pristine beauty of the interior of the building and by the hypnotizing serenity of the foot-pedalled organ that was played there. Most important, the children who attended received free sweets. Even though she couldn't understand anything that transpired during the strange, Western-style services, she continued to drop in periodically until the end of elementary school.

Then she began to feel uncomfortable. Church seemed like a decent place and the local Christian hospital provided good services. But the formal solemnity of the Sunday services felt monotonous compared to the vivacity of idol feasts. The dense, unintelligible jargon of Christianity seemed so far removed from the beliefs that her mother lived out day to day. Like a dove trying to fly under water, Christianity seemed to have no place in

Yufen's life. By the time she was in junior high school, she stopped going to church. Besides, it was embarrassing for a child of her age to attend church just for the sweets.

Notes

1. Gary M. Davidson and Barbara E. Reed, *Culture and Customs of Taiwan*, Westport, Conn.: Greenwood Press, 1988, p. 37
2. Kuomingtang – China's nationalist party. After being overthrown by the Communists, party members fled to Taiwan where they took control.
3. Charles B. Jones, *Buddhism in Taiwan: Religion and the State, 1660–1990*, Honolulu: University of Hawai'i Press, 1999
4. David K. Jordan, Andrew D. Morris & Marc L. Moskowitz, *The Minor Arts of Daily Life: Popular Culture in Taiwan*, Honolulu: University of Hawai'i Press, 2004.
5. Stevan Harrell, 'Playing in the Valley', in Stevan Harrell & Huang Chun-chieh, *Cultural Change in Postwar Taiwan*, Taipei: SMC Publishing Inc., 1994.
6. Tudi Gong – one of the most widely worshipped deities in Taiwan, the 'Lord of the Land' is said to look after particular territories he governs and is particularly important to agricultural communities.
7. Taoism – originally referring to a philosophy based on the writings of Laozi, in Taiwan it is commonly used to describe traditional folk religion, and the worship of many gods and ghosts.
8. Joss money – fake money printed on yellow paper; considered the currency of the dead, it is burned as an offering to both gods and ancestors.
9. David Shambaugh (ed.), *Contemporary Taiwan*, Oxford: Clarendon Press, 1998.
10. John F. Copper, *Taiwan: Nation-State or Province?*, 3rd edn, Boulder, Colorado: Westview Press, 1999.
11. Buddhism – a religion of Eastern and Central Asia, based on the teachings of Guatama Buddha, focusing on the

alienation of suffering through mental and moral self-purification.

12. Jones, *ibid.*
13. Davidson and Reed, *ibid*
14. Harrell & Huang, *ibid.*, p. 140
15. Joseph Bosco, *Yiguan Dao: Heterodoxy and Popular Religion in Taiwan, The Other Taiwan: 1945 to Present*, ed. Murray A. Rubenstein, Armonk, New York: M.E. Sharpe, 1994, p. 429.
16. Cheng-hung Liao and Martin M. C. Yang, *Socio-Economic Change in Rural Taiwan: 1950–1978*, in James C. Hsiung (ed.), *The Taiwan Experience 1950–1980*, New York, Praeger Publishers, 1981.
17. Tian Gong – the god of heaven, the highes in Taiwan's pantheon of gods.
18. Face – honour, reputation, dignity. Many social behaviours particular to Taiwan and other Asian cultures have developed in an effort o preserve 'face' which is considered of upmost importance.
19. Confucianism – a Chinese ethical and philosophical system based on the teachings of Confucius. It influences most moral, social, political and religious thought in Taiwan.
20. World Yi-Kuan Tao Headquarters: www.with.org
21. Han Chinese – The largest ethnic group in the world, with a population of 1.3 billion people. The majority of people in China and Taiwan are from a Han Chinese background.
22. George W. Carrington, *Foreigners in Formosa 1841–1874*, San Francisco, Chinese Materials Centre, Inc., 1978.

Chapter 2

The children fixed their eyes on the glowing red trail of hot embers. As the men carrying the idol started to walk barefoot upon the firey path, Ling Hu flinched. This was only the beginning.

The spirit mediums that led the procession had already begun to shake violently. These *tang-ki*, some of whom were not much older than Ling, usually behaved this way when they approached temples. It was a sign that the spirits had entered their bodies.

Wielding long needles that they carried underneath their ceremonial cloaks, they started to pierce their faces. Blood spattered across their bodies. Yet the *tang-ki* appeared to be oblivious to any pain.

Tang-ki who were more dramatically inclined often carried around swords about fifty centimetres long, wooden batons covered with nails or triangular bits of copper, large axes, or balls of nails nicknamed 'heavenly red tangerines'. The *tang-ki* would then use these to strike themselves on their upper backs or foreheads.[1] Spectators rarely noticed that the grotesque instruments were specially designed to produce bloody, yet superficial wounds. It was said that once, a bystander tried to stop a *tang-ki* who had hit himself three times. The *tang-ki* jumped up and shook, holding out his weapon tenaciously. Then he continued to thrash himself.

After enough blood had been drawn, the *tang-ki* sprayed wine on their wounds. The bleeding stopped. The crowds stood in awe, expressionless but profoundly engrossed. To them, the power of the gods was clear – they could both inflict pain and heal.

This power made many people revere the *tang-ki*, who might have otherwise been 'nobody's' in their communities. Ling had heard that *tang-ki* had to maintain pure lives, free of sexual relations, when serving the gods. She had also heard that they could see ghosts as they mutilated themselves. Try as she might, she couldn't manage to see anything. But this did not hamper her faith.

'If the gods didn't exist, how could these miracles happen?' Ling thought.

In more rural areas like Yufen's hometown of Ming-jian, townspeople often felt proud when the *tang-ki* would visit – a symbol that that their town was still under the protection of the gods. In some towns, particularly memorable visits by *tang-ki* would be recounted for years to come. Did they remember the time when an over-zealous *tang-ki* almost cut his head open with an axe? Thanks to the heroic intervention of a bystander, he only lost an ear.[2]

For Yufen Wang, Ling Hu and Mei Chen, these bloody performances were not the only religious images they would remember for years to come. Throughout their childhoods, there were few memories that remained untouched by the spirits.

* * *

The doors of hell had swung open. For an entire month, gui,[3] or ghosts, would roam the earth, feasting among the living and haunting the unfortunate. Every year, during the seventh lunar month, the Taiwanese were filled with fear. Superstition, integral to Taiwanese thinking, would reach an all-time high. Swimming, for example, would be avoided at all costs, despite the temptation of the scorching summer heat; people who had died by drowning would roam the waters as ghosts. Few people were willing to risk becoming substitute bodies for these wandering ghosts.

Other activities, ranging from planting crops to hanging clothes outside to dry overnight, were also discouraged. One could never guess when a ghost would sneak by and try on some clothes. It was better to be safe than sick. Even people who were not particularly religious would make special offerings during this time of year.

This fear of ghosts, which still permeates Taiwanese society today, is derived from a complex view of the soul. A person has at least two souls.[4] One soul, the lower one, lingers in coffins or around graves after death. Devoid of life, it eventually burns itself out and disappears. The other soul, immortal and ethereal, is believed to have different possible destinations after death.

In one view, it suffers hideously in the courts of hell. According to one depiction, the third hell alone consists of sixteen 'wards', where tormenters continuously pierce their victims through the ribs, scrape the fat away from their bodies, pull out their finger- and toe-nails, scratch their hearts, and more. In the last court, the victim would drink a liquid that would make him or her forget the tortures. This way, the soul could be reincarnated into an earthly form. Such would be the fate for wives who offended their husbands, sons who did not complete their filial duties, and careless people who lost the records of their family burial grounds.[5]

To keep naughty children from forgetting the consequences they could face in hell, temples would pass out macabre comic books.[6] Sometimes religious parades would feature young men dressed as representatives from the courts of hell, coming to seek the souls of the damned.

In another view, souls face a different destination – a ghostly world that overlaps with the earthly world in time and space. This existence could be rather comfortable, as long as the deceased soul's descendants provided it with adequate food, clothing, housing and, most important, money: hence the need to burn paper joss money. Some families even burn exquisitely crafted paper houses equipped with furniture, gardens and a staff of servants.[7] Ghosts that receive nothing from their descendants start to go hungry until, in frustrated rage, they attack innocent humans.

'Watch out: If you're naughty, the gui will get you!' children were often warned. And it wasn't difficult to imagine the kind of havoc a hungry ghost could wreak. After the 1960 premiere of Enchanting Shadow, the first Chinese ghost movie, the subject became a popular one. In the 1970s one Taiwanese director, created more than twenty films about ghosts.[8]

The festival that welcomed gui into the world on the first day of Ghost Month did not always feel like a harbinger of fear. For Yufen, it felt like going to see a movie, since her family couldn't afford to see real movies. At around two in the afternoon, everyone in Ming-jian would gather around the temple near her house, toting glutinous rice-flour cakes and an assortment of dried food to offer the ghosts. Each family would mark their offerings with a triangular flag and place the food on a large bamboo altar. Few townspeople did not participate.

The townspeople took turns chatting, burning incense sticks for the ghosts, and catching up on the latest gossip. Certain townspeople would use various methods of divination to ask the ghosts if they had had their fill. If the answer was yes, the townspeople could eat the food and go home. If the answer was no, as Yufen so often hoped it would be, the festivities would continue – sometimes until midnight. Perhaps the ghosts didn't have much to eat, she thought. She liked to think that the hungry ghosts appreciated their acts of benevolence.

Ling Hu enjoyed giving offerings during Ghost Month, for doing so gave her a sense of peace. She took comfort in the idea that if she had done something to offend the ghosts or gods, there was a way to make up for it. She revelled in the idea that she could communicate with unseen powers.

Every year, during the fourteenth day of Ghost month, Ling's family would make paper lanterns designed to float. They would then take their lanterns to the Tamshui River on the western edge of Taipei. After the procession of lanterns prepared by the local temples had meandered by, the Hus would let their own lanterns set sail. The lanterns supposedly served as signposts that would help lost ghosts find their way back through the human world.

As Ling gazed at the flock of lanterns floating in the water, she hoped that her family's lanterns would float far away – a sign of good luck.

* * *

Red and yellow lanterns lined what would have otherwise been a nondescript dirt road. It was the fifteenth day of the first lunar month, the day of the Lantern Festival, which followed closely after Chinese New Year. Together, the two holidays formed an Eastern holiday season, full of gaiety.

Yufen patted her belly, thinking about the sweet soup dumplings she had just consumed. Her stomach rarely felt this full. The dessert symbolized unity and peace, and, with her stomach being as full as it was, that's exactly how she felt. She recalled the soothing sensation of kneading the soft, glutinous rice dough in the palm of her hand. She loved to watch her mother fill pieces of dough with sweet bean paste and shape them into perfectly round, white balls.

That was the easy part. Now that all the dumplings were gone, her mother headed off for her annual visit to a nearby Buddhist temple, with two teary-eyed sons in tow. When she entered the temple, she picked up a pair of *bwa-bway*, or divination blocks, and knelt before a statue of Buddha. Looking up at the idol with pleading eyes, she gently rubbed the red, crescent-shaped, wooden blocks between her fingers, as if doing so would increase her chances of getting the answer she desired. Curved on one side and flat on the other, the blocks were said to convey the will of a god, depending on how they landed when tossed. Several rumours surrounded their origin. According to one story, derived from the ancient Chinese book Twenty-four Filial Exemplars, 'an unfilial son who, having caused his mother's drowning and failed to find her body, in repentance cut a floating plank into two halves to divine his mother's will.'[9]

Mrs Wang closed her eyes and began to mouth her request: her son's school fees were due, and would the god please help her by letting her borrow money from his temple? She would pay him back in a year, with some interest, of course. Would he please let her get the loan this year?

She focused all of her energy on the question. Then, holding the blocks in her palms, she raised her hands to her forehead and let both blocks drop onto the ground. One flat and one curved side up – it was a yes! If she were to use the blocks for more mundane decision-making, like determining whether her food offerings were enough to fill a deceased ancestor, one yes might have been enough. But in this case, she had to get an affirmative answer three times in a row.

She concentrated on her question again and tossed the blocks. Two flat sides up. No. She had to start over. After a few hours of humiliating tossing, she could hear her sons bawling outside the temple.

Yufen's feverish cries pierced the night air. Her mother ran across the cold cement floor to her side and, despite the lateness of the hour, decided to use the only affordable remedy she knew of. She removed Yufen's sweaty clothes and took them to the nearest Tian Gong temple to be blessed. Some Taiwanese people would have gone there to seek out a *tang-ki*, who would cut his tongue and blot his blood on a sheet of joss money. The money would be carried around to ward off spirits.[10] In this case, Mrs Wang enlisted the service of a *sai-gong* who had mastered the art of writing out blessings in elegant calligraphy. The *sai-gong* said that Yufen had been exposed to a spirit of the dead and had offended it. She had to be blessed immediately in order to counter its anger.

Mrs Wang handed the spiritist a few dollars – a reasonably low price since this particular spiritist was less experienced in the art than others. Usually, the *sai-gong* would take the child's clothing and stamp it with the name of Tian Gong. The parent would then put the clothing back onto the child as a means of protection. But this sickness was different – more severe. In sweeping strokes, the *sai-gong* artfully wrote some blessings on a thin, yellow slip of paper, burnt it, and solemnly scattered the ashes into a cup of water. Mrs Wang took the cup home and told Yufen to drink.

The little girl obeyed. By now she had mastered the art of pursing her lips so that she could avoid swallowing the little black flakes that floated in the water.

* * *

So severe was Mei's illness that a herd of villagers gathered around, offering to carry her to another village where she could receive treatment. Along the way, she weakly closed her eyes. When she opened them, she saw a monstrous green snake, more than an arm's length in diameter, hanging on a tree. With what little energy she had left, she cried out, trying to warn the others. But nobody else saw it.

It was not to be the only unusual 'sighting' during Mei's childhood. Once, as she stood outside of her house, she spotted an elderly neighbour making her way to a nearby outhouse. Mei didn't think much of the incident – until she discovered that the neighbour had died many years before.

But Mei's early contact with the spiritual realm paled in comparison with that of her father and great aunt, both tribal shamans. While her father tended to conduct his duties discreetly, her great aunt openly exercised her spiritual powers.

Once, one of Mei's few friends asked to be taken to this great aunt. 'I like this boy,' she said. 'Can your great aunt cast a spell to make him like me back?' By the time the two girls arrived at the woman's house, they were filled with anticipation. Upon hearing the request, Mei's great aunt started dancing, circling, sweeping her arms up and down. Her fingers sprinkled rice and water into the air, as if she was sowing seeds. Then she waved around some leaves and began to moan in the unintelligible language of the gods. Finally, the gods were pleased with her offerings, and the spell was complete.

To Mei's delight, the boy started taking interest in her friend soon after. Unfortunately, the feelings were fleeting. After six months, the boy virtually hated her. This didn't lessen Mei's faith in her great aunt's abilities, however. She just figured that certain powers of the spirits had an expiration date.

Mei would never forget the day she discovered that these powers also had a dark side. Her father was telling her how someone asked him to kill a person from another tribe and, reluctant to do it himself, he sought out Mei's great aunt. Solemnly, the woman put a knife inside a box and started to chant.

A few days later, the box was opened. The knife dripped with blood. Rumour had it that by this time, its victim had already died.

* * *

The Hu family temple, designed to venerate all the dead ancestors of the family, was simple and neatly kept. Located on a hill in Tucheng, the place of Ling's birth, it featured a pond and a garden – evidence of the family's wealth. On the anniversary of each ancestor's death, at least one Hu family member would visit the temple to burn incense and appease the ancestor's ghost. And during Chinese New Year, the whole extended family would congregate there to worship the deceased.

Thanks to generations of prosperity, Ling's family had financed the construction of another temple as well – a major Mazu temple in Panciao. Religious contributions like these helped their family gain social prestige and religious merit. Since more Taiwanese were striking it rich, the competition had become fierce.

As with the Hu family temple, Ling's entire extended family would worship together at this Mazu temple at least once a year. They would also convene on the first and fifteenth of every month at a small Mazu temple closer to home. Occasions such as these were not only times of worship. They were also family reunions.

* * *

On a normal day, Yufen would have skipped with excitement at seeing so many of her older brothers and sisters return home to Ming-jian at the same time. Because of the age gap between siblings, the oldest four grew up separately from the youngest five. She knew little about her three oldest brothers and her older sister, because they had long since moved away. Like most rural families at the time, the Wangs didn't have a telephone, so a visit from an older sibling was always delightfully unexpected.

But this time was different. When her older siblings came home no one celebrated. Their fifty-something father was ill – so ill that most of the family thought he would not survive. With a situation this dire, everyone knew only one thing could save him.

By midnight, all the out-of-town siblings had arrived. Mrs Wang brought out a worship table with two high platforms on top. Then she brought out the offerings. Solemnly, slowly, she placed dishes of fruit, sweets and other snacks on the lower two levels, as well as a 'holy' selection of meats: one whole chicken, one fish, and a hunk of pork. Candles sat on the top level. The silence thickened as the children focused all their attention on their mother's movements. Yufen couldn't remember ever being more afraid. Her only hope, their makeshift altar, loomed above her like the Towel of Babel, reaching towards Tian Gong – their most high god.

In the flickering candlelight, Mrs Wang started muttering prayers to Tian Gong. Yufen's oldest brother knelt before the altar, his eyes filled with humble tears. His nose almost touched the ground as he bowed. Again. Again. And again.

'Please!' he cried out. 'Please give my father ten more years of life. You can take away ten years from my life. Please give him ten more years!'

Yufen felt shocked at her brother's behaviour. At the same time, she admired it. At the age of twenty-five, he had become like a second father to her. So riveted was she on his slouched figure and tear-stained face that she didn't notice the tears filling her own eyes.

Mr Wang's health eventually improved, though only gradually, and after much care. Around the same time, Yufen stopped going to church. She was in junior high school.

* * *

In junior high, one of Ling's friends, knowing Ling's fascination with religion, introduced her to Yi Guan Dao, the Way of Unity. The sect was organized in China in the 1920s and was brought to Taiwan by Yi Guan Dao missionaries after World War II. Yi Guan Dao got its name by integrating elements of Confucianism, Taoism, Buddhism and Islam, as well as minor ideas from other faiths like Christianity. The Yi Guan Dao missionaries taught that all people would be perpetually trapped in a cruel cycle of death and rebirth – unless they became Yi Guan Dao members. Then they would have the chance to earn their way into the Western Heaven by atoning for the misdeeds of their own past lives and the lives of their ancestors.[11]

Although Yi Guan Dao would not be considered legal until 1984, it had already begun to spread like an epidemic throughout Taiwan.[12] Press reports released in 1984 would suggest that, shrouded in secrecy but highly organized, Yi Guan Dao lured in as much as 20 per cent of Taiwan's population, including Ling.[13]

In accordance with its supposed inclusiveness of all religions, Yi Guan Dao regarded the scriptures of all major religions as sacred texts – though the followers of such religions were believed to be seriously misguided.[14] Yi Guan Dao included all major Taiwanese gods in its pantheon – though Ji Tian Lao Mu reigned at the very top.

The Yi Guan Dao shrine that Ling visited was on the roof

of a neighbour's house. Any person who earned the sect's approval, mobilized eight followers, and became a vegetarian would qualify to open a temple in his or her home. Furthermore, such a person would be worshipped like a god after death.

The neighbour's temple featured a traditional altar with elaborate brass oil lamps[15] and the statues of several gods, including Guan Yin[16], the goddess of mercy and childless women, who would come to be Ling's personal favourite. Incense sticks were burned there every day, and offerings of fruit that had been placed on the altar would be changed about once a week. Since Yi Guan Dao was technically illegal at that time, only initiated members could take part in its ceremonies, Ling was told by the ageing man who owned and ran the temple. He urged her strongly to initiate.

Although Ling was eager to do this, she knew that such a decision – like most major decisions in a Taiwanese person's life – required parental approval. Surprisingly, her mother agreed without any hesitation.

'Really? Have you been before?' Ling asked curiously.

'Well, I once joined a Yi Guan Dao shrine that one of your great uncles had in his home,' her mother answered.

Only one thing held Ling back. She would have to become a vegetarian and give up her favourite food – chicken. So she decided to be initiated, but not as a full member.

'Anyway, I don't think what I do or don't eat makes any difference to my beliefs,' she reasoned. Little did she know that her love for chicken would change her life.

The day of the initiation ceremony arrived, and Ling felt energized. More than fifty members attended the event. The master of another temple – a title supposedly granted to him by the gods – had been invited to conduct the ceremony and deliver a sermon. Ling listened carefully as he described the three kinds of money gods: gods of heavenly money, gods of earthly money and gods of human money. He demonstrated Yi Guan Dao's 'three treasures': a mantra, a secret hand position and a symbolic opening of a door in the body so that the soul could depart properly.[17] Then members of the congregation, supposedly inspired by the gods, stood up and shared stories about the initiates. Ling hoped that no stories would be told about herself. At last came the time of confession.

'Are you willing to become a follower of Yi Guan Dao?'

'Yes, I am willing to become a follower,' Ling answered.

In the following weeks, Ling attended classes that taught her such secrets as the meaning of the secret hand position that had been demonstrated during her initiation. Ling was required to attend these classes at least once a week – a light load, compared to the requirements of other Yi Guan Dao shrines.

Even though Ling was too young to have a job, she tried to donate as much money as she could to the shrine. Worship ceremonies were held twice a day, and snacks were provided for all who attended. From what little knowledge Ling would retain about Yi Guan Dao, it didn't seem all that different from popular Taiwanese religion.

So during this time, Ling continued to worship at other temples. After all, Yi Guan Dao claimed to be generally compatible with all other religions – except for Christianity. Ling could set foot in any Buddhist or Taoist temple that she wished. But church was strictly prohibited.

*   *   *

Mei's mother forced her to go to church – a rather odd occurrence, she always thought, since her father was a tribal shaman. When her parents' first two children died at a young age, her mother came to believe that the devil had taken them away. Soon after, some foreign missionaries with the True Jesus Church came to their village. Mrs Yang was more than eager to see what their religion was all about.

The True Jesus Church,[18] which was established in Beijing in 1917 and came to Taiwan nine years later, claimed to be the one and only true church. It taught that all real Christians would have the ability to speak in tongues, so Mrs Chen frequently muttered her prayers in a way that Mei could not understand. Several times, Mei tried to imitate the unusual sounds that came out of her devout mother's mouth.

'Stop it!' her mother scolded. 'The spirit's not in you, so you just can't imitate it!' Mei scowled.

'Do these prayers have any meaning?' she thought suspiciously. In addition, she thought it odd that, despite her mother's devotion, the woman still went to Mei's great aunt for help on occasion. Once, Mrs Chen asked the great aunt to cast a spell on Mei when she was sick. The woman complied. Chanting in the gods' language, she lightly scratched Mei's body with a tree branch. Mei still couldn't figure out why her mother would call on a shaman. The doubt gave her one reason to avoid her mother's religion.

Of course, there were other reasons too. The True Jesus missionaries strictly prohibited all smoking and drinking, which were deeply rooted habits for the Tso people. Although Mei was too young to take an interest in these activities herself, she would sometimes sit outside, casually observing her neighbours as they ate and drank.

'Go back in the house right now!' her mother fumed when she caught Mei in this second-hand sin. She grabbed her daughter by the hair and dragged her home. 'You can't go anywhere near alcohol!'

Mrs Chen's conversion affected her husband as well.

'My god won't come near me, and it's all your fault!' he would lament. 'I'm still learning about being a shaman, and you're keeping me from developing my supernatural powers! The spirits won't come to me when you're around.'

Then when Mei was around seven years old, her father's arm was severely burned by a gas lamp that had tipped over. As he cringed in pain, her mother started to pray for him. The pain subsided. After a night or so, his wounds got better. Touched by the healing power that he was no longer able to conjure up himself, the burned shaman decided to join the True Jesus Church.

It was a decision that meant little to his children because his lifestyle remained virtually the same, apart from church attendance and a hiatus in the casting of spells. Mei would watch him with amusement as he sneaked out of the house to smoke.

Once, when Mrs Chen found a stray cigarette butt on the ground, she hit her husband three times. Expressionless, the man said nothing. Later, Mei asked her father:

'Daddy, how did you feel when Mum beat you?'

'Well, your Mum is right,' he sighed. 'I shouldn't smoke.'

Although Mei had been baptized as an infant, she had never been told that she could have a relationship with Jesus. As often as she could, she ran out of the house as her mother prepared to go to church. On days when she couldn't avoid the matter, she sat listlessly during the sermons.

'So boring ... so strict ...' she would think to herself. 'And I can't understand any of this Bible stuff.'

What made church even worse was that its leader had a knack for fiercely condemning his thirty to forty members during his sermons.

'According to the Bible, you are all wrong!' he would say, often ostracizing individuals in the congregation for petty sins. Mrs Chen, like most of the other church members, was a target of his condemnations, though Mei could only roll her eyes. It all seemed hypocritical to her, considering the widely circulating rumours that the leader was misusing church funds.

Every legalistic tirade augmented the disgust that Mei's siblings felt towards the church. Every rant made them want to rebel. Every experience Mei had with the True Jesus Church justified her conviction that she didn't want to have anything to do with Jesus.

* * *

No sparks flew the first time Ling found out that Christianity existed. She was blooming into an adolescent, and her affluent parents sent her younger brother and sister to a Catholic kindergarten, which indicated to her that the world contained religions other than Taiwanese folk religion, a muddled mixture of Buddhism and Taoism. However, the implications of this realization didn't become clear to Ling until she had the opportunity to attend a Christian high school.

Every Saturday afternoon, her school hosted a student fellowship group, where students would receive New Testaments, read the Bible, sing hymns, and occasionally volunteer at a local orphanage. Anywhere from twenty to thirty students would attend, on and off; like Ling, most of them came from families who worshipped idols. As far as Ling could tell, none of the students who attended were really Christians.

One week, the students were instructed to open their Bibles to 1 Corinthians 13. Ling started to read: 'Love is patient, love is kind. It does not envy, it does not boast, it is not proud. It is not rude, it is not self-seeking, it is not easily angered, it keeps no record of wrongs. Love does not

delight in evil but rejoices with the truth. It always pro-
tects, always trusts, always hopes, always perseveres.' For a
brief moment, she thought about Jesus' love. Then she
thought about the despondent children she had seen in the
orphanage. She struggled to keep tears from coming out.

'That's the kind of love I'm looking for,' she thought.
'That's the kind of love I want to give others.' But before she
knew it, the feeling was gone.

She wasn't quite sure why she felt drawn to the group
week after week. The Bible lessons were interesting
enough. Also, her teachers invited her to the group, and
like many Taiwanese people, she found it hard to turn
down an invitation from an authority figure. Yet
Christianity still seemed like a foreign religion to her – a
religion her parents tolerated, but did not condone. A religion that seemed so different from her other beliefs, which
so readily applied to her daily life. Not once did she tell her
family about her experiences with Christianity. Not once
was she encouraged to believe and be baptized.

The leaders of the fellowship group taught her how to
pray, so when she encountered problems at school, she
would sometimes talk to God about them. She would talk to
other gods too. She became a self-proclaimed expert at
shopping for good, accessible fortune-tellers. Selection
depended on many factors: the nature of her question, the
amount of detail that she wanted in a response, her relationship with various fortune-tellers and temple representatives, the 'preferences' of various gods and, of course,
how much money she had on hand.[19] She used fortune-
telling not only to predict the future, but also to better
understand her life and help her make decisions.

One fortune-teller told her that the spirit of Guan Yin
was within her. If she ever needed help, Guan Yin would be
the god to count on, she was told. At the time, such advice

seemed rather frivolous, for her problems were relatively few and far between.

When Ling graduated from high school, she thought she was ready to dive into the sophisticated intricacies of the adult world. For the next twenty years, she would have no contact with the church.

Notes

1. David K. Jordan, *Gods, Ghosts and Ancestors: The Folk Religion of a Taiwanese Village*, Berkeley: University of California Press, 1971, p. 79
2. Jordan, *ibid.* p. 82
3. Gui – Chinese word for ghost, it describes the lost and destructive soul of a person who has not been properly worshipped after death.
4. Jordan, *ibid.* p. 82
5. Jordan, *Mom's and Moskowitz, ibid*
6. Jordan, *Mom's and Moskowitz, ibid*
7. Jordan, *ibid.* p. 33
8. Taipei Times, October 8 , 2004
   www.taipeitimes.com/News/feat/archives/2004/16/08
9. Mark Caltonhill, *Private Prayers and Public Parades*: *Exploring the Religious Life of Taipei,* Dept. of Information: Taipei City Gort. p. 77.
10. Jordan, *ibid.* p. 68
11. Bosco, *ibid.* p. 434
12. Bosco, *ibid.* p. 424
13. Bosco, *ibid.* p. 434
14. Bosco, *ibid.* p. 434
15. Bosco, *ibid.* p. 430
16. Guan Yin – the 'Regarder of Cries', the Chinese goddess of compassion was originally a male bodhisattva in Indian Buddhism.
17. Bosco, *ibid.* p. 425
18. True Jesus Church: members.tjc.org/sites/en/default.aspx
19. Jordan, *ibid.* p. 60

Chapter 3

'Cities must be full of rich people and dark buses,' Yufen Wang had once speculated. Since she had never been to a major city before, she had all sorts of romantic notions about what city life was like. In fact, apart from rare excursions to her grandmother's house, she had hardly ventured outside of her rural hometown of Ming-jian. Until now.

Yufen was on the brink of graduating from junior high school when her father suffered a massive stroke. He was sent to the hospital, and his speech became unintelligible. The shock of the incident had barely set in before Yufen and her siblings realized that, if they wanted their family to survive, they would all need to start working immediately – a tragic irony, considering how Mr Wang continually emphasized education as the only way out of their dire poverty. One of Yufen's older brothers didn't even have time to celebrate his high school graduation; he left for work before he could receive his diploma.

Because Yufen had no high school education, it became clear that she would have to find a job at a factory. Due to a recent boom in industrial development, demand for unskilled factory workers was so high that Taiwan's unemployment rate, which had hovered around 20 per cent when Yufen was born, had fallen to 5.2 per cent by 1963.[1]

In the end, Yufen found herself on a bus heading to Taichung, a major city in central Taiwan. It had been decided that she would work at a plastics factory there. For the next one to two hours, a plethora of feelings boiled within her. On the one hand, she tried to relish her antici-pation and excitement at having the opportunity to start anew, to see the world outside of Ming-jian. On the other hand, she felt bitter about not being able to finish school, and being forced to leave home so suddenly. She felt like a baby bird, booted out of its nest before learning to fly.

Yet, according to Confucian ethics, which emphasize group interests over personal interests, co-operation over competition, and obligation over rights, Yufen had no choice in the matter. She knew that this was her duty.

Little did she know that her predicament was not at all unusual. In 1965, only 3 per cent of employed people had received any higher education, and 22.9 per cent were illit-erate.[2] Yufen was just like thousands of other children who were migrating to the factories: children who, due to a lack of education, would grow up to be more influenced by tra-dition and idol worship than their upper-class counter-parts.

Yufen hadn't yet arrived in Taichong, and she already missed home. She was sixteen.

* * *

The factory resembled a concentration camp, jammed with a thousand or so workers donning drab grey or blue uni-forms. Most of the workers were between seventeen and twenty-seven years old. Yufen felt as if she had been swal-lowed up by a corporate giant.

The plastics factory manufactured raincoats, rain-boots and other goods carrying the label 'Made in Taiwan', which was quickly becoming a household term world-wide.

When Yufen first arrived, she tried to cling to the one person she already knew – a classmate whose family situation in Ming-jian also forced her to begin work at the factory. But after being assigned to work in separate parts of the factory, the two rarely saw each other again.

Yufen's job was to inspect the merchandise coming down the assembly line and to remove faulty items. Day in and day out, she would fix her eyes on the passing items and set her fingers in monotonous motion for a length of eight hours, interrupted only by one thirty-minute lunch break. Stern managers kept a watchful eye on the workers, and as Yufen avoided their accusing gazes, she found herself trapped in a constant state of anxiety.

Despite all this, she actually enjoyed the work. Because it was her first job, she didn't realize how low her salary was – a little over 600 Taiwanese dollars a month (about 18 US dollars today). Although she sent most of it home to pay for her father's medical care and only kept $200 a month for herself, she felt rich. When she was little, she had been plagued with the insecurity of having nothing to offer her family, since many of her brothers and sisters were much older. She had felt like a negligible member. Now, at the age of sixteen, she could finally make a contribution. And since her company already provided her with housing and meals, she had spending money for the first time in her life.

The factory dormitories bunked six people in each room. 'Very good,' Yufen thought, considering that this would be the closest thing to university life that she would ever experience. The dorms even had lounges equipped with newspapers and televisions – luxury items in those days. Even though all the employees had to rush through their mealtimes, Yufen enjoyed them, for each meal usually included three small dishes and a soup – a feast compared to what she typically had received at home.

Since the factory adjoined a cultural district full of roadside food stalls, Yufen and her youthful co-workers would sometimes go exploring after work. Her favourite pastime was buying a bowl of noodles for $4 or $5 (about 15 cents today) and devouring it bit by bit.

The factory was also near Tunghai University, a Christian college known for its architecture and landscaping. Sometimes Yufen and her friends would relax by strolling under the cool shade of the campus' mighty acacia and ficus trees. The Luce Chapel, built only a few years earlier in 1963, also served as an amusing attraction on campus.

'How do you think this was made?' Yufen's friends would ask, pointing at the building, which resembled an enormous tent. They would then eagerly peek into the dark interior through the front windows of the building. Rows of pews faced a golden cross, which hung over the pulpit. They figured that, since they weren't students, they were not allowed to go inside.

In her spare time, Yufen also frequented a forty-year-old Confucian graveyard that she considered beautiful in its naturalistic disarray. There, she would prance about among the osmanthus bushes until the sweet aroma of their tiny white flowers released her from all her worries.

Although Yufen went home just about every weekend, she still enjoyed the feeling of being independent from her mother and father. With this independence came her abstention from religious practice during the week. This was not an active decision of unbelief, but rather a sign of nonchalance. Taiwanese religious customs were time-consuming and expensive, and she had no interest in taking part when it was not required of her.

During this time, Yufen functioned largely like a robot, programmed to follow orders. She never thought about the meaning of life, never thought to analyse the world around her, never thought to ponder over spiritual matters.

One night, she woke suddenly, startled by a feeling of being pinned down to the bed. She opened her mouth to scream, but no sound came out.

'Is it a ghost?' she thought momentarily. But after calming down, she deduced that her stressful work environment, not a spirit, had caused the panic.

The poor working conditions began to take their toll on her youthful body. A haze of dust constantly filled the factory, making it difficult for Yufen to breathe properly. She developed a sinus infection, and as she worked, she struggled to keep her head lowered enough to see the assembly line and raised enough to prevent the smelly pus in her nose from dripping out. Eventually the problem became so serious that surgery would be necessary. She had no choice but to retire from factory work – at the age of seventeen.

Newly fitted with an armour of self-reliance, Yufen felt ready to become a real city girl. By this time, Taiwan's economy had begun to show signs of preparing for flight. Per capita income was increasing,[3] and throngs of young people from the southern part of Taiwan were migrating to Taipei to find work.

Among these were Yufen's oldest sister and two of her older brothers. They already lived in a long, narrow apartment building that housed five families on each floor. Like most of the other families in the building, the three siblings all lived together in one small room. Since there was no space for beds, they all slept on the floor. The Wangs felt lucky to live in such a place since, at the very least, it adjoined a balcony. Though their quarters were cramped, they invited Yufen to live with them while she looked for a job.

Yufen's sister had heard all kinds of stories about naive young women from the countryside who found work in seemingly harmless restaurants or hair salons, only to discover that sleazy business was conducted behind the facade. To avoid all risks, Yufen's sister advised her to look for a job at a stationery store – simple, stable and sinless.

Every morning, Yufen would scour the newspaper for job listings. Before long, she found a job as a stationery store clerk, which paid a whopping $800 a month. She would have the luxury of two days off each week, and would live and eat at the store – a relief, despite the hospitality of her older siblings.

Yufen soon discovered that, although she would no longer be lost in a labyrinth of nameless workers, this job was just as stressful as the last one. Her boss, Mr Huang, took his Japanese education very seriously and, like the Japanese, considered orderliness to be a supreme virtue. From 9:30 a.m. to 10 p.m., he would sit on a chair behind the clerks, eyeing them closely as they spoke with customers, counted change and brought out items from behind the counter, as in a pharmacy. Mr Huang's iron grip even extended beyond business hours, for he often prevented his employees from leaving the premises or spending money.

'If you go out, you'll just buy anything. Then you won't have enough money,' he said, eyeing his clerks distrustfully. 'This is a bad habit to have.' As he disapprovingly examined whatever they managed to purchase, Yufen came up with a hypothesis: Mr Huang feared that his employees would start stealing money if they found their salaries to be insufficient.

However, not every aspect of the job was so strict. Like most Taiwanese businessmen, Mr Huang encouraged the clerks to offer discounts and throw in free items in order to maintain good relationships with the customers. In Taiwan, good relationships were, and are, of utmost importance. Yufen enjoyed the sense of empowerment that came with this part of her job. She no longer served as an expendable cog in an industrial machine. For the first time in her life, she came in daily contact with white-collar people. She learned how to serve people politely, and she learned about the world through the stories her customers would tell. She loved to chat with them.

She harboured very different sentiments towards the family she now lived with. Mr Huang's daughter, who was around the same age as Yufen, looked down on the clerks as if they were of an inferior species. Mrs Huang was the same, holding her head so high that Yufen often caught sight of the bottom of her nose.

Every night at the dinner table, Yufen and the other clerks were not allowed to eat until every member of the Huang family had had their fill. Yufen swallowed familiar feelings of envy as she remembered the idol feasts of her childhood – feasts that only her father's friends enjoyed. After watching the Huangs devour the choicest parts of the meal, Yufen nibbled at the food that was left, trying to disguise her injured pride. Anger bottled up inside of her as she fantasized about the sheath of stinging words she would use to attack the Huangs if circumstances had been different.

Her only ally was Mr Huang's oldest son who, several years older than her, had got into Tamkang College. Yufen had heard that the college was founded by Christians. Unlike the rest of his family, Mr Huang's son chatted cordially with her, and one day invited her out to a movie.

Yufen rarely went out with men because, even if they were 'just friends', she knew that things could get complicated. For her, going out to a movie with a boy required a great deal of consideration, but this time, she was unusually trusting.

'He just wants to be friends,' she thought to herself. Besides, she appreciated the fact that this Huang was willing to treat her more like an equal.

The evening started out like any other as they walked to the theatre together. Yufen avoided the back row as they found a spot in the dark theatre and sat down. Before long, he started to touch her. She tried to squirm away.

'We're watching a movie!' she thought, annoyance swelling up inside of her. 'Everyone behind us can see what's going on.'

He grabbed her hand and pulled it towards himself. Frightened, she tried to pull away.

'I can't believe this is happening! What should I do?'

She resisted for what seemed to her an eternity. He pushed her head down. She fought back angry tears. She wanted desperately to slap him, to run away.

'But what about my job? I can't lose my job!'

Yufen's heart pounded furiously as Mr Huang's son passed by at work. He glanced at her, acknowledged her presence, and walked away. He acted as if nothing had happened. Revulsion filled her heart.

She also began to despise herself. She wished that she had resisted him, that she had cried out for help.

'I'm such a stupid girl,' she thought to herself. 'So stupid, so stupid, so stupid ...' The self-effacement would continue like a broken record for years to come.

A year or two before the incident, Yufen's father had died. Although she had grieved, his death, which had been imminent, provided one consolation: finally, Yufen was freed from the responsibility of having to send money back home.

After the incident, Yufen lost all interest in keeping her job with the Huangs, especially since she had saved enough money to quit her job and look for a new one. She had endured the condescension, the distrust, for more than four years. But now the daily discomfort of seeing the boy, the shame in wondering why she didn't do more to fight back, was more than she could bear. Since elementary school, she had been all too familiar with the feeling of degradation – from begging for food to working under the whip of strict managers – but this agony was the worst of all.

Then came a way out. One day, a relative asked her, 'Would you be willing to work outside of Taipei, in Yungho? I know of a job at a stationery store there.'

'Well, at least I'll be far away from the Huangs,' Yufen thought. Little did she know that in escaping from one man who had devastated her life, she would land on the doorstep of another.

Mei Chen

Mei ran and ran, haunted by the lustful gaze of her twenty-four-year-old brother.

'I won't let him get to me this time,' she thought, running to a storeroom. Once inside, she locked the door and started to cry. She thought about the times he had grabbed her while nobody else was home. Locking the doors, he would try to overcome her again and again. Mei's sister had long imbued her with the importance of saving herself until marriage, and the words had sunk deeply into Mei's heart. Protecting her virginity with all her strength, Mei would always manage to fight her brother off until the return of her parents. The sound of their approaching footsteps would be music to Mei's ears, for immediately her brother would let go and run away.

Mei hated her brother. She hated waking up, only to face another day of fear. She hated being home alone, which was why she took refuge in the storeroom, reeking of hay. When her mother returned from work, Mei tentatively emerged from her hiding place. She knew that her mother would not be pleased.

'Why haven't you cooked?' Mrs Chen demanded. 'Why haven't you at least started a fire?' Livid, Mrs Chen started to beat her daughter. As Mei endured the blows, she reminded herself that her virginity was worth it all. She wished that she could tell her mother the truth about her brother – but, in her mind, this was simply impossible. These things could not be discussed.

One morning, around four o'clock, Mei was sleeping soundly while her mother started to prepare breakfast. Ever since her parents had partitioned their house so that her older brother and his wife could sleep in a separate room, Mei had slept more peacefully. Although it was challenging to avoid him during the day, at least she did not have to share his bed at night.

Yet on this morning, she felt something. She woke up with a start. And she shockingly discovered that the attacker was not her brother. It was her father.

Sensing that Mei had woken, her father removed his hand from her, as if nothing had happened. Mei's virginity was still intact. Her faith in her father, however, was not. Now she knew why she had always been a bit suspicious of him.

Mei hated home. She much preferred going to school, where she could spend time with people who couldn't hurt her. Among them was her younger brother, a simple-minded boy who understood her well, though she never told him about the attacks. One day, he discovered that Mei's period had come and, as usual, she didn't have the money to buy sanitary napkins.

'Here's some money,' he said, handing her a few coins. 'I don't need it.'

As Mei neared the end of her last year of elementary school, she began to see junior high as her only escape; then, she could live in a school dormitory far away from the home she so desperately wanted to escape. Freedom seemed so close at hand ... until she suddenly fell ill. It was then that her parents broke the news: since they were getting old and their financial troubles had worsened, Mei would have to stay home and work with them in the fields instead of continuing her education.

All the quiet rage that had pent up inside of her erupted. Her childhood innocence had crumbled before her eyes, and her school life was the only thing left standing. Now, her parents wanted to take that away. Mei wanted to provoke them. To make them feel her hurt.

'Why can everybody else go to school and not me? How come my older sisters can go to school? WHY? I don't want to work! I DON'T WANT TO!'

'You just don't understand things,' her mother retorted. 'When your sisters were in high school, we were younger then. We could work hard to support them. But now we can't. You're just going to have to work,' she declared, sentencing her daughter to a few more years of misery.

In 1968, Taiwan's Kuomingtang Regime extended compulsory education to include three years of junior high in addition to six years of elementary school.[4] Also, one of Mei's older sisters had recently graduated, leaving the Chens with one less tuition bill to pay for. After one year of working in the fields, Mei would get another shot at education after all.

Despite Mei's victories in athletic contests, her battles at home began to eat away at her self-confidence. When she started junior high, she was second in her academic class, but soon she dropped to the bottom.

Because her mother's cough had worsened, Mei returned home every weekend to help out with her family's farming work. She convinced her parents to let her sleep in a room by herself. Although the room's thin Japanese-style paper door did little to protect her from the other family members, it at least gave Mei a semblance of security. At night her overworked muscles enjoyed the respite offered by her bed.

One night, Mei buried her problems under a heavy blanket of sleep. Even an earthquake would not have been able to wake her.

Suddenly, pain seared through her body. It felt like a knife had been shoved between her legs. She shrieked.

Opening her eyes, she caught a glimpse of her oldest brother climbing off her. She shrieked again. He ran out of the room. She couldn't believe it. For more than four years she had resisted his agonizing advances. And yet it still came to this.

Despite her cries, nobody came to console her. Her parents probably thought that she was having a bad dream.

Mei's brother never touched her again. But her life had already become a nightmare. The memory of the dreadful night haunted her, and she guessed that her brother had wanted nothing more than to be with a virgin. Then again, it was only a guess. At least it gave her a reason – any reason – for what had happened.

She became obsessive-compulsive, washing herself as often as possible. Even after many years had passed, she would wipe down the tables and windows in her apartment several times a day.

After the rape, Mei mostly kept to herself. While all the other tribal villagers celebrated their harvests with singing and dancing, Mei stayed at home.

'I'm not good enough to be with everyone else,' she thought. 'I'm dirty. I'm ugly. I hate myself.'

Mei's self-inflicted introversion led to profound loneliness, but she just couldn't stand to be around people in her tribe, especially the men. The fear of her childhood had turned to hate, as it appeared that she had nothing left to protect. Aggravated by constant hunger and fatigue, she stopped listening to her mother and started throwing temper tantrums. Her mother, without asking for a reason behind Mei's sudden change in behaviour, would simply yell at her for being disrespectful.

There was one person who knew about and shared in Mei's grief. A friend next door had been raped by her own brother many times over several years. One day, thirteen-year-old Mei was talking with her cousin and her neighbour behind a small clinic. All three were noticeably depressed. Although Mei's cousin had not been sexually abused, her uncle was forcing her to marry a man she despised. As the girls shared their woes, it became clear that none of them wished to continue living.

'Let's die together,' the other two girls resolved. One of them produced a bottle of fertilizer. Realizing that she could not deter them, Mei ran to enlist help. When she returned with several other villagers, they found that the two girls had already ingested the poison and were writhing on the ground. Since the teeth of Mei's cousin were grotesquely crooked, someone was able to shove a spoon into her mouth in order to induce vomiting. Another person grabbed Mei's neighbour and tried to do the same, but to no avail. As she clenched her teeth together, blood started oozing out of her ears, her eyes, and the corners of her mouth. Then she started to scream.

'May my whole family be cursed!' she shouted. 'I will get revenge!'

Soon after the girl's death, her family's house burned down. Mei figured that the curse had come true.

By the time Mei turned fourteen, she had experienced more anguish than some adults experience in their entire lifetimes. She had lost all hope for the future. With no goals left to achieve, she stopped doing her homework.

'What's the point of living, anyway? Why am I so messed up? And if I just die, then where would my spirit go?' she would ask herself. In stark contrast to her explosive nature at home, she became a pensive, quiet loner at school. Perceiving this as good behaviour, one of her teachers began to favour her. The teacher occasionally asked her to help correct other students' tests after class, an honour usually reserved for only the best students. The teacher also invited Mei to her house on occasion. Sometimes Mei would go there with another classmate, who would eventually land a solid job as a physical education teacher, and together they would sample their teacher's homemade cooking.

'Why do you get to go to Teacher's house?' other students asked jealously.

'Because she wants us to help her with things,' Mei replied. Influenced by Confucian thinking that highly values the teacher–student relationship, Mei took great pride in the favour she had earned. A flame inside her was rekindled as she started dreaming about one day becoming a teacher too.

The dream was short-lived. Eighteen years earlier, in 1953, among the estimated one million students enrolled in elementary and junior high school across the island, only 7.2 per cent were granted secondary education.[5] Now, an increasing number of Taiwanese students were enjoying access to secondary education, but the privilege was still determined by highly competitive entrance exams. In Mei's class, only one student passed the exam to get into a high school for training teachers. It was not Mei.

So after Mei graduated from junior high at the age of seventeen, she looked for another way to escape from home.

'I hate how Mum and Dad don't take good care of us! It would be better to get married quickly or find some other way to leave this place,' she hoped bitterly.

She got her wish. Soon enough, she found work at one of Taiwan's largest fabric factories in Tainan. Like Yufen, she didn't mind the monotony of the work – in fact, she enjoyed it. Although she used to be self-conscious about the thickness of her meaty hands, roughened by years of hard labour, she forgot all about them in the factory. Her job was to carefully watch over the machines that spun the cloth, and whenever it was time to switch threads, she would nimbly remove the bobbin, throw it into a basket, and replace it before the machine could make any mistakes. Her job was so specialized that she never had the chance to visit other parts of the looming factory, where clothes were actually made.

In years to come, she would remember little about the experience, perhaps because her heart was busy mending its past hurts. When she wasn't working, she occasionally joined some of the other girls in making flowers for fun, using thin pieces of sponge. Mostly, though, she didn't make the effort to form any special relationships, even though she lived in the factory dormitory and had plenty of opportunities. She was so lonely that she even started to miss her family.

Two years later, Mei heard that a co-worker was planning to move to Taichung. Mei decided that she was ready for a change as well. This factory, though smaller, was similar to her previous place of employment. Aside from the musty smell that always lingered in the air, Mei enjoyed virtually every aspect of the job – the work itself, the managers, the environment, and, most of all, the steady income, which gave her a sense of stability that she never had when growing up. She felt satisfied doing something that her parents could not do – paying the tuition that would allow one of her brothers to attend a private technical college. When he started taking classes there, he hoped that his training would someday land him a stable government job as a physical education teacher. In the end, though, he was forced to drop out. Mei's meagre salary simply wasn't enough to keep him in school.

In years to come, Mei would continue to feel guilty about her inability to fund her brother's education. She knew all too well the feeling of giving up.

Ling Hu

'Girls don't need so much education,' Ling Hu's grandparents used to say. Ling's mother might have agreed with the statement when it came to other people's children; after all, she personally kept an apprentice around Ling's age, who had to quit school to work in her clothing shop. But Mrs Hu had a very different attitude towards her own children.

'If we have the financial ability to educate our children, we should do it,' she believed. When the children wanted to take music lessons, she bought a piano. When Ling began to prepare for her entrance exams, her family let her take expensive after-school classes in order to get ahead.

While many of Ling's classmates didn't make it to high school for financial or academic reasons, Ling enjoyed the benefits of a generously endowed education. Thanks to the after-school classes, she managed to pass the entrance exams for all three forms of secondary education: high school (the only route to university), technical college, and junior college. Since Ling's relatives, owning soda franchises in three cities, had been successful in business, her mother urged her to choose a two-year technical business college over high school. This would heighten her chances of finding a practical job, argued Mrs Hu.

Ling's mother was a practical woman who, after starting her own business, worked from 10 a.m. to 10 p.m. and had little time to look after her children and do housework. Though Ling nearly worshipped her mother, she secretly hoped that her life would be different, that she would find a husband who would provide for her financially and let her stay at home.

In the meantime, she had her parents, whom she could rely on. When she found out that she needed to find a business internship to complete the course requirements for her degree, she turned to them for help. Although her school offered her a prestigious internship with the government, she followed the example of her parents who would, without blinking, give to those in need: she shrugged and told the school to let her classmates take the opportunity. Her family would help her. And sure enough, they found her an internship at a bank belonging to a relative, as well as a subsequent job as an account clerk at her uncle's soda company.

Listening to her mother's advice truly paid off. At the He-Song Soda Company, Ling earned $3,000 a month, three times the average salary of her friends. Ironically, even though she had studied business, she knew very little about personal finance – a fact that didn't bother her at all. As a child, she had never worried about money. Not once. The very concept of saving money was foreign to her. Whenever her monthly pay cheques arrived, she would give them to her mother, who handled the family finances. Life was good.

At the soda company, Ling worked with three other account clerks, all relatives of her uncle. Nepotism had its benefits: her boss was straightforward yet easygoing towards her, her workload was light, and she got along well with her co-workers, who would often pass the days talking about every topic under the sun. When they didn't feel like eating the lunches provided by the company, they would plan their own menus together, go out to buy vegetables, and cook up a feast.

Ling got along so well with her co-workers that sometimes they would plan short holidays together. Once they went on a three-day tour to a destination known for its spectacular sunrises: Ali Mountain, Mei's childhood home.

Ling's job entailed answering the phone, arranging soda distribution routes, and writing up bills and receipts. She took special care to make the customers, mostly owners of small shops, feel comfortable with her.

Although Ling respected her uncle, she noticed that he had a nasty temper, especially when they had to deal with a surge of clientele during the hot summer months. At times like these, his wife, who also worked at the company, still treated him warmly and supported his leadership. Ling firmly believed that her aunt's attitude played a major role in her uncle's success, and Ling hoped that, someday, she would be just like her. In fact, she thought, she was already well on her way to becoming that kind of person – considerate, humble and ready to stand behind a man.

Although Ling loved her job and couldn't imagine working anywhere else, she began to feel restless. Living with her parents, was becoming an increasingly frustrating situation. Space wasn't the problem; after she graduated from junior high, her maternal grandfather had built several apartment blocks and gave each of his children an apartment. By now, Ling's parents owned not one, but two apartments.

But a seedling of jealousy had taken root in Ling's heart. Ever since her younger brother was born, Ling had cooked, cleaned and done everything she could to help her chronically busy mother. Ling was a traditionalist who believed strongly in the Confucian idea, 'Recompense kindness with kindness.'[6] She expected her mother to treat her well as a result of her hard work.

But in Ling's mind, it appeared that the very opposite was true. Not only did she feel that her efforts were underappreciated, but she also felt that her little sister, who was relatively apathetic in the department of household help, actually received more love. Perhaps, Ling guessed, her own independent, sometimes rebellious spirit had struck a dissonant chord with her mother.

She began to daydream. She would meet a responsible man, get married, move out of the house, and quit her job to raise children. She would be an excellent mother and an adoring wife. Sometimes, when she would turn on the television and see spouses fighting over money or a host of other things, she would sigh with relief.

'Thank goodness those things don't happen in real life,' she thought, smiling smugly. 'Thank goodness those things won't happen to me.'

Notes

1. Copper, *ibid*
2. Harrell & Huang, *ibid*, pp. 100–102.
3. Per capital income in 1952 was $186 and $203 in 1965. Shambaugh, *ibid*
4. Shambaugh, *ibid*
5. Shambaugh, *ibid*
6. www.quotationspage.com

Part 2

Love and Hate

Daughters of Jerusalem,
I charge you by the gazelles and by the does of the
    field:
Do not arouse or awaken love
until it so desires.   Song of Solomon 2:7

Chapter 4

Nothing about the tall, lanky man had caught twenty-five-year-old Ling Hu's eye, though she had seen him many times in passing. She was an account clerk for her uncle's thriving soda company; he was a delivery man. In her estimation, Yan Zhang was a man of unimpressive social stature.

One of Ling's relatives, however, saw something else. She saw that the man was hard working, raking in a decent salary. His hauntingly large eyes were set above high cheekbones, giving him a look of maturity that reminded his He-Song Cola co-workers that he was approaching middle age. As expected, the thirty-three-year-old was eager to find a wife, settle down and start a family.

'Why don't you two go out sometime and see what happens?' Ling's relative suggested. Ling figured that she had nothing to lose and agreed.

Growing up, Ling had tasted virtually every material pleasure a Taiwanese child her age could reasonably ask for. She was even used to seeing Taiwanese films for free at the movie theatres that her grandfather owned. But on their first date, Yan and Ling went out for a special treat: an American film. After the movie, the two chatted amicably about nothing in particular at a coffee shop. The whole evening was rather nondescript, though Ling did find Yan to be a kind man.

From then on, Yan walked Ling home after work almost

every day. Since Yan used to work with Ling's father at the Taiwan Tobacco and Wine Monopoly, Mr Hu grew so fond of Yan that he encouraged the suitor to come into their home. The two men talked mostly about work and trivial topics, and often watched TV together. Occasionally, Mr Hu even invited Yan to join their family for dinner.

As Yan and Ling started to date more seriously, Ling, who was rather pragmatic when it came to love, felt besieged by qualms. Yan did not enjoy studying, so he had dropped out of junior college as soon as his father died. Unlike his older brothers, he had no interest in higher education, which severely impeded his opportunities for advancement. In addition, he had no retirement fund and no long-term job security.

'You can do better than that!' Mrs Hu reprimanded when Ling started to mention her feelings towards Yan. Her mother's view of her boyfriend contrasted starkly with that of her father. 'You could marry a bank manager, or someone like that. Someone of the same class.' She reminded Ling that Yan was, of all things, a delivery man, a working-class labourer unworthy of her affections.

But the more her mother objected to the romance, the more Ling felt determined to continue in it. Subtle seeds of resentment that had been planted during her rebellious adolescence now sprouted into weeds that choked her relationship with her mother.

'You've always loved my sister more than you loved me,' Ling thought bitterly. 'You've never understood me. That's why you're criticizing me.'

Ling thought about how hard she had strived to help her busy mother with housework. Her younger sister, on the other hand, tended to evade chores, stating matter-of-factly, 'Why should I do it if you or Mum will always take care of it anyway?'

Despite years of cooking, scrubbing and washing, Ling

felt as if she received no appreciation in return. Her mother still seemed to love her sister more. Granted, Ling knew that her sister tended to be more submissive and compliant when family conflicts arose. Nonetheless, she was tired. Tired of feeling like Cinderella. Tired of living with her family. And she could think of only one solution: 'I might as well leave this family. Then we'll see who else will do the work.'

That was how Ling Hu propelled herself into love.

She tried to list off Yan's good qualities: A decent man, he worked hard, didn't come from a terrible background, and made enough money to support a small family. She found him to be physically attractive, and she believed that he would turn out to be a good husband and father some day.

Eventually, Yan and Ling's relationship progressed to an important juncture: It was time for their parents to meet each other. Ling knew that a positive outcome was unlikely, considering the depth of her mother's disapproval, yet she still hoped beyond hopes that the meeting would at least be a pleasant one. Then the day came.

When the doorbell rang, Mrs Hu refused to answer the door. She headed for her bedroom, saying to Ling along the way, 'Why are you in such a hurry to marry him? You should be able to find a better man who can give you a better life. This is all too rushed. Too poorly planned. You should act in a more dignified manner than this.' She shut the bedroom door.

Ling seethed with fury, unable to remove from her mind the image of her mother pleasantly greeting her sister's boyfriend when he had come over for a visit.

'Ma even took him out to dinner. She took him out to dinner,' Ling remembered, fighting back angry tears.

In the end, Ling's father managed to arrange a second meeting. But the damage had already been done.

* * *

When Yan's mother came all the way from Chiayi, a city in
the southern part of Taiwan, to pay a special visit, Ling
knew that the time of decision had come.

'Will you consider getting engaged to my son?' the
woman asked, in step with a traditional Taiwanese proposal. 'Will you please consider doing it soon?'

Ling paused. She knew that, since Yan was past the normal age of bachelorhood, his mother was eager to see him
married.

'I think it's too early,' Ling replied. 'My mum is still busy
working, and my little brother is only in elementary
school. Since I'm the oldest in the family, they still need me
at home.'

'That's OK, but ... why don't you just get engaged first?
I'll be so relieved if you do.'

Ling thought about Yan. Then she thought about the
glories of being a full-time housewife. Finally, she thought
about home – and how much she wanted to escape from it.
So after more than a year of dating Yan, she agreed to the
engagement.

In keeping with Taiwanese tradition, Yan's family then
confirmed the couple's compatibility with a temple fortune-teller, who performed a calculation based on factors
including their names and birth dates. Since the resulting
figure was even, they concluded that there were no cosmic
impediments to their marriage.[1] After receiving this
'divine' assurance, Yan's family sealed the engagement by
presenting Ling's family with betrothal gifts: engagement
cakes and 100,000 Taiwanese dollars – an extravagant
dowry that would traditionally be either refused, returned,
or saved for the couple's future family. Each family also
was expected to provide the other with twelve gifts: a hat, a
shirt, a suit, a watch and a pair of socks for the groom; a

coat, a purse and a pair of shoes for the bride; engagement rings; and other miscellaneous items.

'The whole thing doesn't have to be too luxurious,' Ling magnanimously assured her future mother-in-law. 'I'll understand.'

According to Taipei customs, the bride's family was responsible for hosting the engagement lunch banquet. The Hus picked an auspicious day on which to hold the ceremony, and when the day arrived, twenty tables of guests gathered under a neatly erected roadside tent in order to eat, drink and celebrate the occasion. Of all the tables, one was reserved for the groom's family, several of whom were stunned by the event, which seemed to overflow with extravagance, compared to a typical banquet in their hometown, Chiayi.

Before noon, an engagement ring had been placed on Ling's finger. By the end of the banquet, she had donned five different formal gowns that, to her, made for the most enjoyable part of the whole ordeal.

But after the excitement wore off, Ling was left with a hodgepodge of mixed feelings. On the one hand, she knew that Yan bore no resemblance to the ideal husband she had long envisioned. On the other, she felt that now that the engagement banquet had taken place, there was no way to avoid a wedding.

Mr Hu, still fond of Yan, sensed his daughter's apprehension in following through with the next step. 'Don't just delay the marriage and have this relationship drag on,' he said to her. 'If you really don't want to marry him, just end the relationship now.'

'He's right,' Ling thought to herself. 'I picked this man myself, didn't I? I was the one who made the choice.'

Only five months had passed since the engagement banquet, and the Hu's home again bustled with activity. The carefully chosen wedding date had arrived.

Since Ling had to be ready by 6 a.m., she slept little and rose early to get her makeup done. Many people assisting with the wedding preparations had been busy all through the night, and when Ling got out of bed, the sweet aroma of rice-ball soup lingered in the air.

The beautician who had done Ling's make-up for the engagement party was not available so early in the day, so Ling's cousin had referred her to a nearby salon. When Ling arrived, however, she was shocked by what she saw: the beautician was pregnant. It was said that having contact with a pregnant woman on one's wedding day would bring bad fortune and, for a moment, Ling felt convinced that her marriage would be doomed. Already, her wedding had displayed telltale signs of bad luck: several people on her guest list had been born in the Chinese zodiac's year of the tiger – a 'curse' which would have normally prevented them from attending a wedding if it weren't for the fact that Ling was a close relative. But to sit in front of the beautician's bulging belly while her face was painted ... Ling could not imagine a more distressing turn of events – that is, until she looked into the mirror.

The face staring back at her looked nothing like what she had expected: Her eyes looked flat and plain, her cheeks over-dramatically pink. On this critical day, the day on which she wanted to present her best to her new family, she looked like this. She began to weep. As her make-up started to smear, relatives gathered around and tried frantically to fix the damage. But the tears continued to slide down her face, taking with them bits of make-up, slivers of past hopes.

After Ling had regained her composure, she returned home to meet up with the groom, who was ready to drive her to his family's home in Chiayi. It was time to formally say goodbye. Ling stood in front of her family altar, which had always been a significant fixture in her life. Standing in that familiar spot helped calm her nerves.

As she had done so many times before, she presented offerings of incense to her ancestors, but on this morning, she prayed a different kind of prayer.

'I'm getting married today. So from now on, I'll belong to Yan's family. Goodbye.' After she had parted with her ancestors, she knelt before her parents and said an official farewell. Then the wedding party packed into three cars and headed off to Yan's childhood home in Chiayi.

Upon their arrival, Yan and Ling headed straight for the Zhang family altar. A senior family member lit some incense sticks and passed them to the couple, who worshipped the ancestors, announcing that they had arrived and were about to get married.

Although this supposedly came as breaking news to Yan's ancestors, the gods had purportedly been aware of the situation for a long while. Yan's mother had long ago approached Tian Gong, the patron god of Yufen Wang's rural childhood village, begging him to provide a bride for her son, who was approaching middle age. The night before the wedding, she had expressly worshipped Tian Gong, thanking him for answering her prayers.

Once Yan and Ling had completed their worship rites, several of Yan's closest relatives and family friends filed into the house, which had been specially decorated for the occasion. Ling handed red envelopes filled with cash to the children who were present, as well as gifts of underwear for the boys and handkerchiefs and soap for the girls. She served thickly brewed sweet tea to the guests, and by the time she returned to pick up the teacups, the guests had already placed money-filled red envelopes into their empty cups, as tradition dictated.

After the official wedding ceremony was complete, the guests went to the restaurant where the banquet would take place. The groom's family, remembering the lavishness of the engagement banquet, had accordingly upgraded their plans for the wedding banquet by serving ten tables of guests instead of the originally planned eight. Still, the Hus regarded the meal as relatively simple; in Taipei, families usually celebrated weddings over dinner rather than lunch, and with more guests.

Ling had only bothered to bring one engagement gown to the wedding, in addition to her wedding gown. She had figured that, considering Yan's family background, the wedding would be a rather modest affair. Of course, the professional wedding photos would cost Yan's family more than $50,000 which was no meagre sum. Then there was still the seven-day honeymoon. Not to mention another ten-table banquet in Taipei that Ling's parents would be responsible for. But Ling figured that, everything considered, she really hadn't asked for much.

Ling was in the middle of cooking yet another meal for her mother and father when it dawned on her: Nothing had changed, really, since the wedding. She slept in the room that her husband had managed to rent, of course, but something always drew her back home, which was conveniently located nearby. Perhaps she preferred having a home that consisted of more than one room. For whatever reason, she spent most of her free time at her parents' house, helping out with the very chores that had precipitated her decision to marry. After work, she and Yan would eat dinner there every day.

Although Ling saw her new in-laws far less frequently than Yan saw his, she enjoyed her mother-in-law's company on the rare occasions when they would get together. The very first time Ling had gone to visit her husband's family in Chiayi, she had tried her best to make a good impression. Since girls from Taipei were rumoured to possess feisty temperaments, she wanted them to rest assured that she was polite and considerate. She chose her outfits carefully to prove that she was not spoiled or greedy. She wanted them to know that, despite her family background, she did not look down on them because of their lack of wealth and social position.

Whenever the newlywed couple spent the night in Chiayi, Ling rose early with prototypical obedience in order to prepare breakfast for Yan's family. When her mother-in-law woke up, Ling would chat with her like she would with her own mother. In years to come, Ling always sent her mother-in-law a gift on Mother's Day – a holiday that was not customarily celebrated in Taiwan at the time. Ling had grown up with the financial ability to habitually give gifts.

Although the monetary cushion that Yan offered her was not as snug as the one she had grown up with, Ling felt that she was comfortable enough. By this time, thanks to sky-rocketing inflation, Ling and her husband earned a combined salary of $97,000 a month when business was good. Their rent was only $2,000 a month, and they had few other major expenses.

The excess income gave Ling the means to exhibit generosity to the gods, whose favour she greatly depended on. She bought clothes and fresh flowers for the gods. She donated thousands of dollars to temple building projects, though her donations paled in comparison to the tens of thousands of dollars that her parents would give towards such endeavours. She sponsored the publication of 100 to 200 religious books a month. She bought and burnt heaps of paper money on a regular basis. And whenever she went to a temple, she would empty all the change from her purse into the temple's collection box. She did all of this with the belief that her efforts would be abundantly rewarded in the next life. She also believed that her good works were earning her the right to a fruitful life, good health, intelligent children and a happy marriage.

Before getting married, Ling and Yan had envisaged owning a house someday. After the wedding, Ling avoided major spending, apart from her religious donations, in hopes that their bank account would bulge with savings. She chose not to complain about their cramped living situation, even though they could have afforded to live in a bigger place. Yan believed that living minimally at first would pay off in future dividends, and Ling, who was used to letting her mother handle all her finances, believed him.

But for some reason, the couple barely scraped by. Every once in a while, the disconnect befuddled Ling, but not enough for her to demand control of the family finances. She had neither the time nor the desire to learn the ins and outs of financial planning. So, blinded by what she thought was love, she quenched her desire to pry.

Ling thought gallantly: 'We're young, and there's only the two of us. We can live simple lives. As long as there is a roof over my head and we both work hard, I don't care if he doesn't have a penny to his name. As long as we go through the hard times together, that is enough.

'As long as we love each other, I'll be satisfied.'

Mei Chen

The man gazed at Mei Chen's large, expressive eyes and heart-shaped face. His own face, usually filled with joy, bore a momentary look of grief. He let out a sigh.

'You know ... I really like you.'

Mei's eyes widened. It was one of those rare and fleeting moments when Mei got a taste of genuine love – love that didn't desire to manipulate or conquer. If she had known how the rest of her life would play out, she might have savoured the moment. Instead she was like an aeroplane passenger too tired to notice a fleetingly spectacular view below.

'I like you,' the man continued in his confession. 'That's why I kept on coming over to Auntie Wu's house.'

Auntie Wu, a woman from Mei's tribe, had moved to Taichung after marrying a man of Han Chinese descent. This 'aunt' – an ambiguous Chinese term used in reference to any female family friend, happened to live right across from the thread factory where Mei worked, and so she invited Mei and several other young women to live with her for a relatively low fee.

An active woman, Auntie Wu loved to get out of the house. Every Sunday, Mei and the other tenants would take time off work to accompany Auntie Wu on various excursions throughout the town. They largely depended on taxis for transport, and Auntie Wu had already befriended several taxi drivers.

Among them was Dawei, a polite Christian who would often take the young ladies from place to place. He served Auntie Wu so regularly that she would sometimes invite him into her living-room for a chat. Although he was generally pleasant to be around, he seemed unusually distant towards Mei – for a reason she couldn't explain. Around her, he exuded an aura of aloof propriety.

One day, Auntie Wu lifted her hand to hail a taxi in what normally would have been an act of little significance. The taxi that approached at that moment belonged to a driver named Lo, a middle-aged aboriginal from Taitung. Just as Mei had done with Dawei, she paid little attention to Lo.

From then on, Lo drove past Auntie Wu's house every day, hoping that he would find a chance to give Mei a lift. For the most part, the two said little to each other. Since he was thirteen years older than Mei, they had little in common. On the rare occasion when Lo would talk, his open mouth would reveal a set of blood-red teeth, stained by betel nut, an Asian version of chewing tobacco. They would chat a little about their families, but not much more.

Mei discovered that, even though Lo was old and not particularly attractive, his years of experience had led him to be quite skilled in the art of seducing women, of making them feel beautiful. Two months after first meeting Mei, he led her to a bedroom in Auntie Wu's house, where she half-willingly slept with him.

Soon, her fears were confirmed – Lo had got her pregnant.

All week at the factory, Mei busied her fingers to keep up with the quick pace of the assembly line, paying little attention to anything else. Similarly, the judgmental gazes cast upon her ballooning belly led her to focus all her energy on one question, and one question only: 'Should I get married?' Her mind never strayed to other, related questions: 'Do I really love this man? Is Lo the kind of man I really want to marry?' Her mind never conceived that marrying the wrong man could have negative consequences.

'Don't marry this man,' her parents urged. They strongly opposed her relationship with Lo because he was so much older than her. 'Just get an abortion.' But, as with Ling, their resistance only strengthened Mei's resolve. She despised her memories of being under their care and yearned to sever her ties with the past.

For as long as Mei could remember, she was always running away from something. She had never really thought about what she wanted out of life; rather, she simply knew that she did not like things the way they were. Wounds from her childhood had not yet healed, and disquietude filled her heart whenever she thought about home. She assumed that marriage would bring her a semblance of stability that the status quo did not seem to offer.

Eventually Mei decided to quit her job at the factory and move to Taitung, a small city on the eastern coast of

Taiwan, where she would join Lo's tribe and live with his family. Then she would get married and, eventually, give birth to her child.

Almost immediately, warning signs began to emerge: The unusually high number of single men and women in Lo's tribe; the fact that many married men in the tribe beat their wives. Yet she did not waver in her decision to marry the man whom she still barely knew.

One day, Mei was paying a visit to Lo's younger sister when she spotted a familiar face. Dawei.

'Oh! You live here,' she said to him.

'Yes, I do.' By an ironic twist of fate, Dawei's family lived right across the street from Lo's sister. 'When did you arrive in Taitung?'

'I came here with Lo.'

Dawei looked at Mei and sighed. As he confessed his feelings for her, her heart sank. If she had only known, she might have liked him. He was kind, polite, talkative and optimistic. Even though she harboured a hatred for men so deeply seeded that she couldn't even recognize it within herself, this man seemed different. He was certainly different from people like Lo, and even different from the other 'Christians' she had seen in her mother's church.

As it turned out, Dawei had intentionally kept his distance from Mei, treating her with cautious respect and guarding his own heart until their friendship had time to ripen.

'But you decided to get married so quickly,' he continued. 'And since you've already made your decision, I hope you have a blessed marriage.'

Had Mei and Lo's wedding 'banquet' taken place outside the safe confines of Lo's house, it might have resulted in a dramatic loss of face. The bride was pregnant and the fare was minimal – just enough to serve their immediate families, who simply sat around a single table and ate, just like any other meal. No friends were present to celebrate the matrimony.

Mei remained unfazed. As a married woman, she no longer belonged to her own dysfunctional family, and, in a few months, she would give birth to a son.

For those few months, life was comparatively ethereal. She was nineteen.

Yufen Wang

Yufen's new boss smiled at her. She smiled back. They made a good team.

The first time Yufen had stepped into Kai Lin's stationery store, the place looked like it had just been hit by a typhoon. Kai, as it turned out, knew little about how to organize his shop. After graduating from college, he sailed around the Taiwan Strait while serving in the military, as all healthy young Taiwanese men were required to do. After he was discharged, his family, successful and well known throughout the suburb of Yungho, urged him to start a business – just like throngs of other middle-class Taiwanese were doing at the time. Kai agreed enthusiastically. He enjoyed trying his hand at new things. His uncle, an experienced businessman, initially helped him open the stationery store, which, like most Taiwanese small businesses, would occupy the first floor of the family's residence. But since Kai's other siblings were preoccupied with their own busy lives, Kai eventually had to tend the shop alone.

Kai soon realized that he desperately needed help. His brother-in-law had a good friend from the military who mentioned that his younger sister was employable – and quite attractive. This was how Kai came to hire Yufen, who almost immediately started to tidy up Kai's war zone of merchandise, according to the way she had been trained by her former employer, the fastidious Mr Huang. She even showed her new boss how to improve his sales techniques, as if their roles had been reversed. Kai trusted Yufen to the extent that he often let her run the shop while he took care of outside business, delivering bulk orders of writing utensils to companies and schools. Yufen had never before tasted such privilege. In all her previous jobs, she was a worker of little individual significance who was always looked upon by managers with an eye of distrust. Kai, on the other hand, made her feel like a queen.

From her job at Mr Huang's stationery store, Yufen had learned the importance of having good relationships with customers, and in Kai's store she enjoyed chatting openly with them without fearing the watchful gaze of her manager. Her naturally outgoing personality was finally set free.

Out of all her customers, only one left her with a lasting impression. A graduate of National Taiwan University, the top university in the country, this student had a penchant for novels, and would even bring them into the store to read. With his attention half on the novel in his hand and half on the merchandise, he would 'browse' through the entire store and then leave without buying anything.

One day he entered the store armed with a bow and arrow. He waved them around dramatically, slung them onto his back, and then matter-of-factly left the store. Yufen could scarcely keep herself from bursting into laughter. Apparently, she thought, he took the characters in his novels a little too seriously. She smiled in self-righteous contentment.

'Getting a good education doesn't make you a better person,' she thought.

Kai depended on Yufen, and her salary of $1,200 a month – at the time, a vast improvement from $800 a month – showed it. His family also seemed to respect her far more than the Huangs ever did, for they treated her like a guest instead of a servant. When they ate dinner together, she was the first to eat, instead of the last. For the first time in her life, she was allowed to partake of the best.

At first, Yufen supposed that the Lins' attitude towards her was a result of having tasted the benefits of good rapport with their prior employees. Eventually, though, she realized that this approach was only one of many ways in which their lives displayed a quality of hedonistic nonchalance; they were simply too laid back to bother with patronizing her. At one point, Kai's mother tried to sell Japanese-style glutinous rice balls in front of the stationery store – more of a hobby than a business venture, since she let neighbouring children freely nibble on the snacks until she had nothing left to sell.

One day, Mrs Lin stopped by the store in order to ask Kai for money.

'I want to go buy some vegetables,' she said. When she returned at around midnight, she carried in her hands nothing but some green onions and ginger roots.

'You didn't really buy any vegetables!' Kai laughed. Both he and Yufen knew that she had probably gone out to play mah-jong, a Chinese tile game, or to gamble.

'How can you be so relaxed about something like this?' Yufen thought. 'If that type of thing happened in my family, it would be really serious!'

Yufen thought of such behaviour as irresponsible, yet she was intrigued by how much the Lins seemed to enjoy life. When she was around them, she felt that she, too, could partake in a portion of their happiness. Soon, she and Kai became good friends. Sometimes, when they had both finished closing the shop after nine at night, Kai invited her to go out with him and his wealthy friends.

Yufen discovered that she was in love, just as a butterfly suddenly discovers that it is no longer a caterpillar. As Kai's friend, she had always admired his casual, jovial manner, which was especially useful when he dealt with difficult situations. She wished that she too could possess this quality, since her own personality reflected the austerity of her past. She also admired his love of children and his closeness to his parents, another element missing in her own life. Many girls found him good looking, and he possessed a kind of manly charisma that often brought him to the centre of attention.

One night, more than a year after the two started working together, Kai invited Yufen to go to Bitan, a scenic area in Taipei County that served as a popular hang-out for him and his friends. This time, however, the two would go alone. As she rode on the back of his motorcycle, Yufen was filled with nervous excitement. They had been to the place several times before, but this time the view took on a different quality – the suspension bridge overlooking the lake swung gently to a romantic tune, and the water, shimmering in the moonlight, lapped against steep cliffs. Kai reached for Yufen's hand. As a tingle surged through her body, she knew that her feelings towards him had changed.

Yufen's parents had never taught her about the meaning of true love, so she supposed that she loved Kai. And somehow, he loved her too, though he could never get himself to say the actual words. His family, like many Taiwanese families, had never taught him to be particularly expressive about his feelings.

Afraid of how Kai's parents would react to such a scandalous relationship between their son and his employee, the two started 'secretly' dating. During the day, they tried to maintain a professional relationship so that they would not arouse suspicion. Then at night they would go out together and unleash the feelings they had kept bottled up inside. Little did Yufen know that Kai's grandfather had actually urged him to date and marry her quickly so that his younger siblings would have licence to settle down as well.

Yufen prided herself on having been pursued by someone of such secure social standing, someone with real potential. After all, wasn't she the same girl who used to beg for food and covet other students' lollipops? So she became infatuated with Kai and began to daydream about raising a family with him and riding on the coat-tails of his comfortable life.

Gradually, the couple became more careless in hiding their relationship. It was no surprise, then, that one day Kai's sister came into the store and caught them holding hands, murmuring to each other flirtatiously.

His sister immediately stormed out of the store and rushed to tell her parents the news. She couldn't bear to see her older brother with a woman of such low class. From then on, whenever she saw Yufen, they would engage in a passive-aggressive war that resulted in a household atmosphere that was so thick with disgust that Kai couldn't take it any longer. Unable to comprehend why his girlfriend thought his sister was being condescending, he tried his best not to take sides.

Eventually, the Lins pulled their son aside to talk about the situation privately.

'I just want to get married,' he proclaimed, realizing that if he married Yufen, he could at least move out of the house and avoid future conflict. He also felt that he needed Yufen, especially in a business sense. Seeing their son's determination, the Lins didn't object to the engagement, though they were not pleased with it.

Yufen was glad to hear about the way her beau had

handled the situation, and she agreed with his decision to marry. When he officially asked for her hand in marriage, her older brother and sister agreed; their father had passed away, and their mother lived far away in the country, so the siblings took responsibility over the proceedings. Simple and undemanding, they only asked Kai's family for the provision of traditional engagement cookies for their family and friends.

Yufen saw marriage as nothing more than an obligatory part of life, much like getting up and eating breakfast. So strong was her fear of remaining single – which in her eyes was a sign of abnormality – that she never stopped to seriously think through the commitment. Everyone else around her seemed to be getting married, and she didn't want to miss her opportunity.

'Well, I'm at the marrying age, and it makes me feel really good to be around him – actually, I need him, and I need to get married – so why not?' she had thought in passing.

After two years of impassioned dating, Yufen and Kai got married. Like Ling, they had a traditional engagement ceremony hosted by Yufen's family. When it came to the wedding banquet, hosted by the Lins, so many of Kai's relatives and friends attended that, in addition to serving more than thirty tables in one restaurant, the couple had to rent space in an adjacent restaurant in order to accommodate the overflowing guests. Yufen's family members required only two or three tables. As was the custom for the Lins, the celebration was lavish and elaborate – even more so than Ling's. Many guests didn't leave until five or six the next morning.

In Kai's eyes, the affair was rather simple and ordinary. He had no particular sense of excitement on the day of his wedding, and even experienced a tinge of guilt – though he was not too sure why at the time.

Yufen, however, felt like many Taiwanese people – that

she had managed to achieve a higher social position than that of their parents. The bustling wedding served as a symbol of this achievement. Never before had Yufen imagined that she would someday be at the centre of such opulence. Never before had she experienced such recklessly wonderful feelings.

She felt as if she had been born again.

Notes

1. Carltonhill, *ibid* p. 60.

Chapter 5

Cigarette smoke wafted into the crisp night air as the group of men smoked, drank and leaned over their card tables, engrossed in games of poker and chess. As Ling passed them briskly, eyeing the after-work crowd, she half expected to spot her husband. Their well-to-do neighbourhood was filled with men who would unwind at the day's end through gambling – a form of recreation very common in Taiwanese culture – and her husband was often one of the many pleasure-seekers.

Not seeing her husband, Ling continued walking to her parents' house, where she would spend most of her evening cooking, cleaning and keeping her father company, since her mother didn't get off work until ten. At around eight, Ling might go back home to see if her husband had returned.

Ling found it odd that, even after so many months of being married, she still spent most of her time at her parents' house. Since her husband returned home so late, the rented room they shared felt so empty, as if it was merely a place to sleep instead of a newlyweds' new home.

She found it even more odd that, for the first time in her life, money was not always available in abundance. Although Ling had been trained in accounting, she could never seem to correctly balance her family's own bank account. They always had enough to live on, but the balances on their bank statements would inexplicably peak and plunge like a seismograph reading. Their combined salaries amounted to a generous 100,000 Taiwanese dollars a month, yet where did all the money go?

Ling took another look at the street-side gamblers as one man counted out a stack of bills: $100, 200, 300, 400 ...

* * *

'If you want to gamble, you can, but under three conditions,' Ling asserted. 'You can go to other people's houses to do it, but you can't do it in our home. I'm not going to serve your friends with cigarettes and food so you can gamble. It's too messy and I don't want to have our kid exposed to it.'

By this time, Ling had given birth to a baby girl and was taking time off work to care for little Jun.

She continued, 'As long as they don't come here to gamble, I'll even offer them food.' Although it is common practice for Taiwanese men to invite friends over to play cards and enjoy their wives' food and hospitality, Ling felt that her demand was reasonable. She loathed the thought of spending money on wine and cigarettes, only to let their home become noisy and full of smoke.

'Also, you can't ask me for money,' she said calmly, 'and you can't play so much that you can't work.' She looked at her husband to guage his reaction. He simply smiled.

Ling felt proud that she had made herself perfectly clear. She refrained from telling him to stop gambling altogether, for she knew that it helped him relax at the end of a physically demanding work-day. Besides, many other Taiwanese men were doing it.

Yan suffered from chronic liver disease, and whenever his health started to deteriorate, Ling's uncle gave him a lighter, more flexible workload. Instead of driving back and forth to deliver a constant rush of orders, he would be merely required to stay close at hand after hours, in case a late-night delivery was necessary. Since he and his co-workers had nothing else to do but wait, they would gamble through the night.

Once Ling bumped into one of these co-workers. As they started talking, he looked at her with a wry, mocking smile.

'You'd better watch out,' he warned. 'Your husband and I have worked together for a long time. Don't trust him too much. He's not as well behaved as he seems.'

Ling indeed began to wonder, 'What's going on here? What's Yan up to? Can he really take care of me?' One day, she told a friend about her growing apprehensions.

'Maybe your husband is not even going to work any more,' her friend hypothesized, unearthing more cause for worry. 'Maybe he just gambles all day.'

Ling considered various ways of mitigating her worries. Since, like most Taiwanese women, she held control of the family finances, perhaps she should demand to see her husband's pay-packets right after they were supposedly received. But then she hesitated. Money was an emotionally charged subject for them that sparked irate debate every time it came up. The more she scolded him about his spending, the more he would avoid coming home. She was afraid that someday he would leave the house forever.

Besides, she proudly thought that it was better to use her own money to resolve their problems instead of demanding his help. She started working again, and tried to forget about her dream of being a full-time housewife. 'If my mother could work while raising children, so can I,' she thought.

Soon after returning to work, Ling considered following her mother's example in another way – starting a small-scale clothing factory. After all, Mrs Hu's business had prospered, and Ling felt that she had inherited her mother's sense of style. Yan had grown weary of the heavy lifting that his job required, so they both were energized by the prospect. They figured that having a business of their own would be a wise investment for the future. Yan was particularly enthusiastic when they decided to purchase a vehicle for their new business.

'Let's buy a second-hand one,' Ling suggested, remembering that his family had given him only $400,000 to start the business.

'If you want to buy a car, you have to buy a new one,' he insisted. Ling knew that Yan had a rather unhealthy penchant for glamour and glitter. Before landing a job at the He Song soda company, he had driven a taxi. Unlike the average taxi driver, however, he chose to drive a classy imported vehicle that normally would have been used for private services. Then, in order to protect his precious vehicle, he refused to drive on rainy days. Thanks to Taipei's wet, drizzly climate, Yan did not serve customers for a good part of the year.

'Why buy an old car?' Yan continued. 'It'll break down easily, and the maintenance fees will be high later on.'

'Well ... OK, then,' she said, finally. 'It's your family's money anyway.' Even though Ling knew about her husband's extravagant tendencies, she was easily persuaded by his arguments because of her own inexperience in making financial decisions. She didn't feel peaceful about the decision to spend most of their starting capital on a company vehicle, but she didn't want to argue about it either.

With the money that remained, the couple hired two workers who would assemble garments that Mrs Hu's employees could not finish. As Mrs Hu helped her daughter secure similar contracts with other larger companies, the business started to slowly expand.

Ling's mother proved to be an invaluable resource in other ways too. She taught Ling and Yan how to hire good workers and set up an assembly line that would optimize the special skills of each worker. One, for example, could deftly fashion together a sleeve, while another was good at sewing up the minute details of a collar. Eventually, the company employed ten labourers who lived at the factory and ate meals prepared by Ling. They also employed housewives who worked off-site, operating small machines in their homes, and Yan's primary responsibility was to deliver fabric and materials to these women.

The young couple lived on the floor above the factory, with its nearly constant whir of sewing machines. Their newly established positions of power gave them an initial thrill: In a society where businesses often bore closer resemblance to dictatorships than to democracies, opening one's own business was a sure way to escape the oppression of occupational servitude. But, like many other Taiwanese, Ling and Yan discovered that this freedom came at no small cost. They both were inexperienced entrepreneurs and rather poor managers. They felt as if they had been cast into the ocean before learning how to swim.

Sometimes they had to wait as long as three months to cash a payment from a clothing order, and the frequent delays made it difficult for them to pay their employees on time. Their expenditures mounted. Their incomes did not.

For Ling, these difficulties were compounded by disturbances at home. Yan started to ask Ling for money, sometimes in mysteriously large sums.

'Could you please borrow some money from your relatives?' he asked sweetly. 'I promise that I'll pay it back every month.' He then volunteered to do housework in an attempt to curry her favour.

Indeed, Ling's extended family ran a private loan group[1] that enabled her to conveniently borrow money at low interest. Ling pondered over the proposition. She remembered telling her husband, 'You can't ask me for money,' earlier in their marriage. Yet she disliked conflict, especially from within the family.

'I trust him,' she thought. 'And why shouldn't I trust him? He's my husband, after all.'

Eventually, she agreed to borrow the money for him. He quietly, happily went to bed.

The feeling of trust did not last long, however, as it became apparent that Yan would not pay back the loan any time soon. Furthermore, Yan asked her for a second loan. And a third.

At first Ling paid little attention to the mounting debt, and chose not to demand repayment from her husband. 'I don't want to fight with him. He's my husband, after all,' she thought. After more than a month had passed, she would usually forget about the loan altogether.

Gradually, though, she realized that she could no longer ignore her growing financial dilemma. When her husband approached her sweetly again, she knew the situation would soon get sticky.

'I'm sorry, but I have a problem. Can I please borrow some money from you?' he asked.

'Well ... I have no money,' she tried to say nicely. She felt like a rabbit trapped in its own hole.

'What about the private loan group? Your family has lots of money.'

Ling hesitated. In the end she reluctantly relented. Her apprehension about the mounting debt was overshadowed by a much larger fear – a fear of marital clash.

'Can I borrow some money?' Yan asked on yet another occasion.

Ling glared at her husband incredulously. She could hardly believe that he was asking, yet again. This time, she felt irritated enough to put up a fight.

'I'll give it to you if you give me a reason first.'

Yan's large eyes widened and his lips snarled. Ling felt her body grow cold, her muscles tense.

'Why won't you help your husband out, huh? I know you can get some money, so why won't you just let me have it? What kind of wife do you think you are? You are a stupid woman!' A string of insults followed, and when Ling could no longer withstand the attack, she held up her white flag.

'Fine,' she said, trying to hide the fear from her voice. 'I'll borrow the money for you.'

After Yan's outburst of rage, Ling tried to assure herself that the incident would not be repeated.

'Fighting over money is really a waste of time, and I'm making enough money to pay for these things really, and I didn't want to rely on him for money anyway, and as long as I keep the peace in this house, things will be fine.'

Once, when he was away, Yan called his wife and said with a tone of festive flair, 'Let's close shop early today and let the workers go home. I'm at a friend's house right now, but get Jun ready ... I'll take you both out a little after six!'

Ling waited. And waited. The hours seemed to pass like days as she and Jun waited for Yan's return. At last, Ling gave up, fed Jun quickly, and put the toddler to bed.

When Yan finally came home the next morning, Ling lashed out at him with an evening's worth of pent-up anger. She didn't like to raise her voice – behaviour unbecoming of a loyal wife – but she couldn't contain her frustration.

'Where were you last night?! We waited for you the whole night!' she fumed.

'I was at my friend's house ... So what?'

'Look, I'm not angry because you were over there. I'm angry because you said that you wanted to eat with us, so we waited for you, and then you didn't come home. That's why I'm angry!'

Similar conflicts plagued their business relationship, for Yan had become an unreliable business partner who would go out to 'deliver a work order' to one of their at-home labourers – but then he would not return for hours, or even a whole day.

On busy days when Ling desperately needed Yan's help at the factory, she would call his cell phone in an attempt to track him down.

'Can you come back now? I need your help.'

'OK, sure,' he would reply. But the promise would not be fulfilled. Ling had a sinking suspicion that, during these extended absences, her husband was out gambling with his friends. One friend in particular ran some card tables and often invited her husband to play because he was a reliable customer who would bet high and always pay up.

One day, she called this friend and, as expected, was able to reach her husband there.

'Come back here,' she snapped. 'I need you to deliver something.'

'OK, OK,' came Yan's customary reply.

Ling waited for more than an hour, wondering all the while: 'Why is he taking so long? That place is only ten minutes away.'

She called the friend again.

'Is my husband coming?' she asked.

'Oh yes, he left.'

'He thinks I'm a stupid woman,' Ling thought.

After letting her workers go home and closing the factory, she took a taxi to the friend's house. When she arrived, she saw her husband's vehicle parked outside.

She rang the bell, and when the friend opened the door, he tried to disguise his shock.

'Is my husband here?' she asked.

'Er – yes – yes, he's here.' Without a word Ling barged past the man. She walked up to the card table where her husband sat. He looked at her and stood up. She turned and walked out the door. He followed, humiliated. When she reached the taxi, she finally opened her mouth.

'If you can't come home, just tell me. I was worried that something bad had happened to you. And there's work that needs to be done. You promised that you would do this delivery.'

Yan looked at his wife blankly. No remorse. No anger. He didn't say a word.

Thus started the fights, when Ling and Yan yelled at each other back and forth like a livid ping-pong match. One day, instead of asking her husband to help with an outside errand, Ling determined to do the deed herself because she knew that if he left the factory, he was unlikely to return. Enraged at Ling's distrust, Yan followed her out the door. She crossed the road in an attempt to ignore him. He started shouting, oblivious to other pedestrians, who tried their best not to stare at the spectacle.

'You are such an evil person, and a horrible wife!'

Even as the two returned to the office, his shouting continued.

'Ling,' one of the workers said when Yan was out of earshot, 'I had no idea that the boss could be like that.'

'Yes, that's the way he is,' Ling sighed.

'I thought he was more ... polite,' the worker continued. Indeed, on most occasions Yan treated his workers with courtesy and respect. Talking with his wife, however, was a different matter.

One hot day, Ling decided to buy popsicles for the employees.

'What do you think you are doing? Having fun?' Yan barked at her.

'Throwing your temper isn't going to solve anything,' she replied coolly, attempting to appear calm as she felt the weight of her workers' gazes upon her.

When Ling could not think of a way to end an argument, she would head to her parents' house, which offered temporary respite. Little did she know that the route would become an all-too-familiar one.

Merely two years after Ling and Yan had plunged into the business world, Ling was gasping for air. Among the problems that plagued the company was disturbingly frequent equipment theft. Strangely, Yan appeared calm, and almost indifferent towards the disappearances, even though the problem ultimately led to the demise of the business.

'I'm tired of doing everything by myself,' Ling complained one day to her husband. 'I have a baby to take care of. Let's quit.'

'Oh yeah? If we don't keep on going, I want a divorce,' he threatened.

'I really don't want to fight with you, but if you're going to continue being this inconsiderate, then we just can't be husband and wife any more.' Ling took a deep breath. She had just uttered words that most Taiwanese women at the time could not even conceive.

'Fine. I have some friends who owe me some favours, and I can go to Chiayi to live with them.'

'Fine. If your friends will actually feed you and give you a place to stay, just go. Just go.'

Just like that, Yan drafted up the divorce papers and left for Chiayi. They were only one step away from a legal divorce.

In the meantime, Ling was left with one child and a business that was on its last legs. She decided to gradually downsize the business and live on the same floor as the factory in order to save money.

A month passed. Ling was sick of running the business alone and of hovering at an uncertain point between marriage and divorce. She decided that it was time for closure.

Thoughts sped through Ling's mind as the train click-clacked to Chiayi. She felt like a failure. She was unable to keep the business. She was unable to salvage her marriage. Once she removed her name from Yan's household registration papers, their divorce would be final.

As soon as Ling arrived at the Chiayi train station, she inquired about which bus to take to the house of Yan's family. Never before had she made the journey alone. When she rang the doorbell of her in-laws' house, Yan's brother answered the door.

'Can I get your household registration papers... ?' Ling asked. She thought of how good her mother-in-law had been to her ever since she married Yan. The woman had even called Ling on a regular basis ever since she discovered that the marriage had turned rocky, in an effort to comfort and encourage her. It was as if her mother-in-law was attempting to put out a forest fire with buckets of water.

Ling didn't want to be the one to tell her mother-in-law about the divorce, and was glad when Yan's brother let her take care of the situation quietly. However, when she arrived at the government's Household Registration Office, she discovered that there was a problem.

'If you want to complete this both parties must come to this office together,' the government worker said. 'You can't just take care of the paperwork yourself.'

Ling silently cursed at herself for the oversight. Her heart sank at the prospect of leaving the situation unresolved, but she didn't feel like wandering around town in search of her husband.

She reluctantly headed back to Taipei as a still-married woman. Yet underneath her groans lay a glimmer of relief, barely discernible. All along, she had hoped that things would still work out.

'If you give me money to buy a taxi, I could make $1,000 a day!'

A lot had happened since Yan had decided to rejoin Ling in Taipei, six months after the attempted divorce. Since they no longer had a factory to run, Ling had returned to her former job at the soda company. Yan started working for a taxi company. Even so, he spent a great deal of time lounging around the house, and Ling never saw any of his earnings. Now, he had come up with yet another proposal.

'I'm not making enough, so all that I make goes straight to the taxi company,' Yan continued. 'I know I'm not making enough to take care of the family.' He glanced at her tenderly. 'I really, really want to take care of you, but I just can't. So the only way I can do it is if the car is our own. Will you just give me this chance? I want to change. I want to start over. I want to be a good husband. This is the best way. I'll treat you like my boss and pay you rent for the car.'

'That's reasonable,' she thought. 'I need to at least give him a chance to pick up the responsibility. Maybe then he'll have the incentive to work hard. Maybe this will make him get his act together. Anyway, it would be better than not working and being plain useless at home ...'

So Ling scrounged up as much money as she could manage – more than $100,000 in total. She gave the money to her husband and then waited, hoping that the investment would be the key to release her from her financial quandaries.

Weeks passed. Nothing changed. Finally, Ling decided to confront her husband.

'Where's the taxi, anyway? If you're working, how come I've never seen the taxi?' she demanded.

'It's hard to find an affordable taxi nowadays,' he answered.

Ling said nothing further, clinging to her hope that Yan would change. She wanted to have faith that someday Yan would take responsibility for his family. She wanted to just forgive him and win him over with love. But then she thought about the hard-earned money she so frequently dished out to him – money that was never matched by financial support from his end. She thought about the stark contrast between her husband and her father, who was always there for his family and never seemed to quarrel with her mother. 'Why can't Yan be half the man my father is?' she bemoaned. Every month, Ling's father gave his pay-cheque to her mother, which enabled her to handle the family finances well. Ling regretted that she had not asked the same thing of Yan from the beginning.

Though Ling tried her best not to dwell on her husband's faults, one day her carefully crafted bubble of patience burst.

'Just give me the money back,' she demanded. 'I'll go and buy the car for you. If what I gave you isn't enough, I'll pay the rest.'

He refused. An argument ensued.

'I'll give you one week to either show me the car or the money,' she said finally. She looked her husband squarely in the eye. 'Don't think that I'm a dumb woman!'

Within a week of the ultimatum, Yan called her.

'I bought a used car,' he said.

'Well, at least you can go to work now.' 'And at least you can pay for your own expenses, if not the family's,' she thought to herself.

Even so, she would often pick up her daughter from the babysitter's house after a long day at work and return home to find her husband in bed, still as a corpse.

'It's time to eat!' she said to him in an attempt to wake him up. No response.

Rolling her eyes, she didn't bother to try again. 'He's been gambling the whole night ... again. It's useless to reprimand him,' she thought.

When Yan finally woke from his deep slumber, Ling glared at him.

'We need money,' she said.

'Hey, I'm only a taxi driver,' he retorted. 'I can't support a family.'

'Well, I really don't want to argue with you. We're in difficult times, and we just have to live through it.'

'Look, I'm already working very hard, and I just can't support the family.'

'You have really gone too far,' she thought, both disturbed by and proud of what she planned to say next.

'Fine. Then I'll make sure that we have enough money.'

'I should have been more demanding. He's never thankful for my help. I gave him all that I had. I loved him. But in return, that spoiled man with no self-control just uses me to get money. He doesn't know how to love me, and he doesn't understand my love for him. 'Maybe he's still afraid that I won't be a good enough wife for him.'

She knew that many men from southern Taiwan expected Taipei women to be liberal and bad-tempered – unfit as traditional wives. 'But I'm not that way. Or maybe he's intimidated by me because I'm more educated than him and I have a better family background than he does. I mean, when he first came to Taipei he had nothing – no family, no nothing. Look at all that I've done for him. Why am I so stupid? Why am I letting this happen?'

She fought back tears, reminiscing about her childhood fantasies of being the dutiful housewife of a capable man. But as she thought about the way her life was actually unravelling, she didn't feel pity towards herself. She felt hatred.

Ling remembered that she had made herself very clear during their last spat.

'This is the last time I'm going to help you out. The last

time,' she had said. 'Every time I give you money, you go out and spend all of it on cards and then come to me for help. I just can't borrow money for you any more.'

'That's OK,' he had answered amicably. 'I know you can take care of it this time. And it won't happen again.'

Of course, she had only half-believed him at the time, and sure enough, he had asked again. Even if he could not keep his word, she decided that she would do everything she could to keep hers.

'I'm not giving you the money. I told you last time that it would be the last time.'

'Oh, come on, just one more time.'

'No. I already told you. No.'

'Come on, you're my wife. How could you do this to me?'

'I won't give you the money.'

'I'm telling you, give it to me!'

'No!'

'Well then, I want a divorce!' he screamed, anger burning in his large eyes. Ling normally would have cringed and relented in fear, but she would not let him get away. Not this time.

'You can't do that ...'

'Oh, and why not?'

'Because I'm pregnant.'

Mei Chen

Mei's unborn child had unwittingly shielded her from the reality of her marriage for some time. But now that the bulge in her belly had receded, there was virtually nothing left to protect her.

On what seemed like an ordinary day, Mei stood at the doorway of her home in Taitung, chatting with the cousin of her new husband Lo. She was not used to seeking out close relationships with neighbours, as dictated by the customs of her own tribe, so she had begun to feel lonely and isolated, especially since Lo was out working for most of the day. She was not yet accustomed to her new environment and eagerly welcomed the company of Lo's relative.

Suddenly, their conversation was interrupted by a shout.

'I'm not home, and you're already talking with my cousin?!' Lo exclaimed, swaggering towards them. Prior to marrying Lo, Mei had been completely unaware of his other love: alcohol, a vice that Mei had been trained to avoid as a child. Soon she began to discover that her husband was vastly different from the man she thought she knew – in more ways than one.

'What do you think you're doing, talking to him like that? You can't do that!' Lo continued. He slapped her and shoved her to the floor. As the neighbours started to gather around, he pulled her hair. Then he started to kick her.

Mei's body stiffened. She was too shocked to defend herself from the blows. Amid all the horrors that she had witnessed as a child – the horrors that she had wanted to run away from – spousal abuse was not one of them; not once had she seen her father hit her mother.

From then on, Mei noticed that her husband's breath often reeked of alcohol when he returned home from work. His affinity for alcohol apparently ran through his blood, for his mother also loved her drink, which would often propel her into states of uncontrollable sobbing or shouting.

Even though this behaviour was alien to Mei, she enjoyed an unusually peaceful relationship with her new mother-in-law. Before giving birth to her son, Mei would accompany her mother-in-law to the mountains, where she would help tend the fields – work she was accustomed to doing in Ali Mountain. After her child was born, she stayed at home in order to take care of her newborn and cook for her in-laws. In the meantime, her mother-in-law taught her the dialect of their tribe. The woman made few demands, even when it came to religious practice. Although Lo's family professed to be Catholic, they offered incense to and worshipped Lo's deceased father once a year and asked that Mei do the same.

For a nineteen-year-old, Mei got along remarkably well with older people, and her relationship with her mother-in-law was no exception. Her 'second mother' was, perhaps, better than the first for the lack of beatings.

Whatever blows that would have been expected to come from the hands of her mother-in-law were instead administered by her husband. If Lo came through the door with the slightest scowl on his face, Mei knew that he would find some reason – any reason – to beat her. It was as if he saw her as a punching bag through which he could release all his pent-up aggression.

'You aren't worthy to be my wife!' he shouted during one beating. 'You weren't even a virgin when I met you,' he continued, ignoring the fact that Mei's first sexual experience was not even a consensual one.

After merely a few months of wedlock, Mei had already begun to view her marriage as a regrettable tragedy. Her husband treated her like dirt, trampling her spirit to the ground. She felt helpless against his attacks, which were often intensified by the alcohol.

'How can you just drink all day?' she wanted to scream. But instead, she started drinking herself. Since she was not accustomed to such a habit, she did so only in moderation and with little pleasure, but she figured that if Lo would not curb his own drinking, she might as well join him in his lifestyle. Sometimes the warmth of the alcohol helped her forget the almost constant fear of receiving another blow.

Once, when Lo started to beat her, Mei decided to escape. Freeing herself from his grip, she ran out the door towards the house of a co-worker. Lo followed suit and, despite Mei's physical prowess, he caught up with her, grabbed her, and started to beat her again.

'You are such a bad wo—'

He was interrupted by the unexpected approach of his wife's fist, which slammed into his face. All the wood chopping she was forced to do as a child finally paid off.

Too inebriated to brace himself properly, Lo teetered like a tipped bowling pin and fell to the ground. Mei fled.

When Mei finally arrived at her destination, her co-worker gaped at her body, a rainbow of agony covered in red splotches and various shapes of greenish-blue.

'What happened to you?!'

'Nothing,' Mei replied, trying to remain composed. 'I just fell down.'

'That's not possible,' her co-worker objected. 'Tell me the truth!'

'Really. That's all that happened.' The case was closed, and Mei's co-worker could do nothing more than superficially nurse her wounds.

When Mei decided to return home, the incident had been far from forgotten. Humiliated by the fact that she had the audacity to strike back at him, Lo was prepared to tame his beautiful young wife.

So unbelievable was the image that Mei saw through the outside window of her apartment that she had to force herself to take another look. As she peered out for the second time, her suspicions were confirmed.

There was her husband, with his arm around another woman.

She knew that it would be recklessly unwise for a woman in her position to chase after and confront her husband. She could do nothing but await his return. But as evening came, she became increasingly anxious and decided to search for him. She walked to his friends' houses. She called his company. Nothing. He was nowhere to be found.

The incident would not be an isolated one. Once, from the window that had become like a brutally honest crystal ball, Mei spotted her husband holding hands with a different woman. On another occasion, she saw him putting his arm around yet another. Apparently, his aged, mediocre appearance did not dampen his success with women – women who, in Mei's estimation, were far less conservative and far more promiscuous than those of her own tribe.

By this time Lo was working as a long-distance truck driver, and his job reasonably prevented him from returning home every night. But sometimes he was curiously absent for more extended periods of time. When he did return, he would announce his arrival by scolding his wife, or hitting her, or both.

'Where were you?' Mei asked after one of his extended absences.

'I was out driving,' he answered curtly. Without any semblance of guilt or hesitation, he walked out the door as quickly as he had entered, and drove away.

Mei wallowed in loneliness. She had no close friends. Her only reliable companion, her son, provided little comfort because he was male. On the one hand, she hated men; to her, they seemed to be inflictors of perpetual suffering. On the other hand, she enjoyed the feeling of being able to so easily arrest a man's attention – one of the few things she felt she could be proud of. Even the local grocer was clearly enamoured with her. Though he knew that she was married, he would work slowly when handing her change or helping her carry her groceries. He grabbed any opportunity to touch her hand, even if just for a moment longer.

Lo's absences increased exponentially in length until he would disappear for months at a time. Eventually his family found out that he had settled down in Changhua, a town on Taiwan's west coast. The situation worsened when he neglected to send any money home. Mei was no longer the only one who was worried.

'Go look for him,' Mei's mother-in-law said to her one day. By this time Mei had so little money – certainly not enough to travel – that she hitched a ride with a local man who planned on driving to Changhua.

When Mei finally found her husband, the reunion was far from joyous.

'Why are you looking for me? Are you having an affair with this guy here?' Lo started to hit her. But this time, the force of his blows did not weaken her resolve. She was tired of feeling like an abandoned wife, tired of trying to second-guess what her husband was doing during his absences.

'I'm not going to return to your mother's house,' she stated simply. 'I'm going to stay with you here.'

After Mei moved to Changhua, she became pregnant with a second child. Her mother moved in as well in order to help out around the house, and for a time Mei enjoyed respite from her husband's beatings. He didn't dare lift up his hand against her in the presence of his mother-in-law.

However, his drinking habit persisted and cost him dearly. Because the money he had left could not pay off the bills, it was decided that Mei would start to work at home, much like the out-sourced labourers whom Ling hired. Since Mei was already experienced in operating machinery, her large hands worked deftly and diligently while her older son sat by her side. Her line of work was paid by the piece, and she worked so efficiently that she earned $7,000 to $8,000 per month.

Mei worked. Lo worked and got drunk. Mei gave birth to a baby boy.

One night, Lo and Mei were eating together in a restaurant when one of Lo's friends happened to pass by. The man greeted the couple, looked at Mei, and then smiled. Mei automatically, without thinking, nodded her head in return. The friend then proceeded to sit down at the table next to them. As he ordered drinks, he shot occasional glances at Mei. She, in turn, looked quietly at her food, avoiding the man's subtly flirtatious gazes.

As soon as the couple returned home, Lo punched Mei. The crime: responding, even if only slightly, to his own friend's greeting.

His wife was no longer pregnant and her mother was no longer present, so nothing could hold him back from unleashing his anger. Mei attempted to resist, to hit him back. Despite her athletic ability, she was no match for his strength. Eventually she crumpled to the ground, exhausted, and simply let the blows come.

The irony of the situation was that although Mei's philandering husband had hypocritically accused her of unfaithfulness many times, having an affair had seemed inconceivable to her until she had been beaten to a point of desperation and emptiness that, in her opinion, could only be filled by the love of another man. Desire for revenge seeped into her heart until, ready to burst, she went to the grocery store one day and met a man.

'My husband is so old and I'm so young – yet he's still so unkind to me,' she seethed as she succumbed to the man's advances. They had a relationship. It lasted two to three months, and then the flame of vengeance burned out. Mei, overcome by guilt, ended the affair as abruptly as she started it.

Meanwhile, disquietude continued to fester. Mei thought: 'Other couples seem so happy and don't fight so much. Why do we always fight? Why does he hit me over such stupid, small things?' Two years had passed since Mei signed her wedding vows, and now she was ready to make another kind of commitment. 'I'm definitely going to leave this bad man some day. I don't need to live with this pressure, this kind of agony. I don't need to be beaten by him every day. I'm too young to be treated like this.'

When Mei's youngest son was several months old, she insisted on moving to her family's cabin in Ali Mountain. If they lived on her own territory, she reasoned, her husband wouldn't have the gall to beat her or the children.

Mei's life had circled back around to the point from which she had originally wanted to depart. Like before, she helped her parents with the housework and worked in the fields for income. Unlike before, she had two children in tow, so her mother tended to them most of the time.

Mei quickly found her niche in Ali Mountain, but her husband did not find his. After merely a few months, Lo decided to return to Taitung, where he would be guaranteed more steady work.

'Come back with me,' he insisted. Knowing that nothing in Taitung could protect her from her husband's temper, Mei refused.

Lo and Mei lived apart for about two years, connected by nothing more than a legal document. Lo found work as a bus driver, and Mei continued to work for her family. Though they didn't communicate, Mei was not satisfied with the jagged nature of their separation. Something did not seem right.

Mei asked the police to investigate her husband. Using the phone number that Mei gave them, they found that he now resided on the eastern side of Taiwan.

A police officer accompanied Mei to visit the new address. As soon as the door was opened, Mei discovered that her long-time feelings of suspicion had a reasonable source: Lo was living with a mistress. Lo had got the woman pregnant even before he married Mei, but since the woman's parents were so poor that they could not offer any dowry money, he had refused to marry her. This, however, didn't stop him from continuing to have a relationship with her after his marriage to Mei.

It all made sense now: his coldness, his inclination to hit her at the slightest offence, his obsession with infidelity.

'Living together like this is against the law. You're both committing the crime of adultery,' the police officer said to them. He then instructed Mei to take an article of clothing from each of the accused, which was to be used as evidence.

'Don't you touch my clothes!' the woman exclaimed. 'I'll just go with you to the police station.'

After the arrest of Lo and his mistress, Mei was given the option of filing for divorce. According to the Marriage Law of 1931, Mei and Lo would technically have equal rights in any divorce proceedings.[1] But many women knew that, in practice, this was difficult – if not impossible – to enforce. So they simply responded to abuse with the normative passivity of the patriarchal traditions.

But Mei refused to be passive, she wanted an explanation.

'I went back to her because you weren't a virgin,' Lo said, without a tinge of shame in his voice. Mei wanted to scream.

'Even though I'm still young and beautiful and you're so old, you really care so little for me?! Did you really think that all you ever had to do was put food on the table for me?'

At the age of twenty-three, Mei did what many estranged Taiwanese working-class wives were afraid to do. She filed for a divorce. Lo refused to sign the divorce papers.

'Well, since you two aren't really together any more, you might as well get divorced,' a police officer recommended blandly.

'No,' Lo insisted.

'Look, your wife really wants a divorce. You should just get a divorce.'

'No!'

'Well, in that case, your wife can sue you and this woman. Because what you did is a crime.' At last, Lo assented.

According to the agreement of the divorce, each parent would gain custody of one child: Lo chose the older son, and Mei was left with the younger.

The last time Mei held her oldest son in her arms, he cried himself to sleep. As soon as she saw that he was sleeping deeply, she relinquished the child to his father, who picked him up and took him away. Pain sliced through her heart, and her only consolation was the final image of her son's face, peaceful in sleep. Her precious child had no premonition of what was to come.

Soon after the divorce, Lo remarried – not to his longtime mistress, but to another young wife around Mei's age. Years would pass before Mei saw her son again, and only then would she discover that, because Lo's new wife had despised her son, Lo had often ordered the boy to stand still while he flogged him with a leather belt.

Even without this knowledge, Mei emerged from her divorce with a heart full of bitterness. She was virtually penniless. She had joined the ranks of other Chen family members who, despite being blessed with close relation to a line of tribal shamans, were seemingly cursed with divorces. One of her many divorced relatives empathized with her need to start anew and helped her find a job at a popular restaurant in Chiayi, a city close to Ali Mountain. In an attempt to cleanse herself of past hurts, Mei moved in with the relative and busied herself by waiting tables.

One month later, Mei discovered the key to unleashing the full potential of her new line of work. It started when a customer beckoned her to come to his side.

'Little sister,' he said, 'have a glass of wine with me and I will give you $100.'

'What a great way to earn money!' she thought to herself. 'Just drink a glass of wine and earn $100!'

She sat down next to the man, drank the wine and smiled coyly. Continuing to serve tables, she started to feel tipsy, as she was used to drinking in moderation. As she started to drink more frequently, her body adjusted to the alcohol, and she was able to continue working without feeling inhibited.

Most of Mei's more generous customers came from the dregs of society; many of them were involved in gangs. When a group of such customers suddenly stopped coming to the restaurant, she discovered that they had all been sent to a prison on Green Island, which had detained political dissidents during the Kuomingtang regime and eventually was used to confine Taiwan's worst criminals.

Through observing the charades of her clientele, Mei mastered the art of deception. In Ali Mountain, her family never had enough money to take special note of her birthday, so now she made up for it by telling different customers, on a daily basis, that it was her 'birthday' so that they would buy her cake and treats.

Mei relished this new-found attention like an overnight movie star. One man was so fond of her that, as she weaved around, carrying trays of food, he would jump up and down outside the restaurant in order to grab her attention.

'Mei! Mei! Come out here!'

Tickled by his unconstrained display of interest, Mei smiled.

'Come out here!' he tried again.

Mei's boss, who happened to be standing next to her, looked at her sternly.

'Don't go out with that guy,' he warned. 'He's a gang leader. If you go out with him, you'll just get yourself into trouble.' Mei dutifully obeyed, but only for a time. Eventually, she entertained a short romance with the man – at least until he was sent to prison.

Not all the men she attracted would approach her on such friendly terms. Although she tried not to divulge information about her personal life with her customers, she allowed one man to accompany her when she went to pay for her son's nanny. This man, like many others, eventually tried to convince Mei to live with him. Her refusals only made him more adamant. One day, he tried another tactic.

'If you don't marry me, I'll kidnap your child.'

The threat stunned Mei. She felt as if she was lost within a maze of her own making. She started working for a different restaurant in an attempt to escape, triggering a habit of bouncing back and forth between jobs and apartments like a pinball. Her previous fondness towards her customers turned to fear. Every time a man began to show interest in her, she wondered, 'Will this one take my son away?'

Mei could not easily hide her predicament, especially from a caring doctor who had always been innocently kind towards her.

'You shouldn't drag your child around like this,' he advised once. Mei nodded her head in agreement. Her self-esteem had already been shattered by the divorce. Deep down, she despised herself and felt that she had been a terrible mother.

The doctor went on to mention that he knew of a wealthy couple who were unable to bear children of their own.

'You know, your lifestyle is really too unstable to raise a child properly. Also, since you're so young, you're not going to be able to settle down anytime soon ...'

He had laid out all his evidence and was ready to ask Mei for a verdict.

'Why don't you let them adopt your son?'

Yufen Wang

'Shameless,' Yufen's new sister-in-law said, turning up her nose. The unsightly view reminded Yufen of the days when she worked at the stationery store for the condescending Mr Huang. 'This is just shameless,' the woman continued, shaking her head.

Yufen was so used to being judged because of her poor, provincial family background that she had developed a sort of hypersensitivity towards insult. She could almost always detect a disparaging comment when one came in her direction. This time the word 'shameless' boomed through her mind like a temple gong.

'I bet you think that I "shamelessly" seduced your brother into marriage, that our marriage is a "shameless" one between a high-class man and a nobody. I bet you think I'm a second-class citizen who doesn't deserve your brother. You want to say to me, "What makes you think you can so easily become a part of our family?"'

Time did not weaken the cold war between Yufen and her sister-in-law. A remark here. A glance there. The two women devised subtle ways to criticize each other, often behind each other's backs. Watching the two roll their eyes at each other frustrated Yufen's husband Kai. He felt that negative feelings were beginning to infect his entire family. He attempted to remain neutral and concluded that the two women simply couldn't get along because of personality differences. But his wife remained convinced that the problem lay in his family's inability to accept her – a woman of such 'lowly' status.

As the unspoken pressure mounted, Yufen and Kai started thinking seriously about moving into an apartment of their own instead of continuing to live with Kai's family

– an arrangement that had been dictated by Taiwanese tradition. Kai's eagerness to move was largely based on his desire to throw parties. Since his grandfather had served as the political head of Yungho, Kai naturally had many friends, most of whom were even wealthier and more hedonistic than himself. He intended to continue his family's influential legacy by earning a reputation as an excellent host.

By the time Yufen and Kai reached their second anniversary, they had already started a small printing business inside their stationery store. Kai had purchased a printing press that produced wedding invitations, business cards and fliers. Propelled by the ongoing conflict between his sister and his wife, Kai came up with a proposal: He would hand the stationery store over to his brother and open a printing store at a different, more advantageous location, which would of course necessitate a move. This gave him a convenient excuse to leave his parents without making anyone lose face or causing undue confrontation, which Kai generally avoided.

With the aid of Kai's parents, the couple bought a new condo located in a building that had been recently constructed by Kai's uncle. Kai, who had an eye for design, took charge of the apartment's interior and used attractive, self-designed bamboo partitions to separate the rooms. Then he moved his printing machine into the condo.

From the beginning, the printing business ran in fits and starts. Kai prided himself on possessing a strong work ethic, yet this was primarily fuelled by the thrill of having started something new. When the novelty wore off, Kai discovered that, despite his innate creativity, the learning curve for operating the printing machine was a steep one because of the attention to detail that was required when arranging the movable type. His products were often flawed in one way or another, and he sometimes delivered orders late. He began to lose patience with his business and with himself, and he kept so busy that he didn't have much time to enjoy his new marriage; at day's end, all he wanted to do was sleep. Like many Taiwanese women at that time, his wife didn't demand that he spend more time with her, and for this he was grateful.

Meanwhile, Yufen was rather oblivious to her husband's professional struggles because she was busy with a new job of her own – being a mother. Gazing at the face of Little Ping, her newborn daughter, brought her delight, as well as a deep sense of responsibility. She was determined to raise the baby well. And she had a rather rigid view of how this was to be done.

While Yufen's ascetic upbringing had taught her to be stern and unyielding with her child, the frivolity of Kai's childhood had taught him the opposite. As the new parents worked through the issue of how to discipline their daughter, they started to quarrel.

'Rice paddy to rice paddy in three generations,' warns an old Chinese proverb, suggesting that a person raised in luxury usually squanders the resources that his parents and grandparents so arduously accumulated, dragging his family back into poverty.

Kai and his friends typified this proverb. Connoisseurs of food and drink, most of them came from well-to-do family backgrounds. They were blessed beneficiaries of Taiwan's blossoming economy.

Yufen and Kai's new home was frequently filled with late-night revelry. Sometimes, Kai's guests would even sleep over. When one of his former co-workers went through a difficult time, he stayed with them for three whole months.

At first, Kai's friends felt like family to Yufen. She admired their general willingness to help each other out and found them easy to talk to – even though most of their conversations were directed towards her husband instead of her. But eventually Yufen grew weary. As she busily prepared food for the throng of guests, she listened half-heartedly to the chatter in the adjacent room.

'I know everything about that,' one man bragged. 'Let me tell you what I think ...'

'Bleh, bleh, bleh, bleh, bleh,' Yufen thought resentfully. 'All these people want to do is show off how much they know. They must like the feeling of moving their mouths. But really, they're just full of hot air. And they're having a bad influence on Kai.'

Yufen was tired of serving guests who would babble about intangible topics like politics and philosophy while skirting around topics like family and relationships – things that she could more readily understand. After all, she was a practical woman who cared mostly about the survival of her family, and she was irritated that her husband, unlike her, did not seem to put his family first. She was beginning to feel alienated, as if she was being ousted from her husband's inner circle. The fact that she had to clean up the mess left behind by these people aggravated her further. Eventually she couldn't keep herself from expressing this displeasure in front of Kai and his friends.

'It's getting late and we need to rest,' she said, starting to raise her voice. Several heads turned. Such frankness was rather rare in the public behaviour of Taiwanese wives. 'It's time for you all to go home,' she continued.

Yufen's sternness seemed to do little to get her husband's attention, though, causing her to churn with anger. Once, when she was chatting with the wife of one of Kai's friends, she became so incensed at the thought of her husband that she grabbed a bottle of strong liquor and jerked off the top. She drank. Repulsed by the taste, she found a lychee – a whitish, cherry-sized fruit – and dropped it into the bottle. Then she continued to drink. After guzzling the whole bottle, she grabbed another bottle of liquor. By the time she had emptied both bottles, she began to feel violently ill.

'I'm going to die,' she thought.

Yufen didn't die, but she did vomit, again and again. And to her dismay, even that didn't attract her husband's attention; by the time he returned home, he, too, was too drunk to care.

When Yufen married Kai, she believed that she would never again have to worry about scarcity; her husband would abundantly provide, as long as he remained passionate about his work. He had won numerous gold medals in school, came from a prestigious family, and was clever and resourceful. A recipe for success. Yufen was so intoxicated by the idea of being married to such a capable man that she tried to ignore her growing disenchantment towards her marriage. 'At least his business is going well,' she thought – that is, until it came to an abrupt end.

Kai came to realize that he would not be able to comfortably support his growing family if he stayed in the printing business. 'Oh forget it. I'll try something else,' he thought, unfazed. Then he announced to his wife that he would try something entirely new: real estate.

Due to Taiwan's soaring economy, demand for real estate was sky-rocketing, and by the mid-1980s, almost 80 per cent of families in Taiwan would become home-owners – one of the highest percentages in the world.[2] For this reason, Kai and several of his friends decided to start their own real estate agency. Kai kept his printing machine in order to print advertisements and fliers, and whenever he needed advice he would simply ask his father, who had also been involved in real estate. Kai enjoyed tackling the challenges of his new job, which felt less mundane than his previous one. Whenever a building was ready for sale, he would print out advertisements and set up flags outside the building. Not surprisingly, Kai's company raked in profits.

Kai's initial financial success enabled him and his family to live comfortably. Yufen could cook and heat water using city gas, which had just become available, instead of having to order bulky gas tanks, which most families still used. Kai also provided his family with a washer, a refrigerator, a colour television and a sound system, though such appliances were no longer considered luxury items. Within the next ten years, the average Taiwanese family would own more washing machines, colour television sets and refrigerators than the average American family.[3]

In spite of these material pleasures, Yufen was not wholly satisfied. Her home, though full of modern amenities, was characterized by a disconcerting coldness. Due to the flexibility of Kai's new job, as well as the good relationships he managed to maintain with his co-workers, he was spending an increasing amount of time in Beitou, a nighttime hot-spot known for bars, clubs and a lively red-light district. At that time, Beitou was known for offering Japanese-style fun, reminiscent of the Japanese occupation a few decades before. After an afternoon soak in nearby hot springs, men would often spend their evenings drinking and being entertained by beautiful waitresses who were hired to sing and socialize, like traditional Japanese geishas. Sometimes Kai and his friends would rent private rooms where they could drink and belt out karaoke tunes without fear of being chastized.

Ostensibly, the excursions were business-related. For instance, sometimes he would invite key government building inspectors out for drinks – a common form of bribery that was deemed necessary for maintaining positive business relationships at the time. Kai, however, thrived on these activities, and his interest in drinking seemed to exceed his interest in his actual job.

Yet Kai and his friends rarely warned each other about the extent of their drinking. 'How much somebody drinks is his own business,' Kai figured. 'Besides, drinking is a part of Taiwanese culture!' In addition, the trips to Beitou helped Kai relax and take his mind off what he considered to be an uncomfortable family situation.

He had begun to realize that, in addition to coming from vastly different family backgrounds, he and his wife also had very different personalities. Before marrying Yufen, he knew that she had a tenacious temper; he had seen her upbraid customers at their stationery store, though she had never treated him with such disrespect. It wasn't until after marriage that he really started to be affected by the repercussions of her strong personality.

One night, when Kai and his friends were joking around about their Beitou adventures, Yufen threw her temper without warning.

'I've had enough of this useless talk, and I don't want my kids to hear it. Just go home – all of you!' she bellowed.

Kai froze, paralysed by the feeling of having lost face in front of so many friends.

'I said, GO!' she repeated.

Another time, on a night when Kai had come home with alcohol on his breath, Yufen threw a fit, though she did not explicitly spell out the reason for her anger. 'Maybe she thinks that I've been with another woman,' Kai thought. Though he felt that she generally trusted him in this area, he had brought home a matchbox from a bar that he had gone to earlier in the evening, and from the look of the matchbox, it was obvious that the women who worked at the venue offered services beyond waiting tables ...

But Kai chose not to dwell on the possibility that he had incited jealousy in his wife. 'Maybe the problem is something else,' he concluded. He much preferred ignoring such matters.

What he couldn't ignore, however, were their continuing disagreements about how to raise their children – disagreements which escalated after Yufen gave birth to a son in 1978. In addition to holding onto a different approach to discipline, Yufen held a traditional Taiwanese mind-set that favoured male children over females. A view that, ironically, her husband despised.

'You just can't raise the children like this,' Kai objected. 'If you play favourites, they'll sense it.'

'But the children are still so little! They still don't understand what's going on.'

'Little?!' Kai roared incredulously. Although he once prided himself in having a mild temperament, he found his wife's feisty demeanour to be contagious. 'Our girl's already in kindergarten. Of course they know what's going on.'

'But ...' Yufen began. Kai, preparing for an onslaught of heated words, started to walk away. Neither one of them knew how to communicate amicably about their differences, and since Kai had already stated his opinion on the matter, he decided to avoid further argument. This blatant indifference infuriated Yufen.

'Where do you think you're going?!' she barked.

'Forget about her,' Kai thought as he walked out the door. 'There's just no way I can talk with this woman in a civil manner. If she doesn't talk to me, I'm not going to talk to her.'

Simply getting through a single evening at home had become so strenuous that Kai lost the desire to think about his family's future. He found two avenues of comfort: drink and work. Although the work itself did not always go smoothly, he enjoyed the relationships that sprang from it, including those with his construction workers, who tended to be straightforward, boisterous and, best of all, laid back – a characteristic his spouse did not possess. On most days, Kai and his blue-collar employees would work at one site for several hours, chat and share a few drinks together, and then move on to another site. Kai began to see these people as his best friends, though he refrained from confiding in them about his family.

'That's one thing they won't understand,' he reasoned.

Hands flailed in raucous confusion as Kai and a friend came head to head in *cai quan*, a bewilderingly complex version of 'paper, rock, scissors' that was often used as a drinking game.

'Wah!' the crowd cried as Kai threw up his hands in momentary defeat. He didn't mind the loss, really. The punishment was beer, his favourite beverage. He took a few generous gulps, and for a moment felt off-kilter. When the sensation subsided, he continued to play.

Hours later, it was clear that Kai had made an impressive come-back and had emerged as the most sober player in the group. A friend took a final, drowsy swig and passed out in his chair. Kai, who had often been in his friend's shoes, volunteered to take the man home.

As usual, Kai had no idea how many beers he had consumed that evening, though he did feel he was sober enough to drive. If the night had been less exhilarating, he might have come home early, perhaps at midnight; or, if the evening had been unusually dull, as early as ten. But this evening, by the time he had dropped his friends off and had returned home, it was past three in the morning. His two toddlers had long since gone to bed.

Apparently Kai had been drunker than he had realized, because his wife could barely manage to wake him up at noon the next day.

'The phone!' Yufen said angrily, pushing him awake.

When Kai reluctantly lumbered to the phone, he discovered that his crew would be taking on a new project in the afternoon. He quickly changed clothes and left the house, and resuming his regular cycle of drinking, working and carousing. As Yufen watched her husband leave, she both despised the friends who were influencing him and worried about the family finances. She could not manage to loosen herself from the grip of her childhood anxiety – the feeling of holding an empty pot in her hands, begging for something to eat.

Yufen did have a basis for worry: Because Kai had such difficulty in getting up, he sometimes worked as little as three to four hours a day. Furthermore, since he went to Beitou several nights a week, he spent a good proportion of his salary on drink. Eventually the family's unhealthy financial situation began to show obvious symptoms. Banks would call, always at 3:30 p.m., to warn them about a bounced cheque or an overdue loan payment. Yufen tried not to let the calls bother her, especially since her husband always managed to resolve the problems somehow. Secretly, he had started to borrow money from his friends.

What bothered Yufen the most was the effect her husband's habits were having on their children. One night when Kai came home, he swaggered to the couch and passed out, too drunk to even greet them.

'You drunkard! You irresponsible man!' Yufen shouted.

Yufen knew that many, if not most Taiwanese men at the time had similar lifestyles. She knew that drinking with friends was an inexorable part of the working man's culture. But as she watched her husband doze on the couch, she seriously pondered for the first time: 'Is this really normal? Or is there something really wrong here?'

On one of Kai's sober days, Yufen reminisced about how, during their courtship, she had admired Kai's natural way with children. His profligate lifestyle couldn't undermine this ability, and she admired him from a distance as he called his daughter over. He hoisted her onto his lap and rocked her in his arms. He told a joke and they both burst out in giggles, as if they had never experienced anything funnier.

Suddenly the phone rang. The beautiful moment was shattered. Yufen could tell from her husband's enthusiasm that a friend was inviting him out for a drink. After hanging up the phone, he immediately changed clothes and walked out the front door, as if the child he had cuddled only moments before no longer existed.

Such things tore at Yufen's heart. Even if her husband chose to spend his free time doing nothing but watching television on the couch – even then she felt she could be happy. Instead, he was hardly ever around. 'How can he be like this, not paying attention to his own family? He has two children at home. How can he pay more attention to his friends?'

When she thought about these things, her body felt like a pressure cooker, stewing up a concoction of anger, sadness and bitterness. Sometimes she would lose control of herself and simply explode.

One day, her five-year-old daughter fell ill. Little Ping was usually a brave girl who didn't make a fuss, even when she went to the doctor's office to get an injection. But when it came to oral medicine, she absolutely refused to open her mouth. When Yufen tried to feed her the liquid, the girl got up and lunged away from her mother's hands. Again Yufen grabbed. Again Little Ping squirmed away.

'You're just like your father!' Yufen thought, muscles tightening. 'It's time you learned a lesson!'

With almost superhuman determination, Yufen picked up a metal coat hanger and brought it down hard upon her daughter's soft skin. Swat! Then she poured the medicine into a spoon. Little Ping tried to get away. Swat, swat, swat!

Finally, Yufen managed to force the spoon between her daughter's pursed lips.

Suddenly, Little Ping bit down, breaking the spoon. As mother and daughter continued to wrestle with each other, blood started dripping out of the girl's mouth.

Kai came home to the sound of his daughter crying. Blood flowed out of her mouth and welts covered her body. He ran to the girl and held her.

'How could you hit the child like this?!' he fumed. It pained him to see his daughter like this, especially since he didn't believe in corporal punishment. 'She's so young! She doesn't know any better!'

'But she wouldn't eat this medicine!' Yufen protested.

'Couldn't you think of another way? You could slowly coax her into eating it. Or just take her to the doctor and let her have an injection. Why did you have to do it this way? Why did you have to force her?'

'But look how stubborn she is!'

'Aiya! It's just wrong to hit her like that.'

'But look at what she did ...' Yufen began, unaware that her husband had mentally left the conversation. 'Forget about it. I can't calm her down,' he thought angrily. He was tired of her incessant whining and nagging, and although he often listened quietly and unresponsively, he seethed inside.

As Yufen continued to shout, Kai perfunctorily turned and walked out. As usual, he would head straight for a friend's house, a haven where he would be safe from these seemingly irreconcilable conflicts.

There, he drank himself into oblivion and, blissfully forgetting the day's heated exchange, passed out on the sofa.

Notes

1. Biaohui – lending groups organized by families and close friends; members make regular contributions and then can borrow money from the pool when needed.
2. Davidson and Reed, *ibid*, p. 185.
3. John F. Copper, *Taiwan: Nation-State or Province?*, 3rd edn, Boulder, Colorado: Westview Press, 1999.
4. Copper, *ibid*.

Chapter 6

Life had become complicated, and Mei Chen was glad that she had freed her infant son from the mess. Actually, when the kind doctor had urged her to give her son up for adoption, she felt it was obvious that this was the right decision. She already felt terrible about her behaviour as a mother.

'I'm too young and too poor to raise him,' she thought. 'These other people will give him a better life.'

Now that she had got rid of her husband and two sons, Mei felt free to continue working in restaurants, where she often had to mix with unwholesome company. This was how she found herself trapped in the entanglement of gangs.

Mei harboured mixed feelings towards the gang members. On one hand, they gave the restaurant good business and mostly treated her well. On the other hand, they had fearsome tempers, exacerbated by the fact that they carried knives and guns. If someone happened to offend them, they would smash their plates and cups to the ground with a roar. Mei and her co-workers would then dutifully pick up the mess.

One evening, a group of customers who were members of a gang invited Mei to go out with them and have some fun. Simply not in the mood, Mei refused.

The rest of the evening passed without incident and after Mei's late-night shift ended, she left the restaurant alone, exhausted and eager to return home. Suddenly, a blue van pulled up. Three men armed with knifes jumped out. They grabbed her and pushed her into the van. Then she recognized them. They were the gangsters whom she had rejected earlier in the day.

Knowing that nobody was near enough to hear her if she tried to cry or scream, Mei kept her mouth shut. She knew what was coming.

'I deserve this, I'm very bad, I've had a bad past, very bad.'

The men drove her to a nondescript building, obscured in darkness. They forced her into a small room. As they took turns raping her, she tried to appear brave, though inwardly she was afraid – afraid of getting pregnant or contracting a disease, afraid of what they would do to her afterwards.

When they had finished, Mei finally broke her silence. 'Now that you're finished, please take me home,' she said, her voice forcibly calm and confident. 'I won't tell the police, because I don't know you at all. But if you leave me here, I might not be able to get home.'

'Fine,' said one of her attackers, wearing an expression that almost resembled – pity? But the other two refused. An argument ensued.

'C'mon, we just wanted the sex, right? We didn't mean to kill anyone,' insisted the first. Finally, his argument prevailed, and the men drove Mei to a remote area near a mountain.

'You'd better not report this to the police,' one of them warned as they let her out.

'I promise,' Mei answered, trying to hide the pain in her voice. 'Just don't bother me again.'

* * *

The next day, it was back to work as usual. Mei had already been sexually abused as a child; she wasn't terribly surprised that it had happened again. And she certainly was not going to quit her job. After all, she earned such an impressive income that she could afford to live by herself, and she was even able to send her asthmatic mother a one-time gift of 70,000 Taiwanese dollars, which would have been an unimaginable sum just a few years earlier. In fact, her relatives in Ali Mountain were still accustomed to cooking sweet potatoes over an open fire for their meals. Mei certainly was not going to quit her job.

The incident didn't keep Mei from continuing to associate with gang members either. In her line of work, there was little way to avoid them. In time, she caught the eye of one particular customer, the leader of a gang. Significantly older than her, Big Brother Cho was not a particularly large or tall man, and one of his eyes drooped ineffectually – the result of being gouged out during a fight. Even so, he managed to exude an impenetrable aura of toughness.

One day Big Brother Cho asked Mei to move in with him.

'He seems decent. So why not?' she thought. Indeed, after they started living together she discovered, with much relief, that Big Brother Cho did not hit her like her first husband did. For this, she felt lucky. Also, his apartment was spacious and tastefully decorated, and guests often streamed in and out. Mei started to feel as if she had finally found a good man.

When Big Brother Cho wasn't at home, he liked to call Mei up and invite her out.

'I'm at a restaurant with some friends. Do you want to come?' he asked. When Mei arrived at the restaurant, he was waiting for her at the door. His one good eye took a careful look at her and stopped at her feet.

'We need to get you some good shoes,' he said, taking her by the arm. After a brief shopping trip, they returned to the restaurant and entered a private room that was reserved for the gang. Mei proudly strutted around in her new shoes. She would come to love the fact that Big Brother Cho wanted to ensure that his girlfriend was always presentable, for his efforts to maintain face led to the immediate expansion of her wardrobe.

Mei knew blissfully little about Big Brother Cho's 'business' dealings. Whenever fellow gang members came to the apartment to discuss serious matters in the living-room, Mei would retreat to the bedroom.

She knew there was trouble when Big Brother Cho started to make frantic phone calls, apparently to arrange meetings. After one such meeting, Big Brother Cho returned home horrifically stoic. In cold, calculated movements, he sat down silently, his muscles tense. Mei wondered what his eye had just seen, what his hands had just done, but she refrained from asking questions. She knew how to detect a potential explosion from the expression on a persons face, and she knew better than to set off a bomb.

When Big Brother Cho wanted to escape from the stress of work, he took Mei on week-long excursions to places like Guanzihling, an area famous for its hot springs, where they would relax and drink together. Although Mei gladly took time off work to accompany her boyfriend on these trips, some of his other demands were not so easy to comply with.

Big Brother Cho was like Mei's first husband in that he was prone to jealousy. He ordered one of his trusted men to follow Mei, even when she briefly left the apartment to buy groceries. Then Big Brother Cho forced Mei to quit her job because there she had such frequent contact with other men. Confined to the apartment while Big Brother Cho was out conducting his business dealings, Mei began to feel lonely and trapped – a state of mind that was uncomfortably familiar.

Mei began to loathe the thought of staying with Big

Brother Cho, but she also feared the thought of leaving him. A break-up could have serious repercussions: She could be beaten by his men or, more likely, killed.

A few months after Mei had moved in with Big Brother Cho, he was caught in a drug deal. When the police arrested him, he possessed several kilograms of drugs – a serious offence that would land him a long sentence in a maximum-security prison on Green Island.

'When I go to prison, will you leave me?' Big Brother Cho asked Mei after his arrest. Seizing the chance to resolve her quandary in a diplomatic way, Mei tried to convince her boyfriend that waiting for him to be released would be too difficult, that she would miss him too much. The stakes were high. She knew that if Big Brother Cho did not agree to the split, then her life would become miserable again after he was released. Finally, after much persuasion, he agreed. Mei applied for a job at a different restaurant, changed her hairstyle, and dressed differently so that she would not be easily recognized. She was finally free.

Less than a year after Mei's nuptial knot had come undone, she was given a second chance. Han, a customer at the restaurant where she worked, was a construction worker who specialized in laying cement. Just as she began to feel lonely and in need of a man's love, he began to show interest in her. They lived together for two years, and during this time Han asked Mei to marry him. She declined. He asked again. And again. And again.

Mei felt increasingly dubious about the idea, especially since he had stopped working, opting to spend her money instead. Even so, the emotional black hole in her heart devoured her sense of judgment. 'Well, he really does care for me,' she thought, her former resolve wearing thin. Meanwhile, Han became more insistent in his proposals, which started to sound more like commands.

'You're already living with me in my house, so how can you not marry me?' he contended.

'Oh ... OK,' she eventually surrendered.

Mei's previous marriage had been so terrible that it was difficult for her to imagine anything worse. Not long after she married Han, however, the unimaginable became reality.

What frightened Mei most was that when her husband was angry, he exercised absolutely no restraint. With one hand, he would hold her hands behind her back. With the other, he would pound her, punching so ruthlessly that it was as if he was trying to win a boxing match. Sometimes he beat her for half an hour or more before he became too tired to lift a fist.

One day Han took Mei to a kind of pub called a *jiu-jia*.[1] As Mei mingled gregariously, Han spoke with the pub manager and then returned to his wife's side.

'Stay and work here today. I'll come back later tonight and get you,' he told her. Then he left.

Mei worked as usual, serving drinks and flirting with the customers. One customer, though, was not satisfied with her service. He wanted more.

He wanted her.

Peeved by the man's insolence, Mei went straight to her manager.

'I didn't say I would do something like this,' she declared. 'I'm only here to drink with them.'

The manager looked at her sternly.

'You've already been left here, so you must do it!' he ordered.

Mei was stunned. She refused to believe what the manager was implying and started arguing with him.

Finally he said, 'If you don't believe me, then call your husband.' Fuming, Mei went to a phone and dialled.

As she held the phone to her ear and listened, she felt as if her spirit was leaving her body. The words coming through the receiver were so unbelievable, so odious, that her mouth froze, unable to respond.

'Just stay there, be good and do what they tell you to do,' said the man on the other end of the line. The man who, for a hefty sum, had sold his own wife into prostitution.

Several days later, Mei's husband returned to pick her up. The whole experience left her body tense with fear, though her husband showed no sympathy.

'There's nothing to be afraid of,' he admonished. 'The most important thing is to make money.'

'What?! How can you talk like that?' she wanted to say. 'How can a man send the woman he cares about into bed with other men?!' But like a terrified hostage, she kept silent, desperately hoping that the incident would not be repeated.

Han took Mei to brothels regularly. Sometimes he tried to stay near her so that he could personally make deals with customers. Sometimes, when only paying customers were granted entrance, he would wait outside a brothel for hours in order to make sure that his wife didn't run away. And sometimes, he left her at a brothel for long periods of time, but not before borrowing an average of $100,000 from the managers and telling them to detain his wife until after the debt was paid off.

Some managers were disgusted by such business dealings, telling Han, 'You have no right to be her master, her pimp!' Many managers, though, eagerly accepted his offers.

'You can't leave,' these managers would tell Mei when she attempted to go home. 'If you leave, then you'll have to return the money.' Mei knew that this would be impossible. She couldn't pay off the debt herself because Han took every cent of her earnings to gamble or buy alcohol. She couldn't even purchase items as necessary as underwear without his permission. Furthermore, if she came home of her own free will, he would surely beat her – perhaps to death. Divorce seemed impossible because Han would never agree to it. And because she knew of nobody who could help her, the thought of running away had not yet seriously crossed her mind. So Mei resorted instead to delicate persuasion.

'I'm too tired to keep working,' she said. 'I need a break, I'm so tired.' Her words spun Han into a rage.

'WHAT?! You good-for-nothing … You're not good enough to be my wife!' he shouted, punching her in the face. He smashed her head against a wall. Mei crumpled, her head throbbing with pain.

'Well, if you dislike me so much, then let's just get divorced,' she moaned meekly.

'It's not that easy!' he rebuffed. 'You can't do that until you make enough money to satisfy me!'

The beatings destroyed what little was left of Mei's self-esteem, which had already been wounded by years of past abuse. Two or three times a week, her body was covered in bruises when she went to work. When people inquired about her injuries, she gave the standard reply: 'I fell down' or 'I had a motor-scooter accident.'

Once when Mei tried to resist Han, he drove her to a deserted mountain and grabbed her roughly, as if she was a prisoner of war. He picked up a large rock.

'If you don't do what I want you to do, I'll smash your head in with this rock! I'LL SMASH YOUR HEAD IN!' Knowing that Han was a man of his word, Mei said nothing. She quaked in fear.

'How did I get married to the devil – no, he's worse than the devil. He treats me as if I'm not human, as if he only married me so that he could control me like this.'

Mei's enslavement was so extensive that she was even afraid of telling her own family about her predicament. Her in-laws were also completely unaware of the situation; in fact, they continued to think highly of their son, especially since he often gave them gifts of money – money earned through the sale of his wife's flesh. For a period of time, Han even took Mei to his parents' house once a month because his mother had complained, 'How come we never get to see your wife?'

The reason, of course, was that Han was forcing her to keep busy. In one particular *jiu-jia*, he forced her to work virtually non-stop and to sleep within the confines of the *jiu-jia*. For more than a year, she hardly stepped outside, and she was allowed to leave the vicinity only when Han wanted to sleep with her or parade her in front of his parents.

Giving birth to two sons did nothing to loosen his grip on her psyche. Until, a flicker of hope: Han won $3 million in the lottery – a sum that would alleviate the need for her to continue working. Or so she thought.

'I don't want to work any more,' she said to him after the win.

'Do you think you're going to get money from me, then? If you want money, earn it yourself!' he exclaimed, punching her.

As the blows fell, she lamented, 'If he kills me right now, nobody will care. Even my family wouldn't know about it. I can't go on. I can't follow this man for the rest of my life.'

Like many young people at the time, Han and Mei migrated north to Taipei in search of a better life; yet even there, Han forced Mei to continue working as a prostitute. By this time, she was sick of supplying her husband's bottomless gambling addiction by selling her own flesh. She was sick of customers who would demand her services when she had already finished work. She felt so sick that she couldn't even cry, couldn't even feel the pain any more.

She wanted to kill the man who called himself her husband. But she found another solution instead. Mei and the other prostitutes occasionally had time to chat on their breaks, and from these conversations, Mei discovered that she was not alone in her predicament. In fact, many of her co-workers were forced into prostitution either by their husbands or by desperate financial circumstances. Many supported children with their wages.

The story of one woman from the southern part of Taiwan had a particularly profound impact on Mei. Her husband, like Han, refused to work himself, but rather forced her into prostitution in order to support their two children. In the end, the woman decided to run away. Since she knew that her husband would literally kill her if he found her, she fled north to Taipei, where she continued working as a prostitute – but on her own terms.

'There's just no other kind of work I can do,' she told Mei. 'I don't have the skills to do anything else.' Mei sensed that instead of feeling trapped by this reality, her co-worker felt liberated. She was allowed to go out by herself and spend her money as she wished.

'Maybe I should run away too,' Mei mused.

So after being married for more than four years, Mei decided to turn her bruise-covered back on Han and their two children, aged two and three. The opportunity came when she started working for a kind manager who refused to give her husband money in advance.

One evening at around midnight, two hours before Mei was scheduled to get off work, she furtively approached her manager.

'Please give me my money tonight,' she said.

The man nodded. For a moment, Mei thought she saw pity dart across his eyes.

'OK,' he said. 'Be careful when you go downstairs.'

At two o'clock, the manager sent one of the other prostitutes outside to assess the situation. She spotted Mei's husband, smoking and waiting for her a considerable distance away.

Mei bounded down the stairs. As she passed a window in the stairway, she glanced outside, saw her husband, and ran faster. She knew that if Han saw her trying to escape, he would chase her down and then – she was too terrified to think about what would happen after that.

She ran out of a back door into a narrow, dingy alley. And she continued to run. Her heart pounded in fear. She could easily imagine the conversation that Han would soon have with her manager. 'Where's my wife? Why did you give her the money without my agreement? Why did you just let her leave?' he would ask.

Mei knew that she needed somewhere to hide, but she feared that if she ran to a family member, her husband would eventually track her down. Mei felt her pockets. They were full of $80,000 in cash – she had almost forgotten what it felt like to have that much money at hand.

Since her husband could control her no longer, Mei decided to take a vacation. Since she had never been taught how to manage money, she could think of nothing more sensible to do. For about a month, she travelled around the central part of Taiwan, wanting nothing more than to set aside her troubled past and have some fun.

In the meantime, Han did some travelling of his own, paying sinister visits to Mei's family members. He threatened them, demanding to know where they had hidden Mei when, in fact, none of them had even realized that Han had forced her into prostitution.

After Mei had spent a considerable amount of her savings, she realized that she needed to start earning money again. Feeling as if she had no other choice, she went back to Taipei to sell the only thing she really knew how to sell.

The tall man leaned over towards Mei's ear. 'Let's go to a hotel,' he whispered. She looked at the customer, carefully considering his proposition – after all, this would be the first time she had the freedom to accept or reject.

When Mei had first approached her manager about the possibility of earning 'outside income', she discovered that she would be responsible for giving $300 of her earnings to her manager for every half-hour she spent with a customer, whether the earnings came from providing a massage or some other service. The rest was hers to keep.

'If you do it, call me as soon as you get to the hotel,' the manager said to her. 'You'll need to let me know where you are in case something happens. So if you run into trouble, you can get help. Also, you have to help us make sure that if we need you back at work, then we won't have trouble finding you.' Mei had deeply appreciated her manager's concern, which far exceeded that of her husband.

And now she had the chance to do what her husband had always done for her: make a decision. She took another look at the customer. He was decent-looking and seemed harmless enough.

'OK,' Mei answered.

When the two arrived at the hotel, Mei immediately called her manager to inform him of her whereabouts.

'OK. Got it,' he replied.

As they walked to the hotel room, Mei looked around surreptitiously, drawing a mental map of the building's layout in case she needed to make a quick getaway. Once inside the room, she continued to scrutinize her surroundings as the man took a shower. When he finished, she showered as well. Then they slept together.

After the man finished, he started to chat, as if he was at confession.

'See, I'm not married and really needed sex, so I bought myself a sex toy. I kept it at home for whenever I needed to use it. But in the end, I got an infection because I didn't clean up after myself, so now I don't want to use the thing.'

Mei laughed out loud. She felt so free. The man chuckled and continued: 'Anyway, doing it with a real person is better. Worth the money.'

He paused. 'So where do you live?'

'I live at the massage parlour,' she answered.

'Next time, can I take you out somewhere?'

Mei hesitated. She had heard from her co-workers that some men were genuinely interested in starting relationships, and that she would have to practise the skill of discouraging unwanted complications.

'Depends on whether I'm in the mood,' she said. 'Well, looks like it's time to get back to the parlour!'

Mei discovered that, when using effective bargaining techniques, she could make a great deal of money through prostitution – as much as $100,000 a month, now that her husband couldn't pilfer all of her earnings. Many customers would be interested in sex after their thirty-minute massage and would offer her up to $5,000 for her services. If she found the price to be acceptable and the man to be trustworthy, she would agree. If she had any qualms about a man's character after speaking with him or simply wasn't in the mood, she would refuse. She would always demand payment up front; otherwise, many men would simply walk away after the deed was done.

Mei became skilled at acting, feigning different personalities in order to suit the needs of her customers. To some men, she would be a tender lover. To others, a witty one. Her personality became as formless as melting ice-cream, and although she was able to maintain peaceful relationships with those around her, she began to lose a sense of who she really was.

Since Mei was young and attractive, she was soon able to find an even more lucrative job at a pub. There, customers tended to be so rich that they would flaunt their wealth by soaking their feet in imported brandy. Most were business owners and other beneficiaries of Taiwan's soaring economy. With these customers, Mei could demand as much as $10,000 for her services.

The polite and refined men who came to the pub would often phrase their propositions subtly and with elegance. Although Mei appreciated the fact that this new breed of customers treated her with such respect, she found it more difficult to discern what a customer actually wanted.

'May I invite you to come out with me?' one customer asked, in what Mei later discovered was a glorified proposition for sex. She was far more accustomed to the straightforwardly vulgar men who frequented the massage parlour.

Post-coital conversations with these high-class men were also different. 'Don't you ever think of getting married?' one man asked her. 'Do you always want to be like this, to live like this?'

'Actually, I got into this whole thing because I got married,' Mei could have answered. Instead, she replied, 'I don't know. Right now I'm not thinking of getting married. I haven't found the right person yet.'

Truth be told, Mei's marriage was the one thing she wished she could get out of her mind. She enjoyed her new-found independence but was plagued by constant fear that her husband would find her. A few months after her return to Taipei, she saw him once in a crowded shopping area. Even though he did not see her, the too-close encounter made her shudder.

To calm her nerves, Mei imbibed throughout her evening shifts, loosely timing her drinks so that she would be sober enough to socialize cogently with the customers. Afraid of bumping into her husband at night, she sometimes stayed at work until seven or eight in the morning. Other times after work, she would go drinking in the safe company of co-workers and friends.

Sometimes these new companions invited Mei to join

them at temples. '*Bai-bai*² will help you make more money,' one friendly co-worker said of idol worship.

Mei gladly tagged along, finding it hard to say no. 'Why not? Besides, it's fun,' she thought to herself.

Mei worshipped almost all of Taiwan's major idols in more than ten different temples in Taipei. She especially enjoyed going to the Eighteen Lords Temple in Tamshui, a considerable distance away from where she worked.

Inside this temple, giant candles lit up the central prayer hall, with several bronze idols in the centre. Less architecturally grandiose than other temples in Taipei, it was always surprisingly crowded, even late at night. According to temple legends, some time during the Qing dynasty seventeen people and a dog were making a nautical pilgrimage to a shrine when their boat started to sink. All seventeen people died, but the dog, while trying to save its master, miraculously survived. Thus the dog earned a designation as the eighteenth god of the temple.³

Despite the temple's tragic beginnings, it was believed that any requests presented there would be fulfilled. For many years, even Taiwanese pop stars would worship at the temple, presenting offerings of incense sticks or cigarettes – acceptable contributions, since these gods were purportedly fond of smoking.⁴

As Mei offered her incense sticks, she prayed, 'Please give me peace. Please help me make more money.' Even though she already earned a sizeable income, she always found a way to spend it all.

Mei hoped that worshipping the gods would help her find spiritual respite amid her muddled life. But instead of quieting her restless spirit, the temple visits contributed to the chaos that had long since brewed within her. Her father's spells, the childhood visions of dead people and snakes – all were haunting premonitions of what was to come. Now, it was as if going to the temples opened a door in her soul, giving her involuntary access to the spiritual realm.

So one night Mei started to hear them.

She was resting quietly in a massage chair, waiting for customers to arrive, when she suddenly felt something pressing down on her, pinning her to the chair. She couldn't move. She heard the muted garble of male and female voices, and as her eyes strained towards the sounds, she saw a dark object, devoid of any recognizable shape.

Then, nothing. The sensations subsided, and she sat upright. The incident was so strange that Mei tried to think nothing of it. Her work continued as usual, and she still went to the temples to worship when she had the chance.

Once, as she entered a temple with a group of co-workers, she heard another voice: 'Those people are here to worship.'

Mei looked around, finding it odd that someone would talk about her and her friends in this way. 'Of course we're here to worship,' she thought.

At a different temple, she heard yet another voice: 'Look, those people are here to worship,' it said.

Mei turned around, expecting to see someone standing next to her. Again, she could not identify the source of the voice, which was so clear, so real. She began to feel uneasy. 'Where are the noises coming from?' she thought. 'A group of people trying to cause trouble? Trying to bother me?'

Then one evening, as she was resting at home, she felt the familiar sensation of something pressing down on her body. She wanted to get up but couldn't. Her body was glued to the chair on which she was sitting. Then she heard some voices. Shoved into a state of partial consciousness, she dreamt.

Many celestial hands take care of a little baby, dark and naked. The baby is naughty, though, and so is cast from heaven to the ground, where it is entrusted to the care of a woman. 'You are this baby,' the voices say. 'You are this baby, you are this baby ...'

The next morning, Mei woke up and discovered that she was still sitting upright in the chair, with her head tilted uncomfortably to one side.

'What happened? Why am I here?' she thought drowsily.

From then on, the voices increased in number and intensity as Mei began to display signs of classic schizo-phrenia.[5] She was convinced that her hallucinations were real, and that the voices she heard came from actual people. On occasion she doubted the latter, but even then she figured that someone conspiring against her had planted a device in her ears, causing the sounds.

No matter where she went, the voices seemed to know her inner thoughts and feelings. Like diabolic sports commentators, they would discuss her every move.

'Look! Now she's changing clothes!'

Mei began to feel acutely self-conscious, particularly about her weight. Naturally big-boned, she was not as slim and slight as most Taiwanese women. Her ears perked up when she heard rumours that she could easily lose weight by taking drugs, and when a drug dealer started to frequent the massage parlour, she took notice. One of her co-workers knew the man well and would eagerly invite him into the parlour whenever he passed by.

One evening, the man walked in and motioned to Mei, beckoning her to follow. He walked to the rest-room and, once they were both inside, he produced a pouch of speed.

'If you take this, you can drink and drink, and you won't get drunk. You can drink all day, and you won't throw up.'

Mei thought about the times when she had indeed failed to properly control her drinking on the job. She remembered how she had to run to the rest-room and throw up before she could resume drinking. She thought about her weight and how the voices mocked her about it. Then she glanced at the white powder that the man was collecting into a line.

'Doesn't smell like cigarettes,' she thought to herself as she bent down towards the powder. Then, with little hesitation, she snorted the drug.

The rest of the day passed in a daze, with dulled senses. Mei had no desire to eat. After work, she collapsed onto her bed, expecting to fall asleep quickly, as usual. Instead, she lay awake, her heart still pounding from the speed.

Despite the frustration of sleeplessness, Mei started regularly purchasing speed and marijuana, as well as a host of other drugs that she took when she felt afraid or upset. Her senses became so dulled by drugs that even her fears dissipated, resurfacing only when a customer overtly possessed a weapon. When things went smoothly, Mei slept with an average of seven or eight men each night. To attract even more customers, she started buying sexy, tight-fitting clothes. All the while, the voices inside her head cheered her on.

'If you keep on working, then you can buy more beautiful clothes,' they urged. 'We know you love to wear beautiful clothes.'

Mei spent at least $3,000 on every article of clothing she bought, and her favourite was a $10,000 velvet suit. She figured that it was a good investment that exuded an aura of class, which attracted her wealthier customers.

By the grace of a higher power, among the hundreds of men whom Mei slept with, none tried to harm her, and she never contracted a sexually transmitted disease. Even so, the drugs made her pale and gaunt, and before long, she lost nearly twenty kilograms of weight.

Mei had never before possessed so much money, so she knew little about managing it. If not for her addictions to shopping, drugs and gambling, she could have saved enough money to buy several condos. Instead, she settled for renting a one-bedroom suite in an apartment complex that housed many young women like her – single and employed at various entertainment venues. She lived alone, afraid that a room-mate would not like her drug habit, which was becoming more and more severe.

As Mei lay in her lavishly expensive bed, her clouded senses detected the sirens of approaching squad cars. Police officers were raiding the apartment complex yet again, most likely to confiscate drugs or break up fights, during which the young female residents would beat each other bloody.

Police officers also made frequent appearances at the pubs where Mei worked. Once, a local policeman she despised started to eye her and asked her to sleep with him. Mei refused. Not easily rebuffed, the officer approached her manager.

'I want this woman,' he said, agitated. The manager walked over to Mei and started to plead.

'If you say no, the police will raid this place. They'll close us down.'

Mei enjoyed having the freedom to choose whom she would sleep with, but now even that was being taken away. Since the policeman did not intend to pay, the manager offered Mei money out of his own pocket and pushed her to say yes. Eventually, she was forced to agree.

Mei had never before felt so utterly disgusted by her job. She felt as if she was being raped. Moreover, the persistent man continued to frequent the pub, so whenever Mei spotted him from a distance, she would look for a place to hide. Once she even ran out the back door of the pub and didn't return to work until the next day.

After encountering an uncomfortable situation such as this, Mei would usually switch jobs. Yet every place where she worked – from the shoddiest massage parlours to the most up-market pubs – would be visited by at least one policeman who would drop by until a particular employee caught his eye.

Some policemen overtly solicited bribes from the managers. 'Give me some money, or else I'll make sure this place gets shut down,' said one.

'If you don't give me what I want, I won't let you continue to run this business,' said another.

Since most policemen would give up after not being able to find a particular woman once or twice, one pub manager constructed a secret room where his employees could hide. Once, when a policeman started to pursue Mei, she hid in a warehouse behind the pub.

Unfortunately, such tactics could not protect her from another kind of enemy. Ever since she had started doing drugs, the voices inside her head had increased in intensity, frequency and clarity, to the point of becoming unbearable. She even disliked taking showers because she despised the thought that the spirits could stare at her nakedness.

'We're going to kill you!' they said to her.

'I don't believe you,' she retorted in her mind. Suddenly, sharp pains shot through her leg.

'They're electrocuting me,' she grimaced.

One night, a customer from Hong Kong noticed that Mei was lost in a daze and gave her a necklace with an idol hanging on the end. He told her that if she wore it, the bodhisattva[6] Ushnisha-sitatapatra, with its 'victorious white parasol' and 1,000 faces, would watch over her, protect her, and give her peace.[7] After taking the necklace, however, she felt even more oppressed by the voices.

Other men gave Mei more lavish gifts, like diamond rings, but none of these things could buy her heart. 'You can find me at work,' she would often say to her suitors. In her mind, a relationship was only worth something if she received payment. She never fully trusted male friends, and whenever a man started to seriously pursue her, she would automatically distance herself from him. A living paradox, she hungered for love, yet hated men. In fact, she secretly enjoyed rejecting men, finding pleasure in their pain.

Sometimes Mei would even switch jobs and move into a different apartment without telling anybody of her whereabouts; she rarely stayed in one place for more than six months before 'disappearing' again.

Through her self-imposed transience, Mei dug herself into a pit of loneliness. She tried to numb the pain through drugs, drinking, smoking and gambling, but nothing could pull her out of the abyss, where the voices continued to echo: 'We're going to kill you! We're going to kill you!'

One evening after work, Mei looked up at the brightly lit moon and cried in her heart: 'What is my life about? Why am I so lonely and empty?'

She started to rummage through her memories, searching for one that would make her happy. Even though she had distanced herself from her family and rarely went home to Ali Mountain, she thought of her mother and her younger brother – two of the few people whom she truly loved. She derived little pleasure from thinking about her father.

By the time Mei returned to her apartment, the good memories had already been swallowed up by a host of bad ones. The childhood abuse, her first husband, the gang rape, her second husband ... Her life seemed to be nothing more than a string of tragedies.

'My whole life, I've been abused by men. I've never had real feelings for any man,' she thought woefully. 'I'm such a disgrace. My life has no meaning any more.'

'We're going to kill you!' the voices cackled in response.

'Then it's better for me to kill myself! Better than letting you kill me,' Mei resolved, still convinced that the spirits were real people who had come to torture her. 'I'm sick of you all knowing all my thoughts.'

Mei went to the refrigerator and grabbed two bottles, full of powdered drugs. She opened them and tipped them into her mouth. The powder, meant to be inhaled in small amounts, burned as it went down her throat. She tried to take a sip of water, but the burning only worsened. Then she passed out.

The phone, ringing. No strength left. Can't move. Then banging. Coming from the front door.

'Mei! Mei! Open the door!' Xi, her older sister. No answer. Footsteps pattering away.

More sounds. The door opening. Xi and a locksmith. A cry.

The emergency room.

'Hmph. Here's another one of THOSE people.'

Who's that? A nurse? Something going down her nose, down her throat, down into her stomach. Churning. Stuff coming out. Foul.

Stuff going in. A black liquid? More foul.

A machine rolling over. A machine for – electric shock?

'No! I'm still alive!' Nobody listens. Can't move!

'STOP!'

A heartbeat. No shocks this time. Relief.

Mei's heartbeat had returned to normal just as the doctor was preparing to jump start her heart with a defibrillator. When Mei fully regained consciousness, her skin and eyes still a sickly yellow, she found herself in the hospital's Intensive Care Unit. And the first thing she heard was a voice.

'Oh look. She didn't die.'

Frightened, Mei looked around for the source of the voice. Nobody but her sister was at her bedside. She started to cry.

'I'm going to die. They're trying to kill me,' she wept.

After she calmed down, she tried to explain to the nurses that she desperately needed to use the rest-room and could not understand why they wouldn't let her go. She remembered the derisive comment one of the nurses had made upon her arrival, and she was filled with a sudden urge to return home, despite her frail physical condition. When a doctor arrived at her bedside, he recommended that she stay in the hospital for two days.

'No,' she said resolutely. 'I want to go.'

After Mei's near-death experience, little changed in work or life until a glimmer of hope entered. She met a drug dealer named Lee, and somehow they started dating. For the first time ever, Mei experienced a feeling akin to love. She was twenty-seven years old.

'Let's go to the hot springs in Beitou,' Lee suggested. The day-long romantic get-away would be their first of many in the months to come.

It was as if a window had been cracked open in Mei's heart. Although she had never before allowed a man to enter her one-bedroom apartment, she made an exception with Lee. Eventually, she even let Lee hide drugs behind her curtains, a location often overlooked by policemen.

'Can I move in with you?' Lee asked Mei one day.

'No,' she answered. 'I don't want to live with anyone.'

Lee persisted. 'But I don't have anywhere else to live.'

Mei still refused. The window in her heart had not yet opened wide enough to let someone actually crawl in.

For a while, Lee stayed with a fellow drug dealer, moving from hotel room to hotel room. Whenever the two began to arouse the suspicion of local policemen, they would move.

'This arrangement is too expensive for me,' Lee insisted once again to Mei. 'Can I move in with you?'

'No.'

'If we live together, we don't even have to sleep together. Anyway, when I'm at work, you'll be at home, and when you're at work, I'll be at home. We can still have our own lives.'

Mei carefully considered her boyfriend's arguments and eventually relented. Lee was right in that she managed to carry on independently after he moved in, and she discovered that their cohabitation came with a bonus: She could now get her drugs for free. Often, they would do drugs together.

The drugs dampened Mei's fear of the spirits that continued to taunt her. She began to accept them as merely a fact of life. The drugs also helped her forget the loneliness and emptiness that lingered inside her heart. Still tormented by past hurts, she often cried over little things when nobody was looking. She felt that her life had little hope, that she was drowning, and she clung to her boyfriend as if he was a piece of driftwood.

Subconsciously, though, Mei still found it impossible to completely trust Lee. Although she cared for him in the beginning, she harboured so much unresolved bitterness toward men, the relationship simply could not work. She loved Lee. But she hated him too. So maddening was the tension that sometimes she simply exploded. In one fit of cursing, she grabbed a kitchen knife and tried to attack her boyfriend.

'You ... ! Get out of here!' she yelled.

'What's wrong with you?!' Lee yelped, backing away.

'Get out!'

'Why are you always like this? You scare me to death when you explode like this!' He started to gather her things and throw them out the front door. He had responded in this way numerous times before, so Mei knew that he would eventually let her back into the apartment – her apartment.

'How come you always throw me out and let me come back again? I don't know what you're thinking! I don't understand you!' she would exclaim.

Again and again, the two attempted to piece together their ever-crumbling relationship. When they were on good terms, Mei would accompany Lee as he drove around the city, selling drugs. She discovered that drug-dealing could be quite lucrative; she could buy a tiny bottle of drugs for $1,500 and sell it for $2,500. She, too, began to sell drugs in her spare time in order to cover her accumulating expenditures.

Once, a customer wanted to buy a large quantity of drugs – so much that even Lee, who feared that he had already aroused too much suspicion, wouldn't take responsibility for the transaction. Mei, however, decided to take the risk.

When the time came to deliver the drugs, she knew it would be unwise to hail a taxi. So with her heart racing, she kept the hefty load of drugs hidden under her coat and skittered through back alleys and side streets until she reached her destination – undiscovered.

Sometimes the danger of getting arrested was closer at hand. One day, as Mei and Lee prepared to do drugs together in Mei's living-room, they were alarmed to hear the sound of heavy footfalls right outside their door. Frantically, carelessly, they tried to hide the drugs. Seconds later, their door was forced open. A lone policeman stood there, glaring at them. Mei quivered.

'Look at you young people not working, just taking drugs!' the policeman rebuked. Then he started to search the apartment. He went into the kitchen and opened the refrigerator.

'Ah, that's bold! Putting drugs in your refrigerator!' he exclaimed, glaring at Mei.

'It looks good there,' she replied dumbly.

'Flush it all down the toilet,' he said. Mei obeyed. He continued to search the apartment, destroying their paraphernalia and pouring out their drugs. Then, to Mei's surprise, he stopped.

'I'm willing to forgive you this time, but the next time, I'm not going to let you go,' he said. 'Don't do it again, or else.'

'OK, OK,' Lee said hastily.

When the policeman left, Lee scowled at Mei.

'You really messed things up this time!' he said angrily. 'Well, now the police have already found you out, so you just can't live here any more.'

Mei, quite used to moving, insisted that they live separately this time. She sought the aid of her older sister Xi, who welcomed Mei into her home.

'Jesus has come! Jesus has come!' Xi announced. In truth, a Catholic priest who had developed a special affinity for her two children had come to visit her home. He did this regularly, but if the family was busy – watching television, for example – Xi wouldn't bother to open the door. Other times, when the mood was right, she would invite him into the living-room.

On this occasion, Mei happened to be at home. Upon hearing the sound of his voice, Mei automatically retreated to her room, where she would remain for the duration of his visit. Her childhood experiences with Christianity were so legalistic that she felt not a tinge of amicability towards the man. She had absolutely no interest in what he had to say.

Yet, for some inexplicable reason, she started to feel as if, in her heart, a tug-of-war had begun between two intangible, inescapable powers. She only knew of one way to alleviate the growing discomfort, and that was to run away.

'I'm going out for a little bit,' she would tell her sister when the voices reached a deafening level.

'We're going to kill you!' they said.

As Mei walked out the door, Xi knew that she would probably not see her younger sister for two or three days.

'This is just not normal,' Xi said to Mei one day. 'Why are you living this way?' She looked at Mei sternly, knowing that she could do little to control the situation.

Sometimes, Mei's disappearances were due to drug or alcohol binges; other times, she would retreat to her family's home in Ali Mountain in order to seek solace from the voices.

Mei's vagrancy irritated Lee, who was unaware of her spiritual afflictions.

'You're acting so crazy,' he said to her worriedly. 'What are you doing, disappearing all day long? I've taken drugs for so long, and you haven't done it as long, and you're already like this. You're a totally different person.' He paused. 'I love you. I care for you. So why are you like this?'

As much as he tried to help, however, Mei remained unstable. She couldn't get herself to reciprocate his affection. And she gradually became aware of the fact that her unresolved past was preventing her from maintaining a healthy relationship with him.

'Let's break up,' she said to him one day. 'We're just not right for each other.'

Lee still would not give up. Despite Mei's attempts to avoid him, he managed to win her back, sparking a seemingly endless cycle of break-ups and reunifications. Mei, deeply entrenched in her personal soap opera, failed to see the much larger problem: Just as she could not resist her boyfriend's advances, she also could not resist the attraction of his drugs.

Xi, troubled by her sister's brutal addiction, had no other choice but to call the police.

Ling Hu

'Surely you won't resist me this time,' Ling thought as she faced her husband Yan. 'Surely you won't leave me, now that you know that I'm pregnant.' She glanced at her belly, hoping that the good news would put an end to their current dispute, which – as usual – centred around her refusal to give him money so that he could gamble. She glanced back up, hoping to see some celebratory compassion in her husband's face.

Instead, Yan glared at her incredulously.

'You liar! I don't believe you! You're just trying to manipulate me so I won't divorce you!'

The sting of Yan's words shocked her. A whirlwind of arguments tumbled through her head.

'I'm not lying! You know, marriage is about both joy and suffering, and getting through them together. But all you care about is sharing the joys! When we're in a tight spot, you don't want to have anything to do with it. You just want a divorce so I'll be responsible for all our debts, all YOUR debts, since I was the one who did all the borrowing for you ...'

Ling paused. Knowing that saying these things aloud would do nothing but provoke her husband further, she chose her words carefully.

'Well. If you don't believe me, let's make it easy then,' she said numbly. 'I'll go live with my parents, and you can go live with those friends of yours. Just let me have the two kids.'

Once Ling had moved in with her parents, her mother sat her down gravely.

'It's not good to have a baby when you and your husband are separated,' she said soberly. 'You already have an older child and you're not working right now ...' She looked at Ling, who nodded in return. She continued.

'You need to weigh this situation. If you have another child, you'll just accumulate more debt. Besides, your husband doesn't even want this baby. The man is plain irresponsible.' Tears started to slide down Ling's face.

'Why do you have to put yourself through this?' her mother went on. 'Why do you have to do this? This will put too much pressure on you, and if you stay pregnant, you won't be able to work ... I think you should get an abortion.'

Ling nodded. She could see her mother's point. But after she had some time to ponder over the predicament, her agreement turned to anger. Anger at her mother. Anger at her husband. 'If I get an abortion, my husband will think that he was right – that I was just pretending to be pregnant in order to threaten him. But if I keep the baby, it'll show him how selfish he is.'

Ling quickly sought the advice of two trusted guides – her doctor, and a fortune-teller. Both suggested that she keep the child, and she gladly complied, though not because of any moral prerogative. She eventually found an apartment in Banciao for her and her daughter Jun.

By the time Ling was six months pregnant, it had become painfully obvious to everyone that Yan's accusation had been unfounded – Ling's undeniable pregnancy became fuel for gossip. One night, Yan sent his older brother to Ling's apartment as a mediator.

'Yan sent me to say sorry. Sorry that he didn't believe you. Will you come back to him? Please?'

'He probably realized that his friends didn't want to take care of him any more,' Ling thought indignantly. 'Well, at least he apologized to me. My children need a father, so it's better to keep this family together, even though I can't stand the man. Maybe he'll stand up on his own two feet. Maybe he will be responsible ... for once.'

Ling agreed to live with her husband again, but continued to feel resentful and suspicious of him. Because of Ling's physical state, Yan assured her that he would take care of moving her things to the apartment they would share. In the end, though, Ling discovered that, in the process, he had taken her former apartment's $20,000 deposit – which subsequently 'disappeared'. Ling never knew when she could trust her husband's words. Was his motorcycle really stolen, or did he sell it to pay off gambling debts? Did he really fail his truck-driving exam, or was he avoiding work so that he could spend time drinking?

They argued often, and if a fight was severe enough, Yan would order Ling out of the house, forcing his pregnant wife to retreat to her parents' place, often after midnight. After a few days, Yan would inevitably show up on the Hus' doorstep, prompting the invariable process of 'making up'.

'Sorry. Will you come back?' he would say.

'I'll go back with you as long as you change and are willing to support the family,' Ling would respond. 'I'm tired of you always asking for money. You always say you're going to return the money and then never do, and I just can't handle this any more.'

'OK, I promise,' Yan would answer.

Sometimes Ling would colour her responses with tinges of retribution. 'You know, before I married you, I didn't even want to eat left-overs or cold rice, but since I married you, I've made so many sacrifices for you ...' or 'My friends and family always wonder why you're so unappreciative and uncaring after I've bent over backwards for you!'

These attempts to make Yan feel guilty did nothing to rectify the situation however. Ling spent so many nights with her parents that she happened to be there, waiting for Yan to come and apologize, when her due date arrived. She sent one of her relatives as a messenger to Yan, in order to remind him about the impending birth.

According to the messenger, a friend of Yan's happened to be present when the news was delivered.

'So?' the friend said, turning to Yan. 'What's that got to do with you?'

Nonetheless, Yan did show up at the hospital when his second daughter, Peijen, was born. When Ling was discharged from the hospital, she went back to her husband's apartment, for she was obliged to *zuo yue zi*, or observe a one-month post-partum period of confinement during which Taiwanese mothers are encouraged to stay within the house and eat foods high in protein and calories.[8] Ling did little but rest after the birth of her first child, for such women are traditionally entitled to the full-time care of their relatives; but this time, Ling did not have this luxury. Aside from having occasional meals cooked by her husband or mother, she was on her own.

Ling felt that her dreams of being a full-time housewife had finally come true. Yan drove a taxi in order to put food on the table, and she stayed home with her two daughters. Her husband seemed less prone to arguments and even helped with the children, especially the newborn, Peijen. Perhaps, Ling guessed, he still felt bad about denying that the girl had been conceived.

Ling's parents offered the family one of their condos, but Yan respectfully declined. Determined to live independently, he decided to rent a small, cheap apartment that shared a bathroom and kitchen with another family. Due to the rather negligent habits of their neighbours, Ling couldn't manage to keep the two dark and dingy rooms clean for long. She eventually gave up, and avoided them whenever possible.

Yan and Ling led a no-frills lifestyle, very different from that of Ling's childhood. Yet she tried to be content, grateful that her husband had finally started to assume responsibility for his family. She even felt sorry for him on occasion, for she knew that driving a taxi could be an arduous job.

But the ceasefire didn't last. As soon as Ling started doing calculations in her head, her suspicions resurfaced. She remembered that when she and her husband had initially discussed the prospect of buying a taxi, Yan had said that he could earn $1,000 a day. Even though he did come home with an armful of groceries every day, where were the rest of his wages? If he was really making money, why was his older brother, a doctor in southern Taiwan, helping them pay their rent? Why were her parents helping them pay for their children's school fees? Why did she have to spend money with such unnatural, painstaking caution?

Yet Ling kept silent about their burgeoning financial quandary, especially when her parents began to express concern. The last thing she wanted to do was to drag them into her whirlpool of worry again. She reminded herself of the Chinese saying, 'When you marry a chicken, you have to follow the chicken. When you marry a dog, you have to follow the dog.' Her mother had told her not to marry Yan, yet she had blatantly disregarded the advice. At that time, she had felt like Snow White, on the brink of being delivered by a prince on a white horse. But instead of kissing her awake, Yan was shoving poisonous apples into her mouth. He continued to gamble and buy lottery tickets, which had become popular commodities by that time.

So she started working again. Their financial situation continued to perplex her but, afraid of provoking conflict on the sensitive subject of money, Ling tried to convince herself that whether or not her husband brought home a steady income was inconsequential.

'I can take care of the expenses for myself and the children. But if he keeps on making me take care of more than that, I will have to say something about it.'

But as Yan started to ask her for money more frequently, Ling decided to break her silence. Since she typically gave her husband a monthly allowance, she tried to threaten him.

'I won't give you any money until you give me your salary first.'

'I can't do that!' Yan answered adamantly. 'And if I could, why would I be asking you for money? Look at how hard I work! How can you even say that?' Ling pretended not to be afraid of her husband's widening eyes and rising temper.

'Then I can't give you any money,' she said, trying to hide the trepidation in her voice.

'You good-for-nothing woman! You can't even earn enough money!'

Yan stormed out the front door, slamming it behind him. Later, when the phone rang, Ling braced herself, half expecting to hear her husband's angry voice. Instead, she heard the familiar, cordial voice of his mother.

'Please be patient with my son. He has a bad temper and a bad mouth.' A warm sense of relief swept over Ling. Her mother-in-law's periodic phone calls often made her feel like she was passing through the eye of a hurricane.

'At least I don't have mother-in-law problems like most wives have,' Ling thought. 'I should at least be grateful for that. If I'm patient, maybe this time will pass.'

The unsteady rhythm of heavy footsteps echoed in the stairwell. Yan was drunk – again. Quickly, Ling made sure that her daughters were sleeping soundly, then turned off the lights and hopped into bed.

'I can handle the money thing, but don't think you can just take your anger out on me!' she thought as she pulled the sheets over herself.

Ling wondered whether alcohol really led to her husband's irrepressible temper, or whether it was only an excuse. Either way, she didn't want to be the target of his rage, especially on nights when the cards had not played in his favour. If he had lost a great deal of money, he would come home in a fury, his large eyes crazed and bloodshot, his breath reeking of alcohol and smoke. He smoked an average of sixty cigarettes a day.

Ling knew that when her husband came home drunk, arguing with him would be a useless endeavour since he would forget everything the next morning. If he came home before she could get under the covers, she would try to avoid him before an argument could explode.

'I'm going to sleep. Let's talk about things later,' she would say.

'Fine,' he would answer.

Gradually, Ling learned to avoid her husband as much as possible. She had grown cold towards him and apathetic towards their endless debates about money. Soon, however, Yan realized that her silence did him no good. The ability to elicit some sort of response from her indicated, at the very least, that she still cared about the issue at hand and could potentially be persuaded to give him some money.

'I need to put the children to bed. Let's talk about it later,' Ling said as one argument began to surface.

'NO!' he said, glaring at her firmly. 'You listen to me now. You are really a useless woman! You ...' As he assailed her with insults, she tried to distract herself by focusing her eyes on the television, which had been left on. She knew that looking at his livid face would bring tears to her eyes and more fear to her heart.

'If I had known how to pray, I would have prayed,' she would later recount. But since her high school experiences with Christianity had already become a distant memory, she could do nothing but talk to herself.

'Please stop.'

'You're a horrible wife!'

'Please make him leave me alone.'

When wishing away the attack proved to be futile, Ling would try to cheer herself up by filling her head with old Taiwanese songs and finding something to do. She headed towards the balcony with the intention of hanging up the laundry.

'You b—!' he roared, stomping towards her. He slapped her. Hard. Then pushed her.

The next day, as often was the case, Yan acted as if nothing significant had happened the day before.

'I was only getting angry,' he said to Ling unapologetically. 'You know that's just part of my personality, right?'

'My husband – your husband's friend – needs surgery,' the woman said, painting a beautifully desperate picture with her words. 'The procedure will not be cheap. Of course, hospitalization was necessary. Could you please loan us $20,000 to help us?'

Ling reluctantly discussed the matter with her husband.

'But ... I don't have the money ...' she said, feeling slightly guilty that she could not be more benevolent.

'How could you not have some sympathy?' Yan interjected. 'They're my friends, and they need it. They'll pay us back.'

After some debate, Ling finally agreed.

'I'll go get the money,' Ling said. She grabbed her savings deposit book and her chop (a stamp used as a signature, especially in business transactions).

'No, I'll go get it myself,' Yan volunteered. 'You need to get back to work. Give me the savings deposit book and the chop, and I'll return them to you later.' Although Ling usually had qualms about letting her husband get anywhere near the family finances, she did, in fact, need to return quickly to work, so she decided to trust him.

When Ling returned home at the end of the work-day,

her husband was nowhere to be found. In fact, he didn't return home for several days. When he finally came back, Ling immediately asked the question that had been haunting her.

'Where's my savings deposit book and my chop?' she demanded.

From the livid look that possessed her husband's face, Ling knew that the damage was complete, and that no amount of arguing could fix it.

Yan had withdrawn all $100,000 from their bank account.

In the meantime, their family's financial situation continued to worsen. Since Ling worked, her daughters needed child-care, which came at a disproportionately heavy cost. So several months after the loan incident, Ling decided to resurrect the issue.

'Ask your friend to return the borrowed money. It's been a while,' she said.

'I can't do that. Right now it's *bu fang bian*. Inconvenient for them.'

'Well, then give me their phone number. I'll talk to them since you obviously feel bad about asking. I'm a woman, so it's easier for me to ask anyway. I could also ask them to pay it back little by little. They don't need to return it all at once. Give me their phone number.'

'I don't have their phone number.'

'You're lying to me. Give me their address.'

'I don't know where they live now.'

Irritated, Ling was eventually able to track down the friends directly. She called the man's wife and asked her to return the money.

'We can't,' the woman said.

'Why not? It's already been months since the surgery!'

All the while, Ling never directly told her husband that

she knew about his scheme – that he had gambled away all the money in her savings account. Since she still saw him as the head of the household, she didn't want to make him lose face.

'It should be the man's responsibility to support his family,' she thought. Yet she didn't want to lose face either, and her pride prevented her from begging for his help, especially since she herself had a job. Besides, she felt that she already knew the response, even if she did ask: 'I can't. I just don't have money to support you all. Be a little understanding, OK? You know how hard it is to be a taxi driver.'

Ling was tired of the excuses but felt powerless to do anything about it. One day when the phone rang, she grabbed it, half-expecting it to be her husband, explaining that he would come home late from his taxi rounds again.

But when the reply came this time, the voice on the other end was unrecognizable. And puzzling.

'I'm calling from your husband's taxi company. We're coming to pick up the car.'

Yufen Wang

Yufen had done everything she could to keep her family's financial situation from going deep into the red. She used up all the money she had saved when she was single – not much, considering her low wages at the factory and stationery stores. She borrowed money from her already poor family. She even sold off her jewellery.

Even so, she could not keep up with the mounting debt that her husband Kai was accumulating through his lavish lifestyle and alcohol addiction. Eventually, they found themselves more than $200,000 in debt. When the due date of their next payment arrived, Kai and Yufen had no choice but to declare bankruptcy.

They had owned their condo for merely ten months, and

already they had to prepare it for sale. Since Yufen did not know how to handle such complicated financial matters, she was guided through the process by her husband's aunt.

When prospective buyers started to come to look at the condo, Kai often found excuses to leave. 'I'm very busy, I don't have time to stick around. I need to take care of something,' he would say. Years later, when reflecting on these times, Yufen would wonder if her husband had merely wanted to run away from the face-losing fact that they could not keep their condo.

After the condo was sold and before the family could move into another apartment, one more preparation had to be made. Yufen set up a table at the doorway of their new apartment and placed on it several plates of fruit. Then she lit several incense sticks, stood by the table, and started to pray.

'Please give us blessings. Please give us peace,' she started to mutter, addressing the gods Tian Gong and Tudi Gong. Since Tudi Gong, the god of the land, ultimately 'owned' the apartment, it was particularly important that Yufen ask for his permission to temporarily inhabit the new place.

'Please give us peace,' Yufen continued muttering into the air. Repeating phrases she had heard her mother speak when she was a child, she spoke softly so that she wouldn't attract the attention of passers-by. For the most part, Yufen felt a bit insecure when it came to religion. She felt like she could never express herself eloquently in prayer to the gods.

After her incense had burned halfway, she started burning paper joss money. As the bundles of yellow crackled in the fire, she hoped that the spirits would make her luck improve. At the moment, it appeared that her dreams of having a good life were like the stacks of paper money – disintegrating into a black heap of ashes.

After about an hour of worship, Yufen had nothing left to burn.

Chic paintings adorned the walls of the spacious restaurant, complete with a basement and several private rooms. The restaurant had room for sixty tables, most of which were full. For Kai and his friend, it was the beginning of a good day.

After the sale of the condo, Kai admitted that he had grown tired of working in real estate – a confession that much relieved his wife, for she never liked the coarse co-workers he had started to associate with. Besides, business had started to sour.

Kai possessed a natural ability to motivate others, so he had little trouble raising funds whenever he wanted to start a new entrepreneurial venture. This time, he decided to partner with a friend in opening a restaurant.

'Maybe now he will make better use of his time,' Yufen thought. For a moment she pictured him wearing a kimono like a Japanese geisha, hired to entertain and drink with rich guests. She chuckled, 'Maybe that's the kind of job he would do well.'

Little did she know that such thoughts would be partly prophetic. Kai ended up managing 'public relations' for the restaurant, and since business success in Taiwan often relies on relationships, the breadth of Kai's social circle had its advantages. In addition to buying groceries and taking care of the bills, Kai had the gregarious duty of welcoming friends and other customers into the restaurant. Then, like a newlywed at a wedding banquet, he would spend the evening hopping from table to table, inviting his guests to drink with him. Outgoing, respected, and known for telling good jokes, he was popular with the crowds. On a good night, he would toast at least twenty different tables.

Although interacting with customers in this way was to be expected, Kai often went too far, swaggering around until he was too drunk to continue. Sometimes, he passed out in the restaurant. Other times, he would wait for a friend or co-worker to escort him home, after which he would immediately pass out on the couch. When he finally woke up late the next morning, he would take a quick shower and head off to work again.

Yufen was not one to simply permit such behaviour. Many mornings, she would nudge her husband harshly while he dozed on the couch. When her attempts to wake him proved futile, she would reproach him during his rare moments of lucidity.

'What do you think you're doing, getting drunk all the time?!' she yelled, consumed with anger.

'None of your business!' he would yell back if he was just sober enough to make himself clear. He rolled over, attempting to ignore her. 'I'm already drunk, what do I care? It's not a big deal. It's not like I've done anything wrong. This is just what happens after men have some fun.'

Unlike other Taiwanese wives, though, Yufen would not let him simply get away with it.

'Don't you ignore me! You irresponsible ...' She started flinging about strings of curses.

'*Woman!* What do you know?!' Kai retorted, wielding a common insult used by Taiwanese men at the time. 'Just take care of the house, woman! That's all you need to do. The rest is none of your business. There's no reason to pick a fight about this.'

Deep inside, Yufen knew that he was partly right – that she did pick fights over small matters many times, though she did not consider the present moment to be one of those times. She didn't want to be a nettling housewife, but often she couldn't help but intervene. In her life, she had seen few examples of healthy communication during conflict, so she tended to address problems by losing her temper in screaming rampages.

Kai didn't know how to communicate with his wife either, so two, three, four, then five days a week, he would come home drunk. Ever since he was forced to sell the condo, he could no longer work for enjoyment's sake; there were bills and rent to pay, as well school fees for his daughter and son.

The pressure was exacerbated by Kai's discontent with his marriage. But since divorce was unthinkable, he sealed up his emotions and let them ferment like a bottle of bad wine. Preoccupying himself with a busy work and social life, he pretended to be indifferent towards the inevitable provocations he faced at home. He mentally justified such absences, telling himself that he had to stay in the restaurant until all the money was counted at evening's end, no matter what time it was. Occasionally he felt a tinge of regret about not being able to spend more time with his children, but mostly he felt the situation was unavoidable. 'Besides, I don't want to be like Yufen, controlling and bothering them all the time,' he thought.

So he continued to drink – just like most of the men he knew. In fact, his own brother drank just as much as he did. Kai resentfully noted that this brother didn't have anywhere near as many conflicts with his wife, for the two were rather similar in personality and background. Unlike him and Yufen.

Meanwhile, new restaurants continued to sprout up throughout Yungho. Yufen suspected that the loyalty of Kai's customers was waning, and that they were growing tired of the insipidly standard fare of his restaurant. 'If only he would put in more effort ...' she thought sullenly.

Kai, however, felt that the restaurant did excellent business until the very end. He and his business partner had only rented the restaurant space, and when they were forced to give up the place, Kai figured that the landlord was just envious of their success at that location.

With utmost confidence in his own entrepreneurial skills, Kai decided to open a roadside seafood stand at the Le-hua Night Market. It was a sort of half-indoor, half-outdoor Taiwanese diner, where customers could order their meals quickly and then sit down at flimsy card tables to eat. Since Kai could only afford to hire two cooks, Yufen began to help out with the business. He also enlisted the help of his mother.

At four or five o'clock every afternoon, Yufen would leave her three-year-old son and six-year-old daughter at home and rush downstairs to help her husband open the seafood stand. Then, when the after-work crowd began to stream by, Yufen frantically served customers, collected money, cleared tables, washed dishes and wiped down the new, shiny counters.

Because Yufen and Kai often served customers until two or three in the morning, one of Kai's sisters moved in with them to help take care of the children and put them to bed. After returning home, Yufen would sleep for a few hours, take her children to school, and then go back to sleep again. The children, who were at the age when they still attended half days at school, often returned home in the early afternoon to find their mother still sleeping. And even if she happened to be awake, she would be too exhausted to help them with their schoolwork.

'I simply have too much work to do,' she sighed. 'Besides, it's the government's job to teach them things like that.' Many times, when her daughter's school hosted an open house or other special event, she was unable to attend. In years to come, though, she took special effort to attend such events for her son, her husband noted cynically.

It wasn't long before Yufen grew sick of her demanding work schedule. She tried her best to refrain from arguing with her husband, but the fatigue made her overwhelmingly irritable. The work environment didn't help either; the canvas roof that only partway covered the stand did nothing to keep out the cold during the winter.

'Why aren't you working?!' Yufen often screeched at her husband. 'Why are you still drinking? Hurry up!'

At home, the complaints continued. 'You're so irresponsible! You're so lazy!'

If Kai was not intoxicated, he would sit silently, without responding to his wife's nettling.

'Listen to me!'

Kai picked up a newspaper and started to read.

'LISTEN TO ME!' Yufen exploded, as if ready to strike her husband. Finally, Kai had had enough. He threw the newspaper onto the couch and started to argue back.

'Why do you keep bothering me like this? This is all none of your business!'

Although Kai was initially enthusiastic about his seafood stand, the passion dwindled quickly, as it had with his previous jobs. His work ethic was like a fireworks display – spectacular, yet short-lived. In Yufen's eyes, he generally started to lose motivation after running a business for six months or so.

The decline in Kai's enthusiasm also affected his attention span, which typically reached its limit at around one in the morning, an hour or two before closing. Yufen learned to spot the warning signs: eyes clouded with boredom, envious gazes at inebriated passers-by. Then,

'Hold on, I need to take care of something.' Kai would make an excuse and disappear as soon as the stand was clear of customers. At first, Yufen would patiently await his return, but as his absences increased in length and frequency, she began to suspect the worst.

One night she decided to leave the stand to search for him, like a policeman hunting for an escaped criminal. When she found him, he appeared to be searching for someone – anyone – to accompany him for a drink.

'OK, I'll come right back,' Kai said when he spotted his wife.

'He's so different from the man I thought I married,' she muttered to herself, doubting his words. She knew that her husband didn't like to drink alone, and that any person he had bumped into on the street a handful of times could easily become his new drinking buddy. He also liked to befriend and drink with owners of neighbouring food stands. He was very good with people. In the middle of a particularly busy evening, one of Kai's many friends passed by the seafood stand.

'Hold on, I'm going to Beitou,' Kai said to Yufen. Then he turned to his friend: 'Let's go.'

'Wait! We're not finished here!' Yufen hollered, pointing to some customers who had not yet finished eating.

Ignoring his wife, Kai calmly walked away. Yufen picked up a rag and started to furiously scrub the counter, fighting back tears.

'There's no use running after him, he's not coming back,' she thought.

Other times, she would not give up so easily. Once when her husband disappeared and hadn't told her of his whereabouts, she decided to call his cell phone.

'Are you coming home for dinner?' she asked.

'I tol you, don call! I'm not coming! I'm jus not coming!' he said angrily, hanging up the phone. Yufen could tell from the slur of his words that he was drinking with his friends. He returned home at around midnight.

Another time, when Kai actually promised to come

home for dinner, he disappeared until seven the next morning.

'I just forgot,' he later explained. But as such excuses became habitual, Yufen lost faith in her husband. And her frustration became uncontainable when he started to blatantly drink on the job.

'Why are you STILL drinking?!' she said, glaring at the beer in his hand.

'None of your business.'

'Stop drinking!' Several customers turned their heads.

Kai's mother decided to intervene. 'OK, that's enough, no need to talk about this any more.' She turned to Kai. 'Don't drink any more, OK?'

'Just leave me alone,' he replied curtly. 'Don't bother me.' Yufen felt her face grow hot with anger. She was so angry that she wanted to die. She clenched her teeth, resisting the urge to pick up something and throw it at her husband.

'That Kai – spoiled by his mother, ever since he was a child!'

Three-year-old Bao Lin hid in a stairway, staring at his parents while they screamed at each other at their seafood stand. A few minutes before, they had been cleaning up a table together – a task that was forgotten as soon as the argument had commenced.

'Why aren't you doing what you're supposed to be doing?' Yufen demanded. 'You don't buy the things you're supposed to buy. You're always delaying things. You don't ...'

'You control freak! Why do you have to nag so much? This is none of your business!' To emphasize his point, Kai picked up a utensil and used it to strike a pot.

To Yufen, the high-pitched clang felt like a battle cry. Incensed, she reached into a plastic bus tray and threw a dirty dish at her husband. Miss. Soon, plastic plates and bowls were being thrown from both ends. Miss. Miss. A glass was thrown. Miss. Bao winced as it shattered on the floor. He wanted to run away, but his little legs wouldn't move. Then he saw his aunt, coming home from work, walking closer, inadvertently stepping into the battlefield until –

CRACK! A hit. Blood.

Thus ended the first life event that Bao, as a grown man, would be able to remember.

Yufen watched the tadpoles wriggle away from the paper net in her son's novice hands. She was glad when her husband closed the seafood stand so that his family could have a more 'normal' lifestyle. She no longer had to spend her evenings toiling away and chastising him. Instead, she could take Bao and Little Ping here to the night market, where they could entertain themselves with dart throwing, play fishing, and other carnival-type games.

Bao dipped the paper net back into the plastic bucket. He swished the net back and forth, and the paper started to tear before he could catch any tadpoles.

Now that Yufen didn't have to work, she also had the energy to take her children to the bookstore; she liked the fact that Bao could sit on the floor and read there for a whole day, and was dismayed by Little Ping's relative lack of concentration.

In the meantime, Kai had started to run a Cantonese restaurant, much smaller and simpler than the first. After serving lunch and dinner, he could legitimately get off work at ten, leaving him plenty of time to go out with his friends. He returned home drunk on most nights and his times of sobriety were rather scattered, with one notable exception.

A particular Hong Kong soap opera had become incredibly popular and Kai, like most Taiwanese people at the time, had got hooked. For a few Sundays, the whole family would gather around the television, watching. For a few Sundays, Kai abstained from drinking. His son Bao had never before been so happy.

Although Kai had not needed his family's help with the Cantonese restaurant at first, his mother, sister and wife eventually joined in the effort, helping him serve customers and clean up. For one year, the business managed to stay afloat. But since the location was not ideal, Kai's customer base became unsteady. His wife's heart began to sink.

'Here he goes again with his "five-minute fever",' she thought to herself. 'If he only worked harder ...' Yufen felt that, with Kai's knack for starting a business and her skills in running one, they could have made a good team – if it weren't for his drinking habit.

When the cooks left because Kai could no longer pay them, Kai started using his personal connections to look for other work. One of his friends, a local politician like Kai's grandfather, owned a nearby luxury car dealership. The two men were so close that their children played together. It was no surprise when this friend, impressed by Kai's sense of humour, confidence and talkative but relaxed demeanour, offered him a job in his sales department. There, he was put in charge of organizing promotional events in scenic locales.

Kai excelled at his job, even earning a gold medal for his sales. Like most salesmen, he employed a tactic that he had learned from working in real estate: he would take his customers out for a meal or, better yet, a drink, and once they were sufficiently inebriated, he would casually pop the question: 'So how about if I order a car for you?'

The one disadvantage of Kai's new job was that it required him to get up in the morning, and if he was late to work, there was no way to rectify the situation.

'Why didn't you wake me up?!' he often said to his wife on days when they both overslept.

Kai sold cars for a little over a year, but then his efforts puttered to a stop. Staying out until three in the morning and then missing work the next day was no longer acceptable.

By this time Kai had become shrewd with money, and he devised a way to start a business with virtually no cash. Using his skills as a restaurateur, he set up a catering service for outdoor banquets that are traditionally held to celebrate birthdays, weddings and other major events.

'If you hire me then you don't have to worry about all the details,' he would tell his friends whenever he discovered that they wanted to host a banquet. He would then ask them for a deposit, with which he could hire cooks, as well as buy food and equipment.

After running a successful event, Kai could come out with an ample profit of $20,000 to $30,000. But after some time had passed, problems started to arise. On the morning of an event, for example, Kai would have to wake up before dawn to buy fresh groceries at an outdoor market so that his cooks could start preparing food by nine. Sometimes, when Kai forgot to buy certain items, he would have to make multiple trips to the market. Other times, he would chit-chat with friends while doing his errands, delaying the entire process and irritating the cooks.

'This is no good!' the cooks said once to Yufen as they impatiently awaited her husband's return.

'Why is the guy like this? Why is he always late?' she seethed. 'Thirty minutes late is OK, but two hours ...'

When Kai came back, late, he immediately spotted the familiar look of disdain on his wife's face and, as usual, attempted to lighten the mood.

'Oh, don't be so upset.' Hoping to assuage her, he handed her a frozen treat he had bought at the market.

Ironically, when Kai performed his job well, another problem would arise. Satisfied customers would often express their gratitude through a traditional act of appreciation: 'Good job, Kai! Let's drink to it,' they would say.

As in his previous jobs, Kai saw drinking as an important part of building good relationships with customers. Sometimes he drank so much that he would struggle to wake up the next day. Once when he was hired to cater for a small lunch party, Yufen received a phone call from a cook at nine in the morning.

'Nobody has showed up yet with the food. The tables are ready. The tents are all ready. But there's no food!'

It wasn't until two hours later that Yufen managed to wake up her husband.

'Why can't you be responsible for once? Why do you have to get drunk all the time?' she yelled as soon as he opened his eyes.

'You b—!' he replied. 'I just want to do this, OK? It makes me happy. Why do you have to bother me about it?'

On the morning of one engagement banquet, Yufen once again tried to shove her husband awake – to no avail. He was still drunk. Seething, she waited for him to wake up naturally, but as precious time passed, his body remained limp. Yufen clenched her teeth. She wanted to kick him.

'What am I supposed to do now?' she thought. 'I can't even drive a car!' Indignant, Yufen reached into her husband's pocket and pulled out a wad of bills. Then she drove her motorbike to the Wanhua morning market and bought the groceries herself. She was glad that she had accompanied her husband on such shopping trips in the past and so knew it was important to keep detailed records of her expenses.

'Kai's one lucky man!' she thought to herself. 'Not many women know how to do this kind of thing. He is lucky to have me.'

Two and a half hours later, Yufen had purchased so much food that she had to hire a truck driver to transport the groceries to the banquet location.

'There goes $300 down the drain,' she sighed. She was sick of having to intervene when her husband's work life went awry. Sick of hearing his cooks complain. Sick of everything.

Yufen's heart started to pound as she waited for Kai to come home from another presumed evening of drinking. Heat rose from within her chest, exploding through her entire body. She began to feel faint, as if she could no longer control herself. As if, at any moment, the agony would kill her, and the hate would start to possess her lifeless body. 'You're the kind of man who should just stay single!' she wanted to scream at her absent husband. 'Why did you marry anyway?! Why did you have kids?! It's completely irresponsible!'

She heard slow footsteps in the stairway. Her head felt even hotter. When her drunk husband finally opened the door, everything boiling inside of her spewed out.

'YOU! You only think of yourself!' she shouted, her voice piercing through the apartment. Her two children, sensing an onslaught, cowered into their room. 'Why can't you think of your family for a change?'

'I'm jus' this way. What you want me do 'bout it?' Kai drawled.

Yufen exploded. 'Go to hell! I HOPE YOU DIE!'

Normally, when Yufen reached the height of her anger, she would pick up a nearby piece of clothing and throw it to the ground. But this time, she grabbed a glass ash-tray, and before she could feel the weight of it in her hands, she pitched it at her husband. Miss. Her hands, fumbling for anything nearby, started to hurl things across the room.

Kai slammed at the wall with his fist. 'Yoou ... !' he cursed. 'If you go on like thi', I woll hit you!'

'Oh yeah? You wanna try?'

Kai swaggered towards his wife and started swinging his fists at her head. He was so drunk that Yufen easily dodged the blows.

'You wanna hit me, doncha? You wanna hit me? C'MON, HIT ME!'

The heated exchanges that so frequently occurred at home only intensified Kai's burning thirst for alcohol. When he came home drunk – usually five nights a week – Yufen would immediately start to yell at him. Kai was never in the mood for confrontation, no matter what state he was in, so he would often head back out the door as soon as his wife opened her mouth. Then he would escape to a friend's house. Though he never told his friends about his family problems, they often offered him drinks to assuage his misery and uplift his gloomy countenance. Then they would chat and drink until he passed out in a state of blissful forgetfulness.

During Kai's absences, Yufen found a scapegoat: her daughter, who was now in junior high. Once when Little Ping disobeyed her, Yufen picked up a bamboo stick.

'You're just like your father!' she screamed, beating her daughter with the stick. 'Your father is just like this! JUST LIKE THIS!'

Occasionally, when Kai was able to observe an interaction between his wife and daughter, he noticed that, as soon as Little Ping started to talk, her mother would scold her.

'No wonder she doesn't dare to talk,' he thought sadly. He had always felt that a mother should be trusted with her children, and he hated the fact that his daughter was being treated in this way.

But this paled in comparison with Yufen's hatred of the facts that suffocated her own life. She was tired of worrying about money and tired of relying on her husband's unsteady income to make ends meet. Impressively, Kai had always managed to feed his family, even after spending a large proportion of his income on alcohol. But he had also accumulated an impressive amount of debt, largely due to his business ventures. The loan payments far overshadowed the family's living expenses – a fact that made Yufen feel uneasy, as if she was always on the brink of poverty.

So at the age of thirty-six, she decided that it was time to look for a job of her own. Her older sister, who had successfully started a small long-distance bus company, offered her a position as a driver's assistant. Every other day she worked sixteen-hour shifts, which entailed taking two round trips between Taipei and Kaohsiung, Taiwan's two major cities. On the way, she would collect tickets, attend to customers, and pick up any rubbish that they left behind. Although the trips tended to run through the night, neither Yufen nor her bus driver had time to sleep between trips.

Despite the exhausting schedule, Yufen enjoyed the feeling of having money at her disposal. She earned $30,000 to $40,000 a month, which allowed her to pay for food and rent. She let her husband take care of his own mounting debts. Although Yufen had little time to spend with her children, now aged ten and thirteen, at least she had money to buy them things. So she often bought them souvenirs during her out-of-town trips: a piece of cake here, a trinket or T-shirt there. She particularly prided herself on buying clothing that looked good, but wasn't too expensive, as well as storybooks for her son.

Although Yufen knew that this was not the best way to raise her children, she took comfort in the fact that Kai's sister lived with them and could help out.

'Must be boring, having a mother around only half the time. But at least I make sure they get fed,' Yufen rationalized. On her days off, she would cook for her family and leave them with left-overs for the next day. If not enough food was left and Kai's sister had not yet returned home from work, the children would simply eat out by themselves. Like many Taiwanese children in similar circumstances, Bao and Little Ping did not complain about the way they were forced to live. They had never known any other way.

In 1988, a year after Yufen re-entered the work-force, she was riding back to Taipei on the last leg of her shift. It was around 2:30 a.m., and all was silent in the two-storeyed bus as the passengers dozed. Seated next to the driver, Yufen struggled to stay awake as she watched roadside signs zip by in hypnotic motion. She looked forward to the fact that, in less than an hour, she would be able to collapse onto her bed and not have to ... keep her eyelids from ... shutting ...

Suddenly, a jolt. A crash.

'What's going on?'

Light.

'What's happening?'

Scenes. Her life in rapid rewind, like a broken video-cassette. Scenes of her doing many things. Things she regretted. Fights with her husband.

'Am I dying? Where will I go if I die?'

But as she felt her body weakening with pain, an image. Of her children.

'I can't die now! I don't care what happens to me after this as long as I don't die. My kids – they're still small, they still depend on me. There are too many things I haven't done in life. There are people I haven't thanked. People I've hurt. People I haven't said sorry to ...'

Light-headed confusion. Fear. It was as if her spirit had become lost during its last moments on earth, just before spiralling down to hell.

Notes

1. A venue that is like a pub and brothel combined; waitresses there are expected to sell themselves as well as drinks.
2. A term used to refer to both the worship of gods and ancestors in Taiwan
3. www.chinapost.com.tw/travel/detail.asp?ID=67547&GRP=g
4. www.chinapost.com.tw/travel/detail.asp?ID=67547&GRP=g
5. www.schizophrenia.com
6. Bodhisattva – a buddhist deity or being that has attained enlightenment worthy of nirvana but remains in the human world to help others.
7. www.museum.oglethorpe.edu/TibetGallery/Ushnisha_page.htm
8. www.gio.gov.tw/taiwan-website/5-gp/q&a/page_17.htm

Part 3

Snared in Darkness

Where then are the gods you made for yourselves? Let them come if they can save you when you are in trouble! For you have as many gods as you have towns, O Judah.   Jeremiah 2:28

Chapter 7

'Over here! There's someone hurt over here!'

Yufen's eyes shot open. Blood streamed down her ears and face as she assessed the situation in a moment of unexpected calmness.

The back of an enormous trailer truck had pummelled through the bus's windshield, not far from her face, and shards of glass were strewn everywhere. Pain blasted through the lower half of Yufen's body, and she felt as if she was being enveloped by indistinct noise.

She looked down. Her thighs were intact, but beyond that all she could see was a mishmash of flesh and bone. The dashboard appeared to have severed her legs.

'Be careful!' rose a voice above the din. 'I see someone's bone sticking out over here!'

Yufen started to feel faint.

*   *   *

Ten-year-old Bao Lin was given no explanation as to why his father was withdrawing him from school in the middle of the day, except that his mother was in the hospital. He didn't know how badly she had been hurt, or that she had even been in a road accident. He certainly didn't know that, despite the severity of her condition, she had already been transferred from two other hospitals. The first one was only equipped to take care of her most immediate needs, and the second had no room to accommodate her.

Once at Taipei's Tri-Military Hospital, Bao and his older sister could only see their mother from a distance as she was pushed on a gurney down a long, greyish corridor. Though Bao could not see her clearly, he could hear her. Her torturous screams ripped through the corridor, even after she had been pushed through three sets of doors. The sounds and the uncertainty reminded him of his parents' fights. He felt too petrified to move.

Doctors operated on Yufen's mutilated legs for more than seven hours. Even though she had been given general anaesthetic, she could still hear the crunch of metal breaking bone.

When Yufen regained consciousness, her entire face was swollen. She hadn't lost her legs entirely, but what was left of them was a horrific sight. Two rods had been inserted into her left leg and were connected by six nails to an external metal cage. Yufen looked up. Among the host of relatives who had rushed to the hospital, her husband was nowhere to be found.

Hours later, while Yufen lay in bed, trying to take her mind off the pain, a whiff of alcohol sauntered into the hospital room. She knew then that her husband Kai had finally come to see her. He arranged to have Yufen transferred to a luxurious private suite, complete with a kitchen and a living-room. Even so, the comfort did little to improve her mood.

'Where did Kai get the money to pay for this place?' she thought angrily. 'This place is fit for a general!'

Because Taiwan's hospitals did not provide extensive nursing services at the time, Kai came regularly to bathe Yufen and help her relieve herself in a bed-pan. But instead of appreciating the effort, Yufen bemoaned her husband's lack of emotional support.

'Can't you see that I'm an emotional mess?' she wanted to tell him. 'Can't you comfort me a little?' She felt that Kai hardly cared about her predicament because when he visited her, he often brought along friends – men who had the audacity to get drunk in the presence of a bed-ridden woman, men whom she grew to hate. On more than one occasion, a nurse would walk in to find the floor littered with bottles, cans, and even drunken men. Even though Yufen had a cage attached to her leg, she felt that what really ensnared her was the irresponsible behaviour of her husband. Her condition hardly affected her ability to yell at him when his drinking frustrated her, and she never considered the possibility that other tactics might be more effective in curbing his addiction. Divorce was equally unimaginable.

Even though Yufen couldn't change her husband, she decided to use her time of confinement to research ways in which she could change herself. The hospital bookstore sold a number of Buddhist self-help books about marriage and facing difficulties. Sensing that such books could guide her along a spiritual path that she had never fully explored, she asked Kai to buy her a few.

The books gave her a temporary sense of peace and occasionally inspired her to regard her husband with a measure of mercy: 'Even though he's drunk eighteen hours of the day, at least he's sober for the other six,' she thought. 'He's a good person. He can organize things well. He can even decorate, clean the house and put together nice-looking flower arrangements if he puts his mind to it.'

But these efforts to be optimistic were clouded by her recurring memories of the accident. As Yufen lay on her hospital bed, helpless and immobile, ghastly images tumbled through her mind. Along with them came the thoughts:

'What's going on ... Am I dying ... ? Where will I go if I die ... ? I can't die now ... I don't care what happens to me after this as long as I don't die.'

Confined to her bed, Yufen could no longer preoccupy herself with a long list of daily responsibilities. For the first time in her life, nothing could take her mind off what she was really looking for – truth. She found herself wandering through a maze of questions: 'Why am I here on this earth? Where do I want to go after death?' And her Buddhist books could not provide her with satisfactory answers.

Shrouded by fear and uncertainty, the days started to smear into one indelible grey stain. Yufen's legs were in so much pain that she wanted her life to simply end, and she sank into a quicksand of depression and bleak thoughts. 'Will I be deformed or handicapped forever? How will I be able to take care of my children if my leg doesn't get better? What will I do if I have to be a burden to other people for the rest of my life?'

One doctor's comment exacerbated the torment. 'It might be possible that you won't be able to walk again,' he said, causing Yufen's face to contort with grief. He kindly gave her a special prescription: spending some time in the hospital's emergency ward.

There, Yufen saw moaning patients with unimaginably grotesque injuries and ailments. Some patients had lost their legs completely. Suddenly, Yufen understood.

'I guess I'm not the only one who's in such a mess. I guess bad things can happen to anybody at any time, whether they're ready for it or not. I guess people can never be in complete control of their lives. Things could have been worse for me,' she thought, her misery slightly placated by the realization that she was not in it alone.

'From now on, I'm just not going to let bad things surprise me,' she resolved.

On the day Yufen came home from the hospital, Kai had to hoist her onto his back and carry her up four flights of stairs. Both of them winced in pain. Kai opened the door to their apartment and, to Yufen's relief, the inside was clean and tidy. 'The children must've done it,' she assumed.

Two months had passed since the accident, and Yufen was glad to be home, though the transition offered little more than a change of scenery. The normally strong-willed Yufen could still do little by herself and could only get around if someone was willing to push her in a wheelchair.

Yufen's children, Bao and Little Ping, did their best to help their distressed mother. Taking a bath was particularly challenging, as water could cause Yufen's wounds to become infected. As Yufen painfully attempted to manoeuvre her caged leg away from the water, her children often came to her assistance.

'Mama, where do you want your leg to go?'

'Mama, is this more comfortable?'

The children also helped in the daunting task of cleaning her wounds, since she was unable to reach them herself. As Bao held a cotton swab between his fingertips, he couldn't help but gape at the six steel nails sticking out of his mother's leg. He suddenly felt nauseous. Trying not to grimace, he dipped the swab into a bottle of disinfectant and brought it towards the leg. His hand trembled as he started to swab the skin around one of the nails. His mother flinched in pain. Bao reluctantly, guiltily, continued to swab.

For the most part, Kai was also helpful, though Yufen felt that he gradually began to lose patience with the extra work. He dutifully cooked for the family, but as soon as he finished, he would call up a friend and go out. 'I bet he's really annoyed at this whole thing,' Yufen suspected.

In addition to working sporadically at his catering business, Kai received gifts of money from his relatives in order to allay Yufen's mounting medical costs. Several additional surgeries were still necessary, starting with the removal of the nails.

Because a year had passed since the nails had been

inserted, tissue had grown around them. The procedure would be unquestionably painful, so spinal anaesthetic had to be administered. Everything went smoothly until the doctor started to remove the fourth nail. Apparently, the anaesthetist had made a miscalculation, and pain started to sear through Yufen's leg. With two nails left to go, she started to scream.

Yufen continued to consume a host of Eastern and Western pain-killers after the nails were removed. But the drugs could do nothing to mollify the pain that throbbed in her heart.

'I would do anything to be able to walk again,' she thought, sobbing.

Mei Chen

'Ma'am, are you on drugs?' asked the policeman.

'Yes,' answered Mei with dim-witted candour. She added a few garbled, nonsensical comments.

Her sister Xi sighed, glad that she had finally decided to call the police. Perhaps time in prison would rid Mei of her drug addiction and unexplainable disappearances. Maybe it would even get her to stop talking about the voices.

'Where are you getting your drugs from?' the policeman continued.

'My boyfriend gave them to me.'

'Then give your boyfriend a call and tell him to come over here.'

Mei obediently picked up the phone and called Lee. The phone rang and rang, with no answer. Then the policeman administered a drug test and, to nobody's surprise, Mei tested positive.

Eight women shivered inside the small cell, which reeked of various odours emanating from the communal toilet.

Occasionally, the inmates would shoot suspicious glances at one another, making the wintry air that permeated the cell feel even colder.

Not long after Mei arrived at the detention centre in Tucheng, she had noticed that a fellow inmate wore no shoes, so she offered the woman her slippers in an effort to lighten the mood.

'Why are you giving those to her?' the cell leader barked. 'Give them to the little girl over there.' Mei obeyed.

As a newcomer, Mei was given the unenviable duty of scrubbing the toilet – a job that she performed vigorously, as she detested its smells. Most newcomers were also subject to bullying, but nobody dared to bother Mei. Her well-developed physique, originating from a childhood of hard labour in Ali Mountain, dwarfed the slight frames of the others. Also, Mei exuded an aura of fearlessness, as she was used to harassment by gangsters and other men of questionable character.

Every day, the inmates were given thirty minutes of freedom in the prison yard. Mei always used this time to run sprints. She also tried to exercise inside the cell, but for this she was accused of invading the personal space of her cell-mates. From then on, she invented exercises that allowed her to keep her limbs close to her body. It was all she could do to keep warm, especially after the cold showers that she and the other inmates had to take.

The first time her sister Xi paid a visit, she came with plenty of advice.

'As long as you have enough food to eat, just be satisfied,' suggested Xi, who felt that the prison term was like a hospital stay – necessary, yet best kept short. 'If people do bad things to you, don't think about revenge. Be good. That way, you'll get out quicker.'

One night, a gentle nudge woke Mei from slumber. She turned to find the lucky recipient of her slippers sidling into her bed. The tiny woman started to cuddle in the crook of Mei's outstretched arm.

'What are you doing?' Mei snapped.

'I just wanted to sleep with you,' the woman said innocently. Before Mei had time to react, the cell leader spotted them from across the room.

'You can't do that!' the cell leader yelled, cursing the woman. 'It violates the rules!' Mei sighed with relief. Then the cell leader turned to Mei. 'You can't cuddle with her either. You can't let other people see you like that.'

'I didn't ask her to come over. She did it on her own,' Mei insisted.

'Well, then tell her to leave you alone. We can't have this kind of thing happening here.'

The incident opened Mei's eyes to the homosexual behaviour that often occurred around her. She looked forward to being released. One day, she heard a voice:

'You will get a chance to appear in court,' it said, softly but clearly. It then told her a date.

Mei turned to a fellow inmate and matter-of-factly passed on the message.

'How do you know?' asked the woman.

'A spirit told me,' Mei murmured.

'Ha! You're lying!'

'No, I'm not.'

'Well, I guess you're like E.T. then,' the woman laughed.

Undeterred, Mei started counting down to the date specified by the spirit. Indeed, when the day came, a policeman came to escort Mei to a courthouse in Taipei for evaluation.

After more time passed, Mei heard from the voice yet again.

'You will be released,' it said in the same soft tone. As before, it revealed a date.

Mei turned to her fellow inmate. 'I'm going to be released. I just know it,' she said confidently.

When the date arrived, the police prepared Mei to leave the detention centre for her third evaluation. She was convinced that it would also be her last. As she stepped out of the cell, her previously sceptical cell-mate motioned to her.

'When you leave this place, you aren't coming back, are you?' the cell-mate remarked.

'That's right,' said Mei, pleased by her little victory. 'And how do you know?'

'Just like you said – the spirit told you.'

At the conclusion of the evaluation, the judge turned to Mei.

'I'm going to let you off, but you can't take drugs any more,' he said, dismissing her.

During Mei's three months in prison, she had been clean of all drugs and experienced not a hint of withdrawal. Exhilarated by the thought of being free, she intended to follow the judge's orders. Yet soon after her release, she met another drug dealer. Before long, Mei was spending 2,000 Taiwanese dollars a day on drugs, and in order to fund her habit she returned to the pubs to find work. She also returned to prostitution.

As before, Mei switched jobs often to avoid complications with customers who had become infatuated with her. Some customers showed their interest by giving her clothes, though the more expensive items often 'disappeared' before she had the opportunity to take them home. She suspected her co-workers of stealing but paid little attention to such petty theft; with the income she earned through prostitution, she could easily buy clothes more valuable than those that her suitors gave.

Other customers pursued Mei through words instead of gifts. 'Leave your job,' one particularly forthright customer said to her. 'Leave your job and come live with me.'

'Oh, but I'm in a lot of debt,' she lied.

One persistent customer even followed her home after

work. When she refused to let him up into her apartment and told him to leave, he refused to go. To show his resolve, he spent the entire evening in a nearby park, waiting for her.

The messiest and most frightening situations emerged when a co-worker would start to like her. This happened most frequently with the managers of massage parlours, for they tended to be younger and less established than their counterparts in the more up-market pubs.

One manager often chatted with Mei outside of the massage parlour when she wasn't working. One night, he decided to broach the unmentionable subject.

'Anyway,' he started, 'you don't have a boyfriend now, so ...'

'Rabbits don't eat the grass in their own nests,' Mei interrupted, quoting a traditional Chinese proverb, 'and I'm not attracted to anyone I work with. It's just not right.'

It was a problem that Mei could hardly avoid. After one exhausting evening at a different massage parlour, she fell asleep in one of its upstairs rooms. While she slept, her manager opened the door and tried to join her in bed.

'You can't do this,' she said. Although his impudence infuriated her, she chose her words carefully. She knew that the man could overpower her if he was determined enough – that was an experience she was all too familiar with. 'You'd better think clearly about what you're trying to do,' she continued. 'If we do this, we won't be able to see each other ever again.'

'But I've liked you for a long time.'

'I'm tired right now, and you're disrespecting me. Besides, I really don't have feelings towards you.'

At this, he left.

'You men are really bad people,' Mei thought to herself. Though no longer in prison, she still felt trapped. 'Men are not to be trusted.'

Ling Hu

Ling Hu could hardly believe what the man on the phone had just said.

'I'm calling from your husband's taxi company. We're coming to pick up the vehicle.'

'But why?' Ling asked. 'It's ours.'

'Your husband didn't pay rent.'

'It's our own car. Why do we need to pay rent?'

'Your husband didn't buy a car,' the man said. 'He rented one.' The company representative went on to explain that Yan had agreed to pay $3,000 a month to rent a vehicle, but had failed to pay for the past three months. Ling thought about how she had given Yan more than $100,000 to buy a used taxi. Although he didn't make the purchase as quickly as she had hoped, he presumably did so eventually. If he was renting a car instead, and was even behind on payments, then where was her $100,000?

'This is just too much!' she fumed. 'Why does he keep on lying to me? And why do I keep on believing him? I'm such a stupid woman!'

Irritated by her own naivety, Ling hoped to furtively extract a confession from her husband.

'The car company is looking for you,' she said to him when he returned home. She scrutinized his face for tinges of guilt.

'Why? What for?' Yan asked. He paused. 'Oh, I know what it's about. I'll take care of it.'

A few days later, the taxi company called again. The situation had not been resolved. Outraged, Ling called her husband's older brother in Chiayi and told him about the problem, hoping that he would intervene. To her dismay, she was met with judgment rather than sympathy.

'It's not that I don't know how to manage money,' she finally said. 'It's because Yan never gave me any of his earnings to begin with! How can you blame me? Anyway, the taxi company wants the vehicle back, and we still need to pay them $10,000 worth of rent.'

Eventually, Yan's brother came to Taipei to help settle the issue. A wealthy doctor, he gave Yan enough money to make the payments and buy his own taxi.

Ling warned her husband, 'You'd better buy it this time! You'd better not con your own brother!' She half-expected him to ignore her and use the money to gamble – which he did.

Ling hoped that her husband would give up his 'dreams' of taxi driving and eventually return to her uncle's soda company. Then his gambling would be naturally limited by a set work schedule. One day Ling decided to make the suggestion.

'You used to be so good at your job at the soda company. And you really have experience in that kind of thing. Will you think about going back there?'

To her relief, he agreed. During the subsequent period of bliss, she got pregnant, and when she found out that she would give birth to her first son, she was ecstatic.

'Surely, having a son will make my husband change,' she reasoned.

'Hi, I'm the wife of Yan's friend. Is your husband around?'

'No, he's at work. Can I help you?' Ling replied cheerfully into the telephone receiver. It felt good to be at home full time.

'Well, I was just wondering if my husband could borrow some money. He really needs it.'

'OK. How much do you need?'

'$50,000.'

The figure slammed into Ling's chest. It was more than twice the amount that had been requested by Yan's 'hospitalized' friend.

'That's ... a lot of money,' Ling said, attempting to disguise the intensity of her shock. She was afraid of losing the money altogether, like so many times before. She was also afraid of losing face, especially since her family had such a generous reputation. 'But ... you can borrow it,' she decided.

'Thanks! We'll write you a cheque as collateral, and you can cash it later when we have the money.'

'OK. Just come over and get the money, then.'

A pause.

'My husband was out late playing mah-jong and is too tired, so he can't go over there. Could you bring it over?'

Ling felt her face get hot.

'Why don't you come and get it?' she seethed. 'You're the one who wants to borrow the money! Just because your husband is too tired from gambling with those tiles ...'

Ling stopped herself. After all, she was a decent Taiwanese woman, wasn't she?

'Well, I'll ask my husband about this when he comes home for lunch,' Ling replied in measured calmness. When she put down the phone, she was incredulous. She tried to do some housework but couldn't remove the disturbing conversation from her mind.

Then the phone rang. It was the woman again.

'My husband's still working,' Ling said, increasingly irate. 'And of course we can't just bring you the money. You'll have to come and get it sometime. Goodbye.'

Right then, Yan came home. Eager for a sympathetic ear, Ling quickly explained the situation, but at the end of her rant, her husband looked surprisingly unperturbed.

'I'll bring the money to them,' he said. 'I'll deliver the money during my afternoon rounds.'

'What?! I know you always treat your friends well, but this is too much!' she thought. 'Well, since you're willing to deliver it, I might as well ...' Grudgingly, she opened her purse. She could hear rain start to hit the pavement outside, and a feeling of dread poured over her.

But nothing could prepare her for the news her husband brought when he returned home, drenched.

'I lost their cheque,' he said.

'You what?!'

'It was windy and wet, so when I passed a bridge, I lost their cheque.'

'Why didn't you put it in your pocket, then?!' Ling wanted to cry out. Instead, she responded with silence.

Yan continued nonchalantly, 'If someone finds the cheque, they should return it. It should be OK.'

'For you, it's OK. But not for me. Besides, who would return it when they could just cash it themselves?' Ling decided to take action. She picked up the phone and called Yan's friend.

'Please cancel that cheque you gave my husband. It's missing,' she said.

'Oh, is it ... ? But I can only do that if it hasn't been cashed for six months. If that's the case, I'll give you the money then.'

Ling felt helpless and confused, as if a dam inside her heart had been breached, causing all of her pent-up expectations about marriage to cascade into oblivion. 'Why doesn't any of this make sense?' she wanted to cry out. 'Why do I feel like you're all not telling me the truth?'

Sensing his wife's gloom, Yan attempted to console her.

'It was for our friends,' he said. 'So it's all OK.'

A few months after the birth of their son Matai, the baby suffered a relentless coughing fit and a dangerously high fever. Ling and one of her friends anxiously took the infant to a clinic that delivered grim news: the child was near death and needed to be taken to the hospital quickly. Ling panicked. She was accustomed to only keeping small sums of money in her purse so that her husband wouldn't take it while she slept. Now she didn't have enough money on hand to pay for a hospital visit. And time was running out.

Ling rushed to tell her husband about the predicament. She almost tumbled over her words, and when she finished, he glared at her with disdain.

'No need to take him to the hospital. I don't have any money to pay for that. He's just a kid. Let him die.'

Ling stared at him vacantly, as if numb to the torment of his words. Her friend, however, immediately stepped up to battle.

'If you were my brother, I'd punch you right now! How could you say something like that?! HE'S YOUR SON!'

In the end, the friend let Ling borrow $5,000 and went with her to the hospital. Matai survived.

As Matai grew older, his father grew exceedingly strict towards him, hitting the child at the slightest offence. While many Taiwanese parents tended to favour sons over daughters, Yan appeared to do the opposite. Once, when Matai was still a toddler, Yan started pummelling the boy as if he was a punching bag – for no apparent reason. Ling was so distressed by the desperate cries of her little son that she blurted out:

'He's your own blood! He's your own son! If you want to hit him, just hit him to death! It will save you the trouble of finding something wrong with him everyday and taking out all your anger on him!'

The punches continued to fly. Matai screamed. Ling stepped in and shoved her husband. 'I refuse to give you another son! I've already done my part by giving birth to a boy! Just hit him to death and save him from all the suffering!'

As Yan's gambling debts continued to accumulate, his compassion towards his children appeared to dwindle.

Once, he punched his oldest daughter Jun in the face, causing her nose to bleed sporadically until the following day.

'How can you hit kids like this?' Ling had protested in vain. 'If you want, you can spank her ... Why do you have to hit her on the face?'

Despite such behaviour, Ling continued to pay off her husband's debts whenever he came to her for help. Eventually, she began to run out of sources from which to borrow money. Even though she preferred to stay at home with her children, she decided to join her husband at the He-Song Soda Company.

'I'm not going to pay for a babysitter,' Yan said when Ling told him that she intended to re-enter the workforce.

'What? How can I take the kids to work?' she shot back in disbelief.

'You have to pay for it, then. Look at all the children you've given me to raise. I didn't want you to give birth to Matai.'

'I have not done anything to hurt you. I'm your wife. If you're happy, then I'm happy. If you're an emperor, then I'm an emperor's wife. If you're a beggar, then I'm a beggar's wife.'

'And what a wife you are! All you've done is brought me bad luck and money problems! When my friend got married, it was so great. He got a big dowry and bought a house, and look at you – you have nothing.'

'What are you talking about? If I wasn't married to you, I would have saved more money than that friend of yours. You'd better be clear on that! Besides, I'm the one paying for everything. Family, kids, everything.'

Inspite of this Yan continued to compare Ling to other women. One particular accounts clerk at the soda company became a frequent object of his praise.

'Look at how nice she is,' Yan would say to Ling. 'And look at how much money she's saved.'

Gradually, Ling became suspicious of this co-worker – a single woman who, in Ling's mind, addressed Yan with inappropriate sweetness whenever he passed by her desk. The co-worker also enjoyed probing into Ling's family affairs.

'It's like she's deliberately trying to mess things up between the two of us,' Ling seethed.

One day at around noon, Yan approached Ling's desk and started yelling at her in front of all the other account clerks. Heads turned. Ling fought back tears.

During a pause in the tirade, Ling interjected, 'Don't argue here. We both should get back to work. Please leave.' He didn't move.

'Go home please,' Ling continued. 'If you keep on talking, things will just get worse.' Still no response.

Then, to Ling's surprise, a sweet voice rose above the clamour.

'Go home.' The voice belonged to Ling's meddling co-worker, who glanced pleasantly at Yan. Immediately, he returned the glance and walked away.

The blatant loss of face slashed through Ling's heart. She glared at her co-worker, then lashed out like a wounded animal.

'Don't you say anything! DON'T TALK TO ME!'

Chapter 8

Ling kneeled desperately before the wooden figurine, unperturbed by the pleasant, unchanging grin on the idol's cherubic face.

'Why is my husband like this?' she pleaded, waving a bundle of incense sticks as her offering to Mazu. Her pious eyes drooped with worry, making her look twenty years older than she really was. As her daughter Peijen would later comment, 'She looked like a dead woman walking.'

Ling's quandary had become so exasperating that she sought the only solution she felt she could trust – divine intervention. The Mazu temple was only a few alleys away from her parents' residence, and several other major temples were located within walking distance of her home, so Ling worshipped at these places as often as she could and purchased as many offerings as she could afford. She continued to sponsor temple construction projects and the publication of Buddhist and Taoist literature.

Whenever Ling entered a temple, the mere aroma of burning incense would immediately calm her. Some of the larger temples Ling visited provided worship space for ten or more different gods, though each temple usually honoured one 'main' god. Smaller shrines tended to be more specific, and Ling would have to refer to the black, white or yellow flags that hung outside them in order to remind her which god was venerated there. She conscientiously kept herself up to date on all the latest religious trends: Which

214 Dead Women Walking

temples were the most *ling* – auspicious and accurate? Which gods had the most divine power? Which fortune-tellers were the most popular?

Some temples were so busy that Ling would have to plan her visit in advance. Once she headed to a temple immediately after work in order to present fruit offerings there and sign up for a meeting with its god. As the idol was carried by, Ling and the other worshippers formed a long line so that they could all have an opportunity to reach out and touch it.

Then came the wait. Like a fan eager to get an autograph from a movie star, Ling loitered around the temple, waiting for her number to be called. She fed her growing excitement by asking others about how the god had blessed them in the past. This time, though, Ling's evening ended in disappointment. By the time the temple was ready to close, she still had not been granted an opportunity to receive the god's counsel, and had no choice but to return the next day.

Four or five times a year, Ling would take her whole family on pilgrimages to faraway temples. Since many were located on the tops of mountains, transportation alone usually cost at least 2,000 Taiwanese dollars for each trip.

One of these temples made a particularly indelible impression on her son Matai because it venerated the Monkey King, a character from the classic tale Journey to the West, which was 'well known to every Taiwanese from kindergarten upwards.' According to the story, the monkey, as well as several other animals, was sent by Guan Yin – Ling's favourite goddess – to protect a monk during his sixteen-year quest for Buddhist scriptures. Now, as a reward for its devoted service, the monkey was deemed worthy of worship.

The dark, cavernous temple was full of people

worshipping monkey idols, big and small. While Ling consulted with a spirit medium who was dressed like a monkey, Matai squeezed past the crowds, fighting for a good spot in front of an idol. Like his mother, he was eager to worship – especially since it gave him a legitimate excuse to get out of the house at least once a week. When he reached an agreeable location, he held his incense sticks just like he had seen his mother do on innumerable occasions, and prayed to one of the monkeys.

'Please help me with my schoolwork,' Matai began. 'Help me be a little smarter.' He paused before uttering his deepest desire.

'Help my mummy and daddy's relationship get better.'

* * *

Ling strode confidently into the temple, as if she was an Olympic athlete walking into a gym. As she did in most temples, she completed her worship rituals with seemingly professional ease – and was proud of it.

The reputedly auspicious temple was one of her personal favourites, for it was conveniently located in a neighbour's house. Various modes of divination were set up like stations around the temple, and she knew the intricacies of all of them. Offering incense and throwing *bwa-bway*, or divination blocks, was as natural and habitual as brushing her teeth.

As Ling worshipped and prayed, the temple's high priestess observed her from a distance, then approached her.

'You are a kind person who has found favour with the gods here,' the priestess said soothingly. 'I believe you have the potential to serve as a spirit medium.' Excitement surged through Ling's body. She felt moved by the compassion in the priestess's voice and thrilled by the privileged invitation.

The priestess led her to a room where several experienced spirit mediums were meditating, preparing to enter into trances. One of the mediums began to shake involuntarily, indicating that a spirit had entered her body. The other mediums quickly followed. Once in trances, they started massaging their arms and legs. Then they began to dance. Ling watched them carefully, remembering that every god was said to manifest itself in a distinctive way. She noticed that each medium engaged in a different dance.

'Now, close your eyes,' the high priestess instructed. 'Empty yourself of all thoughts. Meditate. Invite the spirits to come in. You must be willing, or they will not be able to enter.'

Ling sat down, closed her eyes and did as the high priestess had instructed. After a few minutes of silence, Ling began to shake. She swooped and swayed, as if performing a Chinese folk dance.

After dancing for about half an hour, Ling's reverie was disrupted by a dash of fear. 'What's the meaning of this anyway ... ? What am I doing ... ? I'd better stop.' And she did.

The high priestess contentedly proclaimed that Ling had embodied the spirit of Guan Yin, the goddess of mercy and childless women. Ling's dance had been characterized by the joining of her third finger and thumb, Guan Yin's sacred hand position.

Ling was elated. She had manifested the spirit of her favourite goddess. From childhood on, Ling had always been well acquainted with Guan Yin's serene, slightly smiling face and slender fingers, always shaped into the sacred position. Originally a male bodhisattva worshipped by Indian Buddhists, Guan Yin had such delicate features that by the time it was worshipped in Taiwan, it had transformed into a female deity.

Thinking about the gentle Guan Yin reminded Ling of her simpler days as a high school student. It was then that a fortune-teller first told her that the spirit of Guan Yin was within her. For a moment, Ling savoured the thought that Guan Yin still favoured her. But the high priestess was not finished.

'If you manifest the spirits inside the confines of this temple, you will be protected by a guardian. But if you do so at home, there will be nobody to protect you, and you may not be able to come out of the trance. It will be like walking into fire, with no way to escape.'

This was how Ling developed the habit of going to the temple almost every night. Sometimes she went to simply enjoy the presence of Guan Yin and join other mediums in dance. Other times, she would utilize her new-found skill to serve others. She did so for the first time when a worshipper came to the temple in order to ask Guan Yin a question. Eager to test her powers, Ling sat in a yoga-like position and started to meditate, with the high priestess standing by her side. She entered a trance. The petitioner said her name, then asked a question.

Ling scribbled the first idea that came to her mind on a piece of sacred yellow paper. The high priestess examined the paper, interpreted the answer, and told the petitioner how to resolve her problem. She then ceremoniously burned the piece of paper, scattered its ashes into a cup of water, and told the petitioner to drink.

Ling's new role at the temple made her feel magnanimous and important. Petitioners came to her with a variety of questions, usually centred around family, marriage, or school, and eventually Ling developed the ability to speak out Guan Yin's answer, which was more impressive than writing it down. Despite her improvement, doubts began to stew.

'If I can help others, why can't I help myself?' she

thought. 'Why is my situation at home only getting worse and worse?'

'I need $200,000.' Yan's requests for money had become like waves, increasing in frequency and intensity. In order to appease her husband's unsettling demands, Ling started taking out loans at the same rapid pace.

'All right, but this is the last time, OK?' she replied, trying to sound convincing.

Before long – before Ling could even repay her previous loan – Yan asked for more. Normally he would manage to coerce his wife into agreement, and the cycle would continue.

But not this time.

'I can't give it to you,' Ling determined.

'You have rich relatives,' Yan shot back. He leaned menacingly towards her. 'I know you can borrow the money.'

'No, I can't!'

'YES, YOU CAN!' he screeched, slapping her across the face.

Such altercations were particularly frequent during the summer, when the heat and humidity of Taipei became almost unbearable. Sometimes, when they were both irritable, Ling and her husband would even fight over religion.

'If we just *bai-bai*, worship your ancestors, then maybe we could change our bad fortune,' said Ling. 'That's what they tell me at the temples.'

'Ha! If people could really change their fortunes by going to the temple or *bai-bai*, then nobody would have to work!' Yan mocked.

When the conflicts became nearly constant, Ling started to avoid the apartment. She trod a worn path to her parents' apartment, where she often stayed for days, weeks, and even months. She also sought solace in temples and hoped to reverse her misfortune through the fortune-tellers who would set up their booths there. Most fortune-tellers – for a fee of $1,000 or more – would give her a reading after knowing nothing more than her name and birth date. The results sometimes seemed accurate.

After meeting a fortune-teller she felt she could trust, Ling would start to disclose her burdens in detail, as if the fortune-teller's roadside booth had become a counsellor's office. In one session, the fortune-teller cried out, 'It's a miracle that you've stayed with a man like that for so long! Why don't you leave him? You should have got a divorce a long time ago.'

'Well, I need to think about my kids too,' Ling replied. She worried that the stigma of divorce would bring shame to her family's name and anguish to her children. Her second daughter Peijen already found it difficult to make friends because of the gossip. And the fights left Matai, the youngest of the three, so distraught that one day he burst into sobs at school.

'What's wrong?' a concerned teacher asked Peijen, who came to his side. Peijen said nothing, too embarrassed to mention the bitter fight that had occurred between their parents the night before. Suddenly, a classmate spoke up.

'I know! I live in the apartment below them. It's because they're the children of THOSE people, Ling Hu and Yan Zhang!'

It pained Ling to know that her children were being ostracized, and she feared that getting a divorce would only make the situation worse. She continued to visit other fortune-tellers, hoping that an alternative solution would emerge.

'Change your name, change your fortune,' one fortune-teller advised, offering her ten auspicious names to choose from. Ling declined and continued in her search.

Eventually, a family friend referred Ling to a

well-known fortune-teller who ran a booth in front of one of Panchiao's main temples. When Ling arrived, she saw two small Java sparrows perched in a tiny cage on the fortune-teller's table.

'I want to know about my marriage,' Ling said.

The plump, white-haired woman asked Ling a few simple questions, rearranged a stack of cards sitting next to the bird cage, and then turned to one of the sparrows.

'Spirit in the sparrow, Ling Hu is here to see you ...' she said with mystical flair. After completing the introduction, the fortune-teller held a piece of bird food between her fingertips and opened the cage door.

The sparrow stepped forward and pecked at three of the cards. After it retreated back into the cage, the fortune-teller rewarded it with a piece of food and then examined the cards.

'Your husband is like a giant snake that is strangling you to death,' she said. 'He's like a bottomless hole that cannot be filled,' she said. For effect, she drew a picture of a snake on a piece of paper.

'Yes, that's it! That's what my heart has been telling me all along,' Ling thought. Although the reading did not provide her with a new solution to her problems, its apparent accuracy bolstered her faith in the spirit world.

So during Ling's visit to a different fortune-teller, she decided to ask boldly, 'Do you think I should get a divorce?'

'One is better than two,' came the answer.

'It's not that I can't let go of him,' Ling explained. 'I'm just worried about the children. I don't know what I'll do if we get a divorce and he gets custody of the children.'

'No matter. If your relationship with them is already good, then it won't be cut off. Don't worry. One is better than two.'

Ling watched the spirit medium slowly, ceremoniously trace out some characters in a rack of sand known as a planchette. She was in one of several home-operated Taoist shrines she would visit in order to gain wisdom from the planchettes.

Planchette writing, dating back to China's Tang dynasty, was originally used to summon the opinion of 'The Lady of the Privy'. In her past life, this goddess was said to have been a concubine who was forced to clean toilets – as her name suggests.[2] But in Taiwan, planchette writing, like many other local religious practices, had broader uses. Through it, one could petition a host of different gods on a range of topics: business, school, marriage, destiny.

Ling stood before the planchette, hoping to find a new answer to her problems. But instead she found herself wrestling with inner disquietude. 'How can I help others when I need help myself?

Ling started telling the high priestess whom she assisted that she was too busy to serve at the temple. But she would feel unbearably guilty after giving such an excuse and, like a lover unable to break off a relationship, she could not stay away for long. 'This is giving me too much pressure, like I'm being forced to do it against my will,' she thought begrudgingly.

Eventually, Ling's conscience found a way of escape. She discovered that the high priestess was living with a spirit medium – specifically, a *tang-ki*, the kind so possessed by the spirits that they would mutilate themselves ritualisti-cally. Ling had witnessed such performances as a child and knew that chastity was required during a *tang-ki*'s term of service, so she was disgusted by the sexual relationship this one shared with the high priestess.

'The gods told us to live together,' the high priestess insisted. But Ling was not convinced. 'If the gods are holy, why would they ask them to do something like that? Really,

I'm too young to be spending so much time doing this. It's time to leave this temple,' Ling resolved.

The temple of Cheng-Huang Ye,[3] 'The City God', resembled an ordinary traditional Chinese house on the outside. But when Ling paid a visit, the courtyard of the small, square compound teemed with more than forty people.

In addition to answering prayers for protection and prosperity, 'The City God' was known for judging the spirits of the dead in the courts of hell. But this did not faze Ling or the other worshippers. What drew her to the temple was that, through a spirit medium there, she could summon the spirit of her husband and speak to it directly about their marital problems.

Ling drew a number and waited for her turn. As she spoke with the others in line, she realized that the spirit medium provided a variety of services. She was even told that a spirit medium had healed a lame person. Of course, such services came at a price, based on the severity of the problem. Hers would end up costing $3,000.

Another unusual characteristic of the temple was its process of membership. In past visits, Ling had refused to become a disciple of 'The City God' because she deemed membership too expensive. Now she was so desperate that she decided to take the chance. She made the required offerings, recited a sombre vow to the god, filled out a personal data form, and then used her chop to seal her decision. Now the god's relationship with her was as official as her relationship with the family bank account. Now she was granted exclusive access to a sacred part of the building, where she could burn sacred offerings and meditate, shrouded by darkness.

*   *   *

Ling gulped the night air in quick breaths, straining from the heavy load. With her son on her back, one hand holding the arm of her second daughter, the other dragging a suit-case, and her oldest daughter trailing behind, she trudged towards her parents' apartment. This was the result of yet another vicious fight with her husband.

By the time Ling and her three children arrived at the Hus' doorstep, they looked and felt like despondent refugees. Ling rang the doorbell. But this time, her mother refused to open the door.

'When daughters are married out, they're like water used to wash your face – once you pour the water out, you can't bring it back in,' Mrs Hu had reasoned. And Ling had tried to come back one time too many.

Ling felt hopelessly abandoned. The last pillar holding up her crumbling life had just collapsed.

The next time she was driven out of the house, she had no choice but to accept the hospitality of Suzhen, a friend from the temple she had once served at.

Since Ling and Yan fought rigorously several times a week, Ling started to spend a great deal of time at Suzhen's house. A single woman in her fifties, Suzhen came from a wealthy family – the recipients of much good fortune. In fact, they were so lucky that they had found a stone statue of Guan Yin poking up out of their yard. They had dug it up and had worshipped it ever since.

'The spirit of Guan Yin is very strong in you,' Suzhen said to Ling one day. 'You should let the spirit of this stone Guan Yin enter you so that you'll be able to go into a trance by yourself.'

Even though Ling had been warned to do this only within the confines of a temple, she felt indebted to Suzhen. Whenever Ling would stay over for a few nights, Suzhen would invite friends and relatives over to utilize her services. Like before, she enjoyed helping people deal with their problems, especially since her own seemed incurable. Like before, she enjoyed having the power to dictate what other people should do. But like before, she began to have doubts.

'Is this all really true?' she thought to herself whenever she was in a particularly candid mood. 'Are Guan Yin's answers really helping people, or are they just making things worse? Are the answers I give really coming from Guan Yin, or are they my own ideas?'

When Ling started to openly express her doubts, however, Suzhen sternly reprimanded her.

'If a god wants you to serve, you don't really have a choice,' she said.

Ling disliked being bound by this sense of obligation, especially when she was already weary from long work days as an accounts clerk. To make things worse, the man who volunteered to drive her to work, one of Suzhen's relatives, began to like her romantically. Snared in darkness, Ling felt that every time she embraced a solution to a problem, it would just deliver her into the hands of another.

Then came two signs of hope. Ling's mother allowed her to come home again. And Ling discovered a way to confront her husband's sea ghost.

She first learned of the sea ghost when she visited a certain temple fortune-teller after work and stayed at the temple until four in the morning.

'Your husband has so many problems because an evil gui, a ghost, is tormenting him,' the fortune-teller said. 'The ghost belongs to someone who died at sea. Someone whose spirit hasn't been worshipped properly by its family. It went through the earth, trying to look for its family, and when they couldn't be found, it followed your husband instead. I tell you, when this bad ghost is gone, your life will change.'

'That must be it!' Ling thought. 'It all makes sense. The

ghost must have followed him when he worked on that boat, before we got married.'

The fortune-teller went on to say that the god of the temple, if properly compensated, could release Yan from the ghost's tenacious grip. Ling was told to prepare a bowl of rice, some joss money, and several dishes of raw food. She would then have to offer them to the god at the side of a major road at around four in the afternoon.

The following day, Ling carried an armful of offerings to an intersection near her house at the appointed time. She gleamed with hope. While vehicles sped by, she worshipped the god with three incense sticks, looked skyward, and prayed:

'Please be the master over this ghost. My husband always argues with me over money and asks me to give him some when he's broke. I don't want to be rich, but I do want to get back what I've lost. I have three children to feed. Help me to not have more debt. Stop my husband from continuing to throw money around.'

Ling left her offerings along the side of the road and walked away, filled with peace. She firmly believed that her husband's spirit was now free. Indeed, his situation did seem to improve – at least for a while. But the relief was as momentary as the ebb of a tide.

'I've already done what you told me to do,' Ling said when she went back to the fortune-teller a few months later. 'Why is this ghost still bothering our family?'

'Our god did help release your husband, but you didn't come back. Haven't you been told that when you receive an answer, you need to come back and thank the god for its help?'

'No. Can I give proper thanks now?'

'Sure. Then we'll see if our god will respond to your gesture.'

Ling walked dutifully to the temple entrance and

purchased $3,000 worth of joss money. Stack by stack, she threw the money into the furnace of the god, then knelt down to pray.

'Is this enough for you? I have three kids and am already working so hard. But I'm willing to borrow money if you think this is not enough.'

Since she had heard that driving out a ghost could cost millions of dollars, she dearly hoped that her offering was sufficient. She picked up a set of divining blocks and let them fall. After several tosses, the god's answer was a relieving 'yes'. Ling left the temple hopeful.

'Come back if you have any problems, and I will help you,' the temple worker said to her pleasantly as she walked away.

In time, Ling found out through office gossip that Yan had won $1 million in the lottery. He was even planning to buy a car. The relationship between him and his wife warmed, and he eventually gave her $2,000 of his winnings.

Ling was happy. The gods were finally on her side.

Mei Chen

Mei's body felt light, almost weightless, as she faced the apparition. It wasn't that of a man, as she hated men. And it wasn't that of a spirit, as she was generally afraid of the spirits. Rather, the apparition bore a haunting resemblance to herself.

'Strange,' Mei thought as the apparition's skull floated out and up, hovering in midair. It drifted towards her. Then it entered her own head. Pain. Her head felt as heavy as a bowling ball.

In the following days, Mei suffered from a dull headache that muddled her thoughts. She lethargically roamed between the massage parlour and hotel rooms, like a wandering ghost.

When Mei turned thirty, her contact with the spirits became more vivid, more disturbing. Manifesting themselves as voices and apparitions by day and menacing, life-like shadows by night, the spirits began to multiply until a whole host of them followed her, showering her with constant taunts and threats.

'We're going to kill you!' they often said. And she often believed them. She continued to work as a masseuse and prostitute, despite the distractions. One tiring evening, during a bathroom break, she closed her eyes and breathed deeply, trying to clear her thoughts.

Then they appeared.

The spirits hovered around and placed a screen in front of her. It was their instrument of torture. The screen lit up and started displaying one of her rapes in sordid detail.

So unbearable was the pain that she looked away and ran. She ran out of the bathroom, out of the massage parlour, out to a small road where nobody could see her. There, she started to sob.

After she had purged herself of all tears, she still could not erase the images from her mind. She asked for a few days off and went home. But even home provided little solace, as the spirits became increasingly intrusive.

'We're going to kill your mother! We're going to kill your father!' they whispered, brandishing electric batons. One of them struck her leg, and pain seared through Mei's body.

'No! Get away from me!' she cried out, trying to will them away.

'We're going to kill your whole family!' More shocks. More taunts.

Desperately confused, Mei felt that she had no choice but to run to the world she had mostly tried to forget – her childhood home in Ali Mountain. Whenever Mei showed up at her parents' doorstep, her pale face always bore a distant, lifeless gaze. She was so absent that she hardly noticed that the village was starting to change. Electricity. Running water. Such developments were mere hints of the transformations taking place across the island.

But if Mei's behaviour served as any indication of how city life could change a person, she was a very unappealing advertisement. Like a walking corpse, she would slowly amble back and forth as if lost in her own world, wandering along the dirt roads of her village until the whole community knew of her plight.

What the villagers didn't know was that behind Mei's apparent languor was a gritty determination to defend herself against the intangible forces that assailed her, to escape from a spiritual realm that seemed to her very much like hell.

'Don't touch me with that thing again! I'm going to run far, far away ... away from you and your electric batons ... Can't take the pain, the shocks ... Have to run away ...'

'Where are you going, Mei? Why can't you just sit down for a moment?' It was a voice not among the other voices. The voice of Mei's older sister.

'Because it hurts. Because my leg is being electrocuted.'

'Oh yeah? How is that possible?'

'They're electrocuting my leg. See, check my pulse ... my heart's not beating.'

'Who are they?'

'Them!'

'Where are you going, Big Sister? Why are you laughing at me? You had to run to the next room just so that you could laugh at me?'

Mei's mother refused to laugh. Her years in the True Jesus Church had taught her to pray for her daughter, but these days, her prayers seemed to go unanswered. So she resorted to what she considered the next best thing: witchcraft.

Mei paced about nervously in the home of her great aunt, the renowned shaman. She refused to sit, so it was only with much effort that her great aunt eventually managed to force Mei onto a chair. The woman's dark, wrinkled hands produced an invisible rope, which she looped around Mei's body while mumbling in the language of the spirits. The spell was meant to still Mei's heart, to keep her from pacing around, and after its last words were muttered ... a moment of anticipation.

Mei stood up and walked away.

'We're going to kill you!' came the cackles.

After Mei returned to Taipei, a male voice encouraged her to buy a lottery ticket by revealing its winning numbers. She listened to the voice carefully, but with some apprehension. 'If I listen to him, I will be selling my soul to him forever,' she thought to herself, though she was still eager to test out the spirit's accuracy.

She got her chance when she overheard some co-workers discussing what numbers they should pick for their lottery tickets. Mei interjected with her spirit-guided suggestion. Since she had been moderately successful in the past by picking numbers at random, they decided to bet a couple of hundred dollars on her number.

The number won. As a gesture of appreciation, Mei's co-workers bought her some things to eat. It was then that Mei had an epiphany: listening to, rather than fighting, the spirits could occasionally pay off.

'Go and study taekwondo,' a spirit said softly to her one day. 'This way, your blood will flow smoothly throughout your body.' As soon as Mei started taking classes, her wiry limbs easily imitated the instructor's movements.

'You're as clever as students who have been here for two or three years!' the instructor remarked. Mei thought little of the compliment, for she knew that the power that blazed within her belonged to the spirits inhabiting her body. As she kicked and punched invisible enemies, she thought of the men in her life. Men whom she no longer cared about, and no longer feared.

'You're being followed by a female spirit,' the temple priest diagnosed. 'She is waiting to enter your body.' Mei's sister nodded, hoping that this was indeed the source of Mei's mysterious behaviour. She prepared a monetary offering for the spirit.

The money did not bribe the spirit into oblivion, however, and Mei was not at all surprised. She already knew that the temple priest had been mistaken, that the spirits following her were mostly male.

This was not to be the only time that Mei would sense something was wrong around a temple. Once as she prepared to enter a temple located on Heping Lu, or 'Peace Road', she felt anything but peace.

'LEAVE THE TEMPLE!'

Mei was accustomed to the ceaseless chatter of the spirits, but this voice still startled her. It seemed to come from above instead of from within. The voice continued.

'If you go into the temple and worship, you will be worse off! More and more evil spirits will be in you!'

Mei was confused. Usually the voices strongly urged her to go to temples, just as they urged her to offer herself as a prostitute and do drugs. 'Go to this temple and worship! Offer incense!' they would usually order.

Why was this voice so different?

Mei gazed out the taxi window at the spirit's long white gown, dangling in midair. The spirit was doing an extraordinary job at keeping pace with the moving vehicle, considering that it casually hovered in the lotus position. Gradually, the outline of the spirit's body faded until it resembled an amorphous cloud. It continued to follow the car, and even wanted to come inside. 'I won't let you in!' Mei resolved.

The spirit stuck a picture to the window, a round picture of Buddha. A ray of light leapt from the picture and warmed Mei's face. 'Now that doesn't make sense,' she thought.

Another taxi ride was equally perplexing. As this taxi bumped through the streets of Taipei, all was silent – aside from the crackle and hiss of the car radio. Both Mei and her reticent taxi driver uttered nothing to each other, lost in their own thoughts. Suddenly, he spoke.

'Your experience in this world is only temporary. Someday you will go to heaven, where you came from.'

The taxi driver proceeded to drive in silence, as if nothing extraordinary had happened. 'Why did he say that?' Mei wondered. 'Was it another spirit?'

In a dream, Mei saw a village that was part of a new earth. A large circle had been drawn, and inside it stood a host of people who had died, including her whole family. Evil spirits tried to attack the people from the outside, but as soon as they crossed the line, ZAP! They died of electric shock.

In another dream she saw a giant balloon that enveloped a beach covered with people. Some had died of poisoning. Others were dying. Still others had been rescued from death by someone in a white robe. Mei frantically looked around for her relatives: Would they be among the dead? Would she?

In yet another dream, Mei's younger brother grew taller and taller at supernatural speed. In yet another, her older brother was covered in skin so dark that he appeared African.

'Strange, my brother doesn't have dark skin.'

'He will be dark in the future,' the voice replied.

A few years later, her older brother's skin inexplicably muddied into a dark brown. Meanwhile, Mei's younger brother started to rise in political power within the Tso tribe. Although such things had little consequence in Mei's problem-plagued life, she mulled over them, regarding them as proof that the spirits were real.

Mei didn't know what was worse, the pinpricks that danced on her skin whenever she arrived at work or the spirit conversations that consumed her free time. Her stretches of unemployment became more frequent, and weeks would pass like one long, torturous daze.

Some things managed to calm Mei's spirit, like strolling around a tea garden she was fond of. Once she spent a whole day amid the garden's comforting tendrils, but as soon as the sun started to hide behind the horizon, her anxiety returned. As she started to walk home, she had a lingering suspicion that the encounters would resume.

When Mei reached the bedroom of her sister's apartment, she heard pounding in the distance. Then gunshots. And explosions. As they came closer, Mei darted to the window and peered outside.

Dark figures, armed with guns, cannons and tanks, cluttered the street below. Something zipped through the window. Before Mei could hide, a barrage of bullets flew in her direction and she cringed in pain, though her body did not bear any visible wounds.

'What should I do?!' she cried inwardly.

As if she had just uttered a magical phrase, the sky outside the window opened up, and a figure started to descend from the opening. Gleaming and clothed in white, its light emanated as far as Mei's eyes could see and even came to fill her own body. It was beautiful.

Then, as involuntarily as her awe-struck reaction to seeing a television for the first time, a thought occurred to her.

'It's the God of righteousness.'

Before Mei could pinpoint the origin of the thought, there came another sound, this time in the form of a voice.

'God said, "Let there be light." And there was light.' Though she could not remember hearing the phrase before, the words enveloped her with peace and warmth. In that moment, she felt as if she had the ability to forget the past, to even forgive. She looked down. The dark figures on the street below had paused, staring at the brilliance in both fear and amazement.

Two other rays flashed in the distance, like brown and black streaks of lightning.

'Don't move. Don't accept those others,' the voice continued. The light within her left as quickly as it had entered and started hurling balls of brightness at the figures below. As the light faded into the distance, it spoke to her softly, filling her with a much-needed inner strength:

'I will give you the endurance to face everything. I'm not saying goodbye. One day, I'll live inside of you.'

No spirits followed her. No voices taunted her. In the remarkable calm, Mei heard a single sound.

'You have a lot of room to grow,' said the barely intelligible whisper. 'Let me teach you some lessons. If you follow these things, you will receive eternal life.'

'Eternal life? What does that matter? What does that have to do with me?' Mei wondered with her usual disdain. 'What I want is to be beautiful.'

'If you want to be truly beautiful, lesson one is that you shouldn't lie.' The image of *huang*, the Chinese character for 'lie', sprung up into her mind.

'OK, I'll do that,' she said, subconsciously knowing that she had lied already. The voice tried to communicate with her two more times, but each time she paid no heed to its words. So it stayed silent.

* * *

The man had taken the woman to a hotel room, only to find that something was dreadfully wrong with her. When he tried to strike up conversation, she seemed incapable of focusing on him, as if she was busy listening to something else. Eventually she closed her eyes and shut him out entirely. Indignant, the man got up and walked out.

'... It's a laser eye,' the voice continued. Mei looked up and saw a massive, gleaming eyeball drift across the wall. As it neared the other side of the room, it got smaller and smaller until it disappeared.

Mei wished that the more malicious spirits would also vanish from her life with such finality, but instead they stayed by her side, allowing her no escape. Mei felt that she had no choice but to pay yet another visit to Ali Mountain, where at least life was quiet and 'normal'. She found, though, that the visions and voices were not bound by space, time, or the laws of the physical realm.

One day Mei was sitting listlessly in her sister's Ali Mountain home, gazing at some clothes that were hung up to dry. Suddenly, a shirt started to quiver. Mei raised a quizzical eyebrow and pointed her finger at the devious shirt. It quivered more. She moved her finger. The shirt took flight, like a kite attached to her hand by an invisible string.

Mei laughed. She pointed at the shirt again and guided it around the room. It levitated to and fro, and as soon as she had had enough, it landed gracefully on a piece of furniture.

Unfortunately, Mei's apparent paranormal powers could not protect her from the spirits, whose attacks she had started to record in a journal. One day, as Mei was reading through her scribbling, her frustration became uncontainable. She smashed her finger into the journal, as if smearing the words could erase the memories.

Mei lifted her finger and looked at the journal again, through tears.

'What's this?'

At the very spot where her finger had been was a charred hole. It looked as if her finger had burned the page. Invigorated by the discovery of another supernatural skill, Mei eagerly showed her sister the evidence.

'Look, I burned this with my finger,' she said, like a child flaunting a prized art assignment. Her sister turned pale.

'Don't play around with that! Throw it away right now!' her sister shrieked, pointing to a small ditch. Reluctantly, Mei tossed her beloved journal into it.

Since Mei's parents lived nearby, Mei went to them, yearning for a warm welcome.

'What's wrong?' asked Mrs Chen when she saw her pale, gaunt daughter. Though the question was an ordinary one, in Mei's case it didn't come with a simple answer.

'Someone is trying to kill me,' Mei said, trying to ignore the threats ringing in her ears.

'Who? I don't see anyone ...'

'You don't understand. If I stay at home, he will kill you too,' she said, suddenly convinced of what she must do. 'I need to go now.'

'Why do you need to leave? You're so pale. You look like a dead person ...'

'I don't know,' Mei answered, walking out of the house.

Little did she know that she was about to embark, quite literally, on a journey through the wilderness.

A journey she would never be able to forget.

Yufen Wang

Yufen trembled as she stood, gripping her two canes as if she was nearing the terrifying peak of a roller-coaster. The journey to the other side of the room looked like an impossibly long one.

Eight months had passed since her crippling bus accident, and since the condition of her legs was improving, Yufen finally felt ready to give walking a try. She glanced at her two children, who stood by her side. Feeling assured of their protection, she let go of one cane. Then the other.

Immediately, her legs crumpled under the weight. As Little Ping and Bao tried to lift her back to her feet, her body heaved with sobs, her every movement conducted a melancholy song of defeat. For the next few days, she felt like she was gasping for breath in an enormous whirlpool of sadness.

Yufen was not one to easily give up, though, and she tried again more than ten times. Finally, she went back to the hospital, where the doctor asked her to try one more time. She let go of one cane, then the other. And collapsed. Yufen was so accustomed to failure that she wasn't surprised when the doctor admitted that her first surgery had not been successful.

Six months after her second surgery, she tried to walk again. This time, she was accompanied by a long-lost friend: Victory. Yufen managed to take a few steps without any assistance, though she still felt more comfortable with a cane.

'At least I don't need to use two canes to walk now,' she thought, contentedly resigned. 'If I always have to use a cane for the rest of my life – well, I can take it. I shouldn't expect a full recovery anyway. As long as I can get from place to place by myself, I will be satisfied.'

During Yufen's years of limited mobility, she satiated her spiritual desires – an appetite that had been whetted during her most difficult weeks in the hospital – by reading Buddhist literature. She remembered how her mother, a devout Buddhist, used to remind her of how well Buddha took care of their family. And Mrs Wang was not merely a woman of words. To illustrate her own gratitude and earn future blessings, she regularly recited *A Mi Tuo Fo*, the auspicious name of Buddha in Chinese, and even took a vow of vegetarianism.

Yufen's childhood experiences taught her that Buddhism was a good religion that helped its devotees avoid suffering and gain happiness. Her growing collection of Buddhist books explained how to spurn greed, foolishness, ignorance, and other moral vices. Inspired by the books, she went further and immersed herself in formal Buddhist texts like The Heart Sutra, many of which deeply influence the Taiwanese worldview. Yufen watched several different Buddhist television channels. She let herself get lost in the soothing melodies of Buddhist music. And after she started walking with a cane, she would occasionally take classes at a Buddhist scripture society near her apartment.

'Since I've been invited to go, why not?' she reasoned. 'Maybe the classes will give me some peace.'

Yufen's cousin also took her to a local Buddhist temple, where a monk happened to be preaching. At the end of his talk, Yufen hobbled up to him, bowed, and presented him with a red envelope full of money. At the time she thought the monk would then give her a sacred Buddhist name, like the one her mother had been given, as an expression of thanks. But the monk did nothing.

'Either he forgot about it or he thought that I didn't give enough red envelope money,' she laughed to herself. She figured that the time had not yet come for her to become a real Buddhist. Undeterred, she continued to engross herself in Buddhist literature. Through their counsel, she felt that she was finally beginning to understand herself and acknowledge her personal failings. She especially began to recognize the implications of her feisty temper. She started to regret the numerous instances when her mouth had spewed insults like a volcano unable to contain its lava.

The books made her feel like a volcano in other ways too. They explained that all people are possessed by insatiable desires, which burn like unquenchable fires in their souls. 'No wonder I'm this way. No wonder I'm so stubborn,' Yufen thought, frustrated by the fact that her books provoked remorse, but not resolution. 'I'm really a stupid person. I'm not a good mother, and I'm definitely not a good wife. But how am I supposed to be any better?'

Yufen started comparing herself to other wives, wondering why she could never be as patient or attentive as they were. She wanted to be merciful towards her husband, but her tempestuous reactions to the mere sight of him flowed as naturally as a lion's saliva at the sight of prey. She wanted to take better care of her children, but apart from spending more money on them, she knew of no other way to do it. She even bought her son a $40,000 encyclopaedia set – as atonement for her nagging guilt.

When she wasn't sleeping, watching TV, or spending time with her children, Yufen passed most of her time consumed by her Buddhist books. But even her ten-year-old son could see that the sense of 'enlightenment' offered by the books was coupled with an even stronger sense of anxiety. He felt sad to see his mother so frustrated with life, so helpless, so empty.

Indeed, Yufen began to feel that she had lived her whole life as a victim of fate. Since she had never been properly taught how to live, she had always made foolish decisions without considering their long-term ramifications. She had hastily pranced into marriage, all the while singing a song that extolled her well-to-do prince. He became her centre of gravity, and whenever his moods swung, so did hers. Just as she couldn't rid him of his dependence on alcohol, she couldn't rid herself of her dependence on him.

Years later, she would compare her plight to that of a trapped bird, violently banging its wings against a window. In its panic, the little bird had not yet discovered an entirely different window on the opposite side of the room. A wide-open window, a way to freedom.

Notes

1. www.taipeitimes.com/News/feat/archives/2005/01/14/ 2003219379, Ian Bartholomew, 'Monkeying around with a classic tale', 14/1/2005.
2. www.eng.taoism.org.hk/religious-activities&rituals/ daoist-folk-customs/pg4-8-13.asp, Taoist Culture and Information Centre.
3. Cheng-Huang Ye, 'The City God'. The 'Lord of castles and moats', this god is said to represent heaven's authority on earth by keeping records of births, deaths and the moral behaviour of humans.

Chapter 9

The village boy who found Mei Chen after her overnight struggle through the mountains took her directly to the house of one of her older brothers. She was clearly incapable of finding her way alone. When Mei arrived, her brother and his wife were astounded by her wild transformation. Her clothes, tattered. Her eyes, dark pools of grief. Her body, a dingy mass of cuts and bruises.

As if reading their thoughts, Mei moaned, 'My body isn't all together ... they took me apart and took out my blood, my heart and my organs.'

Tenderly, carefully, Mei's brother tried to divert her thoughts away from what had happened the night before. Considering the pattern of her recent behaviour, it was probably a story that was best left untold.

'Why don't you go take a shower?' he suggested.

After Mei cleaned the dirt and blood off her body and put on a set of clean white clothes, her brother drove her to their parents' house.

'You are not better yet,' he said as he drove.

'Yes,' Mei sighed.

The car revved up the steep lane leading to their parents' house. As soon as Mrs Chen saw her daughter, her eyes filled with tears.

'I thought you were dead,' she said, embracing Mei. 'Last night a lot of the villagers went to look for you, and we thought you were dead.'

'Yes, we thought you were dead,' echoed Mr Chen, touching his daughter's arm.

Mei's younger brother, her best childhood friend, cringed when he saw her. He walked up to her and took her in his arms.

'How did you come to be like this?' he said, his face twisted in agony. 'I just can't look at you when you're like this.'

'They're trying to kill me,' Mei replied, as if nothing had changed since the day before. Her father started to reprimand her for being irrational, but Mei hardly listened. She could only think about the menacing threats the spirits had made throughout the night, and suddenly remembered one particularly disturbing one. One directed at her older brother.

'They're going to kill me,' she repeated to her parents. 'And they're going to kill Big Brother too.'

'Nobody will kill you,' said her mother, soothingly. 'Please, just don't leave again.' Deeply moved, Mei took a good look at her mother. She suddenly understood: 'Even though I must look like I'm going crazy, my mother really loves and accepts me.'

Mr Chen chimed in. 'We've already been praying for you,' he said – a rare reference to the Christianity he professed to believe in. 'Whatever is controlling you ... we don't know what to do about it.'

So desperate were the Chens that they decided to turn to a technique they hadn't practised since Mr Chen joined the True Jesus Church more than twenty years earlier. They decided to evoke Mr Chen's powers as a shaman.

Mei discovered the heresy when, wandering through the house, she came upon a voodoo doll, tied up to a chair. Through examining the doll, she found that her father's rough hands had crafted the doll in her likeness. She imagined him muttering incantations around it, casting a spell that would presumably stop his daughter from running wild.

The heresy came in other forms too. One day Mrs Chen remarked, with such nonchalance that she could have been talking about the weather, 'If you believe in Buddha, you'll be rich.'

Mei was shocked. Even though she personally did not believe in Christ, she knew that her mother did – deeply – and she felt responsible for the numbing of her parents' faith. It was as if the spirits that hurt her had started to infect her entire family.

After Mei settled down at her parents' house, the spirits that stalked her split into two contingents. One group wielded spinning brown knifes that poked at Mei's skin and cut through her innards. The other group remained invisible, but equally malicious. The pain was constant. And consuming. 'What can I do to get rid of these voices, these spirits? They follow me wherever I go!'

'They're electrocuting me,' Mei said when she could no longer keep her agony to herself.

'There's no electricity,' her mother replied, rubbing Mei's arms to prove it.

Unconvinced, Mei grabbed some plastic bags and tried to wrap herself in them.

One evening, Mei discovered a far more effective form of protection. In the safety of her room, there appeared a spirit that bore an uncanny resemblance to Lee, her drug-dealing ex-boyfriend. The dark, towering, knightly figure seemed to shimmer, and it wore a long gown that emanated bright circles of light.

For once, Mei was not afraid. Seeing Lee like this revived feelings that – more than most of the emotions she had experienced in her lifetime – resembled love. She reached out.

'Go to Taipei,' said the apparition as it walked away

from her. 'I'll wait for you there.' It then stopped and peered at a peculiar object near Mei's bed – peculiar in that Mei never had any interest in it and wouldn't have put it there herself.

It was her mother's Bible.

As the Bible started to glow, the apparition reached out its hand. And touched it. Sparks flew, and the spirit withdrew its hand in wounded horror.

'Don't touch that. It will shock you!' it warned, addressing other spirits that had started to appear in the room. Fascinated, Mei figured that the God in the Bible was some sort of superior spirit. She placed the unopened Bible by her pillow and tried to sleep.

'Go back to Taipei! Go back to Taipei! Go back to Taipei!' The taunts had become like a hypnotic chant that droned on, day and night.

It was obvious that Mei's 'retreat' to Ali Mountain was not having the desired effect. One evening, the whole family gathered together to discuss the situation. Finally, Mei's beloved younger brother spoke up.

'Go back to Taipei,' he said tenderly. 'Your being here is just ... causing a lot of tears. Be patient. Just go back to Taipei. It won't be too long before your pain will get better. Just ... wait.' He handed Mei some money, despite their mother's cries.

'No! Don't go ...'

The next morning, Mei went back to Taipei. Soon after, she received news that her older brother had passed away. He had left the world unexpectedly, yet unremarkably, while sitting in a chair. Rumour had it that he had had too much to drink, though Mei refused to believe it.

'We told you we would kill him!'

Mei wept.

A heavy hand of lethargy enslaved Mei, as she had become too unstable to work regularly for any pub, any brothel. And even when she did work, her money seemed to vanish. Feeling penniless, she resigned herself to living with her sister Xi. The days passed as one unmemorable blur, and she would do drugs or wander the streets in order to escape from the voices and the boredom. Often, her wanderings took place at night, when she was too anxious to sleep, too certain that the spirits would kill her once she closed her eyes. The fact that she tended to stagger around haphazardly didn't keep her from wearing her most expensive clothes during these overnight treks. So precious to her in years past, the clothes meant little to her now, and she simply threw them away when they became too tattered to wear.

Mei's sleep schedule had become so erratic that sometimes she was too exhausted to do anything but sit limply in the living-room, with the drone of the television in the background of her aimless thoughts. One day, the meaninglessness of it all became so intolerable that she decided to try something new – changing the television channels with her mind.

'This is really strange,' said her brother-in-law, who had been peaceably watching the television a moment before. 'Why does it keep on switching channels?'

Wind. As Mei lay in bed, a cool breeze swept over her body. She knew that her room had no window or fan, but by now she had got past questioning such strange occurrences.

The breeze blew into her through her mouth and nose. She started to tremble. She felt as if her body was being filled with water, all the way down to her toes. Then a momentary whirlpool suctioned it all into her stomach, which tightened and locked shut.

'There's only one who can unlock this. Go to the top of the house.'

The brigade of spirits that usually surrounded Mei scattered at the sound of the voice. Mei shuffled to the roof. The moon illuminated the night sky, dotted by only a handful of stars.

'Hold out your hands.'

She extended her arms, her body forming the shape of a cross. Two beams of light came down from the sky and touched her hands, numbing them. Gradually, the light crept onto the rest of her body. The numbness spread.

'I am *huo shen*, the fire God,' Mei thought she heard as she half-listened. Several years would pass before she would realize what had really been said – the difference lying in two typically insignificant Chinese characters.

'I am *huo zhe de shen*, the living God.'

It started out like any other stroll. Mei got off work after midnight, did some drugs, and started walking in no particular direction. As she slowly meandered along the street, she felt as if her mind had dissolved, incapable of holding onto any single thought.

'You want your boyfriend, don't you?' the spirits asked.

'Yes.'

'Then walk this way.'

She walked. And walked. After living in Taipei for so many years, Mei was still rather unfamiliar with the city's roads. As she walked, she felt like she was in a foreign land, with only a few familiar landmarks to guide her. Mostly, though, she followed the voices.

'You want a lot of money, right?' they tempted.

'Yes.'

'Then come this way. We'll get you some money.'

Mei walked until daybreak, then continued walking. She passed more landmarks. The Presidential Palace. National Taiwan University Hospital. As she passed the hospital, some elderly patients who were congregating there started to stare at her. She trudged past, bearing the weight of their gazes.

'They're probably wondering why I'm walking around like this, wearing such beautiful clothes.' Indeed, her appearance was paradoxical. Through she was dressed in formal wear, her pale complexion and unsteady gait made her look like a moving corpse.

'You want to be beautiful? Come this way.'

From the hospital, Mei headed west into Wanhua, Taipei's oldest district. Although it had once lived up to its name, 'A Thousand Glories', it gradually became a hot spot for prostitution and criminal activity as Taipei's city centre moved east. In Wanhua, a man tried to rouse Mei from her stupor.

'Let me take you to a hotel,' he said to her.

'Why?' she asked, confused.

'I have something I want to show you.'

She followed. Once they entered the hotel, the man pulled out a bag. Mei's eyes lit up, as it was filled with what she craved most at that moment – drugs.

'If you sleep with me, I'll give you all this,' said the man. As Mei stared at the drugs, an army of conflicting voices warred inside her head.

'Go on! Do it!'

'Resist it and leave!'

In the end, Mei shook her head.

'I don't want it,' she said, turning to leave. The man started to follow her.

'I said, I don't want it. I really don't want it,' Mei reiterated, continuing to walk away. The next time she turned around, the man was gone.

Mei walked and walked until she reached Taipei's city limits. Her throat felt parched and her stomach growled, but she had no money to buy food or drink. She crossed the

Tamshui River on a bridge that led to a suburb of Taipei, passed through some unrecognizable places, and then returned to the city.

By this time, Mei's body was on the verge of collapse. Her limbs began to feel like immovable weights, and the pain in her stomach began to burn. In a brief moment of lucidity, she decided to call for help.

She walked into a hotel and asked to borrow $2. Then she picked up the receiver of a nearby payphone and mechanically dialled a number.

'Hello?' The gloriously familiar voice of one of her ex-boyfriends.

'I'm in trouble,' Mei murmured weakly into the receiver. 'Can you pick me up?'

'Where are you? What's the address?' It was a good question: Where was she? Looking around, she realized she was lost, and had been for some time. She panicked.

Suddenly the clouds in her mind parted.

'I'm on Jilong Road,' she said, surprising even herself.

When the man came to pick her up, she barely looked human – dishevelled, exhausted and gaunt.

'What happened to you?' he gasped. 'How did you get like this?

Guided by the spirits, Mei had wandered about without any food or drink for three days and three nights.

Yufen Wang

'Go home, all of you! Go somewhere else to eat and drink!' Yufen shouted at the men playing cards in her living-room. Although her deformed legs had not fully regained their strength, she had enough energy to make some noise.

'What's wrong with drinking in your own homes?' she continued. 'Is it because your children need to study, but ours don't? Is it because your children need to sleep, but ours don't? Just go!' Embarassed, the men started to file out of the apartment, leaving behind cigarette butts, empty beer bottles, and Yufen's furious husband.

'What are you doing?!' Kai exlaimed. 'You're ruining my relationships with my friends!'

'Oh yeah? See if I care,' Yufen thought to herself, pleased by her new-found method of ejection. During the most difficult parts of her recovery, Kai had refrained from staying out too late and too often, but eventually he started inviting friends over, like he had done at the beginning of their marriage.

Sometimes he and his friends drank and clamoured late into the night, which quickly wore down Yufen's patience. She had previously tried to rectify the situation by arguing with her husband in front of his friends, but when this proved ineffective, she resorted to addressing them directly. After several such incidences, Kai's friends no longer dared to pay him visits at all.

In some ways, Yufen's accident had – for a time – helped her to view her husband from a different perspective. He hadn't deserted her like she half-expected him to, and had even taken care of her. So when he resumed drinking more frequently, she tried to tolerate it by reminding herself of the Buddhist mantras she had spent so much time studying. For a while there was peace – that is, until Kai started bringing home friends or coming home drunk virtually every night.

The fights between Yufen and Kai became like ritualistic dances that almost always bore the same cruel form. Their son Bao noticed that most of the fights were initiated by Yufen, who would indict Kai with some charge related to his drinking.

'Things were OK before, so why did Mama have to be mean? Why does Mama keep messing things up?' he thought occasionally. Most of the time, though, he shared his mother's sentiments about his father's drinking.

Sometimes Kai would come home drunk, fight with his wife, and then promptly leave again. Sometimes he would return home so drunk that he would swagger into the living-room, mumble a few nonsensical words, and then pass out on the floor. Sometimes he didn't return home at all. And sometimes, his drunken moods blossomed into elaborate displays of rage.

During one of these times, Bao watched in horror as his father violently thrashed their dog Lucky for no apparent reason. From then on, Bao relied on the dog's keen sense of smell to know if his father was drunk even before he walked through the door. As soon as Kai opened the downstairs door of their apartment building, Lucky's stump of a tail would wag upward if Kai was sober and point downward if Kai was drunk. In the latter case, the dog would run to a corner, waiting there in shivering anticipation while his master stumbled up five flights of stairs. As Kai opened the door to their apartment, both Bao and Lucky would eye him tentatively.

'Lucky, come!' Kai called out, blowing out a mouthful of alcohol-sour breath. The dog didn't move.

'Lucky, come!' Kai tried again. Lucky looked perplexed, as if unsure of what to do. 'I know how you feel,' Bao reflected sadly. He thought about his own fears and how he could not share them with any of his classmates. He assumed that he was the only child in his class with an alcoholic father, and that if he tried to make friends, he would risk 'losing face'.

As Lucky continued to deliberate, Bao empathized with the dog, one of his only companions in suffering. He wanted to do or say something but, like Lucky, felt paralysed by indecision.

A few seconds later, Lucky hesitantly walked to his

master's side. As Kai stroked him, Lucky sat as stiff as a stuffed animal, without moving a paw.

During the latter part of Yufen's recovery, Kai co-owned a small restaurant that sold goose-meat noodles. Sometimes Kai would be too hung over to open the restaurant for lunch service at 11 a.m., which, of course, infuriated his wife.

One Saturday, Bao decided to stop by the restaurant after school ended at 12:30. He expected to see his father there, busily serving the lunch crowd. When Bao neared the restaurant, however, he noticed that its steel gates – normally pulled down only after closing time – were halfway shut, like a bruised eyelid. A crowd had started to gather around the restaurant. And there were shouts.

Bao ran to the gates and bent down to see what was happening inside. Numbly, he watched his father pick up a chair and heave it towards his mother's crippled body. She, in turn, tried to wallop him with her walking canes.

'You irresponsible drunkard!' his mother screeched.

A plate flew across the room.

'You ...' his father cursed. Another plate flew, nearly hitting his mother.

Bao felt humiliated. Someone started to pull the restaurant's steel gate completely shut, and as his parents' screams became muffled, he simply walked away.

Drawn to the arcade, he checked his pockets: $15, enough for just a few games. So for the next few hours, he mostly watched other children play – kicking and jabbing at each other with make-believe armed warriors.

Bao and his sister Little Ping were contentedly watching TV in the living-room when their father stumbled home.

'Why do you have to drink so much?!' their mother yelled.

'This is ... none of your business!' he yelled back.

Yufen turned to her two shell-shocked children. 'Go to your room!' she ordered. They immediately obeyed. Kai used the momentary distraction to launch a counter-attack.

'You know, the only reason I fail is because you interfere so much. Every time I try to do something, you mess it up! Yufen Wang, I am like this because of YOU!'

'Don't even ...'

'YOU'RE the one who makes me fail! Every bad thing that has happened to me is because of YOU! It's all because of YOU!'

Even after Kai stormed out, the word 'you' reverberated in Yufen's mind, bouncing across every painful synapse. She thought about taking her children to her older sister's house and leaving Kai for good. But she knew that she could never do it, for her entire self-image lay in her relationship with Kai, as broken as it was.

'How am I supposed to live with a man like this? How am I supposed to leave him? Why is my life so miserable?'

'You drunkard! You can't even support your family!'

'Oh yeah? What makes you think that YOU'RE the boss?'

'Because you're useless! All you know how to do is get drunk! You don't know how to make money, so why do you even bother coming home?'

'And why do you always have to bother me like this?'

'Well, if I'm so bothersome, why don't you just hit me then? No point in shouting!'

'What?'

'If you have the guts, just hit me!'

'You ...'

'Just hit me!'

'Fine!'

Kai grabbed Yufen's hair, dragged her to their bedroom and threw her on the bed. He punched her in the face.

Stunned by the reality of the blow, Yufen tried to get away, but her legs were too weak to pick herself up. He punched her again. She tried to block him with her hands. But he punched her tear-covered face again and again.

Outside the room stood eleven-year-old Bao, angry and tormented. He wanted to say something that would stop his parents from fighting like this, but his jaw felt locked in an indelible frown. He was overwhelmingly afraid. Afraid of them both.

Ling Hu

The shouts exploded from the kitchen like out-of-control missiles.

'What kind of wife do you think you are?!'

'What kind of wife?! I've been married to you for eighteen years, and I've never asked you for one cent! I've raised your children for so long, and I've given you all that I could give! What else do you want from me?'

'The money! I'm trying my best to support this family too, but I just can't get what I need right now!'

'I already told you last time, I can't ...'

'LEAVE THIS HOUSE! YOU'RE RUINING MY LIFE!'

Ling hurried to the living-room, where her three children were trying to work on their homework.

'You have school tomorrow,' she said to them, attempting to hide her fury. 'It's time to go to bed.' They quickly obeyed. Ling rushed back to the kitchen.

'Leave this house! I don't want you any more!' Yan continued. 'I can't live with you around!'

'YOU'RE the one who's killing ME!' Ling retorted. 'YOU'RE the one who won't leave me alone!' As Peijen, Ling's second oldest daughter, tried to get ready for bed, she caught a glimpse of her parents grabbing each other's hair.

'Woman, I may not be able to beat you with words, but I can definitely beat you with –'

As her father raised his hand to hit her mother, Peijen ducked into the next room.

A few minutes later, her mother appeared. 'Stay in your room and don't come out. Just go to sleep,' she instructed, shutting the door.

Matai wanted to sleep but couldn't ignore the racket on the other side of the door. Peijen couldn't sleep either. She was tired of hearing her parents slander each other, and was already beginning to mistrust both of them. Lying awake, she thought to herself, 'Why do you two always fight like this? You're grown-ups. Why do you fight like kids? For once, can you think about us? Can you stop thinking about your ...'

'GET OUT!' their father screamed. Within the safety of their own bedroom, the children did not see their father as he grabbed their mother's hair. In one terrifyingly swift movement, he opened the front door of the apartment and swung her out so that she tumbled uncontrollably towards the edge of the staircase landing.

And stopped just in time. As Ling regained her balance, she took one look at the five flights below and started to cry. Then she ran to her parents' house.

Because Ling fled back and forth so frequently, most of her nearby relatives knew all about her marital problems. Some of them gossiped about the fights. Others tried to nurse Ling's wounds.

Although Ling's mother tried to be sympathetic, she soon grew tired of all the talk. 'It's not such a big deal to get a divorce!' she said sternly to Ling. 'At least if you get divorced, then Yan will really get a chance to start again and change. And you will get the chance to stand up on your own two feet again. But if you stay together, he'll just stay the same. If you don't make a clean break with him, he will still be able to hurt you, because you'll still officially be his. Don't let yourself lose face like this. Let it all be over.'

The days began to blend into a colourless tedium of daily habits. Ling went to work. And ate. And slept. And worshipped. And fought.

One morning, Ling decided to simply ignore her husband as he yelled at her, ordering her to give him money. He shoved his crimson face in front of hers, but she simply strolled to the living-room.

'I'm going to work now,' she said coldly. 'If you don't get to work on time, that may be OK for you, but I'm an accounts clerk. I have to be on time. We can talk about this during lunch, but I can't just stand here forever.'

Ling picked up her things to leave. 'You can't prevent me from going to work,' she said as she walked towards the front door. 'It's just not right.'

Suddenly Yan swung her around. He held a large knife to her throat.

'If you don't listen to me, I'm going to kill you!'

Ling blinked, determined to hide her fear. 'Wait a minute. You need to go to work. I need to go to work. We both need to go to work. Let's talk about this tonight after work and ...'

'No! If you don't listen right now, I'm going to kill you! I'm going to kill the whole family!' He shoved her roughly.

Ling stepped back, swung open the front door. And shrieked.

'YOU WANT TO KILL ME, DO YOU?!'

Their neighbours, whom Ling knew well, cracked open their door suspiciously.

Yan dropped the knife, and Ling went to work.

Nothing remarkable occurred on the day Ling's pillar of optimism finally cracked. It just did. 'Yan will never change,' she realized.

Suddenly the crack spread, causing the pillar to crumble. 'He'll never take financial responsibility of this family. What was I thinking … ? I'm not a bad woman, so why is my life so hard … ? All I've ever wanted to do is keep tradition and keep my family together … I've endured so much hardship, and what do I get in return … ? I'm sick of running away all the time, I'm sick of fighting almost every day, I'm sick of always being the one who has to give in … I just can't stand it any more … I just want to die!'

In the end, Ling decided not to consummate this ultimate act, but she also decided that she could not let the misery go on. She sat her children down for a talk that they had been anticipating all along; after all, they couldn't even remember the last time they saw their mother really smile.

'I want you to know that the next time Daddy gets out of control, Mummy is going to leave this place for good,' Ling told them. 'If Mummy says to Daddy very clearly that she is never coming back, then she will really mean it. It'll be better for everyone if the whole thing gets resolved once and for all. So you take good care of each other, OK?'

The next time an argument showed evidence of extending its gnarly arms deep into the night, Ling knew that the time had come. She decided to give Yan Zhang one final chance.

'Tell you what, since you claim that you can support this family, I'll just let you,' she said, testing him. 'I'll quit my job and come home to take care of the kids. You always say that you want to be the breadwinner of this family, so I'll just let you. And when you come home from work, you'll have a hot dinner. I'll take care of all the housework. Isn't that what you want?'

'You worthless woman …' Yan said, starting to raise his voice.

'Don't talk so loudly. It's getting late. If you're going to talk like that, let's do it tomorrow.'

'No, we need to talk about this NOW!'

'The neighbours are trying to sleep. Our kids are trying to sleep. Let's talk about it tomorrow, OK?'

'You're just trying to ...'

'Look, I need to go to work tomorrow. Let's talk ...'

'No!' Yan blurted. 'If you're going to be this way, just go! I don't want you to live here any more. I can cook and wash the clothes and do everything else myself. I don't need you AT ALL!'

'What are you talking about? I pay the rent in this place, so why should I be the one to leave?'

'I don't care!' yelled Yan. He started to hurl insults at Ling's mother, father, and even her little sister.

'You don't need to talk about them like that!' Ling ordered. 'You're a grown man, aren't you? Talking this way won't help the situation at all.'

'Let's talk about YOU then! YOU only have a job because of your uncle. If you tried working anywhere else, nobody would want you. You'd be just as unlucky as me. Your uncle hired you only because you're related. Because he PITIED you. Who else would want such a stupid woman?!' The words seared Ling's heart.

'Look,' Ling said flatly, 'since you won't shut up, I'm leaving. If you're always going to talk to me this way, just forget about it. Since you want me to go, I'll just go. I don't want to care about you any more. You can just take care of yourself.'

'Fine, just go.'

'I REALLY MEAN IT this time. You have NO IDEA how angry I am.'

'Just go. That will finally give me a way out.'

'Good. I'm leaving, then. And I tell you, I'm not coming back.' As Ling opened the front door, she was chased by cries she had hoped never to hear.

'Mummy! Mummy! DON'T GO!'

Ling wanted to turn to her children and cry back, 'I'm sorry, but I have no choice!'

Instead, she walked out and shut the door.

* * *

A fortune-teller once said that Ling Hu would reach a turning point in her fortieth year, Indeed, by that year – the Western year of 1998 – her life had become radically different. By 1998, she permanently left the soda company where she had worked intermittently for more than twenty years. By 1998, she reached a final conclusion to her marriage problems. And by 1998, she met someone who would save her from the life she had grown tired of living.

That someone was Jesus.

Part 4

Coming into the Light

I will sprinkle clean water on you, and you will be clean;
I will cleanse you from all your impurities and from all
your idols. I will give you a new heart and put a new
spirit in you; I will remove from you your heart of stone
and give you a heart of flesh.   Ezekiel 36:25-26

Chapter 10

May 1988

Elisabeth Weinmann tightly clutched the handles of her two duffel bags as a wave of trepidation crashed into her. The thirty-three-year-old woman had spent the last two years studying Chinese intensively in Taichong. That city had been drastically different from her hometown, a quaint German village called Aach, so the process of learning a complex language and adjusting to an unfamiliar culture had been an arduous one. But in the hard times, the Lord had quieted her worries through the promise of Ephesians 2:10: 'For we are God's workmanship, created in Christ Jesus to do good works, which God prepared in advance for us to do.'

Now that Elisabeth had just started to regard Taichong as her home, it was time to move again – and to start full-time ministry among factory workers.

As Elisabeth sorted through feelings of inadequacy, loneliness and fear, the bus pulled up. She hugged her friend goodbye and said farewell, clenching her jaw to hold back her tears.

'Lord, it will do no good if I cry for the next two hours on this bus,' she prayed. 'I don't have any strength of my own to face this new future, so please give me your strength.'

Sweating, Elisabeth stepped onto the bus and heaved

her bags onto an empty seat. Sensing that she could not contain her emotions for much longer, she shoved her hand into one of her bags in search of a handkerchief.

She touched something gooey instead. Quickly pulling out her hand, she realized that a glass of homemade jam – a present from another missionary – had shattered inside. Everything in her bag was sticky.

Elisabeth swiftly moved her things to the back of the bus, where there was a sink. She meticulously wiped down every single item in her bag, and by the time she settled down at her original seat, she realized that, without shedding a tear, she had reached her destination: Panchiao, a suburb of Taipei.

* * *

When Elisabeth Weinmann was two years old, the doctors were convinced that she would die. A severe bout of appendicitis had spread to her abdomen, they said, leading her mother to a hospital bedroom where she could say goodbye to her dying daughter. Instead, the woman said a prayer.

'Lord, if you heal my daughter, I will offer her to you as a missionary!' she cried out.

Three days after the onset of the illness, Elisabeth recovered.

As Elisabeth grew up, Mrs Weinmann never ceased to remind her of the vow she had taken. Mrs Weinmann belonged to a number of missions prayer groups, and at night she would call her six children to her bed, cradling them and telling them stories from the missions field. Elisabeth loved to listen.

Although Elisabeth's teenage years temporarily blurred her childhood dream of serving the Lord overseas, her hopes were eventually rekindled. She graduated from high school, spent one and a half years at a Bible college and

262   *Dead Women Walking*

then left to study nursing. But after receiving her nursing degree, she felt led by God to finish her Bible college education so that she could serve overseas as a full-time church worker instead of a nurse. She hoped to be ordained, which entailed working for a church for at least five years.

Although Elisabeth was – from a humanly standpoint – shy and unimposing, the Lord told her, through Isaiah 54:2, to 'Enlarge the place of your tent, stretch your tent curtains wide, do not hold back.' He gave her an influential job as a youth work supervisor in her church district.

Five years later, Elisabeth had all but lost her call to missions. She had made significant contributions in the church and rarely entertained thoughts about leaving Germany. Yet somehow she felt that the issue had not been entirely resolved.

'My feelings about missions so long ago – is it God's call for me or just something I wanted back then?' she wondered. She took a day off to ponder the issue, and in her prayers she heard a single resounding word: England.

So lucid was the message that she immediately called a friend who visited England often. As she dialled, she thought excitedly about the prospect of studying abroad to improve her English.

'So ... so where do you think I should go?' Elisabeth asked, filled with anticipation.

'There is only one place you should go to,' replied her friend candidly. 'All Nations Christian College. In order to be accepted, you first have to be a candidate of a missions organization. And there's only one missions organization you should apply to: OMF, the Overseas Missionary Fellowship.'

Though Elisabeth was irritated by her friend's effrontery, she tried to keep an open mind. The next day, as she was reading through her devotions, she came across

Galatians 1:15–16 (KJV): 'But when it pleased God, who separated me from my mother's womb, and called me by his grace, to reveal his Son in me, that I might preach him among the heathen ...'

Memories of her mother's goading flooded into Elisabeth's mind. Then, of course, there was the vow her mother had made.

'I should go to the mission field,' she knew, delighted by the certainty that came with the statement. She suddenly felt as if all the clouds that had obscured her future had parted, whisking away every doubt and hesitation.

That evening, she started writing letters of inquiry to mission organizations. The first organization that replied was OMF, formerly the China Inland Mission, founded by Hudson Taylor in 1865. To Elisabeth's delight, the letter invited her to an OMF conference that happened to be taking place near her village the following week. In the days leading up to the conference, she prayed fervently for God's guidance.

Elisabeth arrived late to the conference, right in the middle of a missionary's presentation. On display was a photograph of beautiful mountains atop an island – the island of Taiwan. A seemingly inconsequential Bible verse Elisabeth had stumbled upon a few days earlier, Isaiah 66:19, popped into her head: 'I will set a sign among them, and I will send some of those who survive to the nations – to the distant islands that have not heard of my fame or seen my glory. They will proclaim my glory among the nations.'

At the end of the conference, Elisabeth approached OMF Germany's Homeside Director and told him that she wanted to apply to OMF.

As they started talking about her background and interests, she asked, 'If I get accepted, where would you send me to?'

'Could be Taiwan,' came the answer. And as if the words had already claimed Elisabeth's heart, no other country would ever be mentioned.

*   *   *

Five years later, Elisabeth arrived in Panchiao, the bustling city that was to become her home. Following her first Sunday morning service at Panchiao Gospel Lutheran Church (the church she was assigned to serve), there was what the Taiwanese call a 'love feast'[1] – though as an introvert, Elisabeth did not naturally 'love' the prospect of lunching amid a host of strangers.

The church was considered large at the time, with about 180 people on its membership roll. Elisabeth knew that the church consisted of mostly working-class people who would have had little, if any, contact with white-skinned foreigners; indeed, many of them gaped at her, fascinated but speechless.

'If I already feel lonely in this church and I'm a missionary, I wonder how many other newcomers might feel lonely here?' she thought. Then she said a simple prayer that she would repeat many times over the next two years: 'Lord, please show me people who are lonely and have no friends, and help me be a friend to them.'

Later that week, Elisabeth started to explore the neighbourhood around the church. Vehicles jammed the streets, and throngs of pedestrians bustled around in zigzag motion, avoiding the food carts that had been pushed onto the sidewalk. Since the church was located near the Panchiao Train Station, the density of everything in the neighbourhood was overwhelming. Elisabeth started to walk, observing her surroundings. Up-market clothing stores. Multi-storey department stores. Hundreds of stores.

Elisabeth decided that she would try to befriend some

people and invite them to church. Although the shoppers seemed too rushed or preoccupied to chat, many store employees seemed open to conversation since their jobs required them to just stand around most of the time. Since Elisabeth's level of Chinese was still rather low, she mostly listened to them, her blue eyes as intense as those of a frightened child. When she did speak, she did so slowly, and with a stammer. She was naturally gentle and unthreatening – an easy confidante for several bored shop-workers. Through their earnestness, she soon realized that many shop-workers worked twelve-hour days, six days a week, and that their days off differed from week to week. There was simply no existing church activity that they could feasibly attend.

On the day Elisabeth was scheduled to meet with the church pastor to discuss her future ministry, she spent the entire morning in prayer.

'I don't know what work I can give to you, really,' Pastor Chang said to her earnestly when she came to his office. Elisabeth understood his sentiments. Her language skills left much to be desired, and she suspected that some of the church leaders thought the same of her level of education. Apparently the church did not expect much from her.

'There's factory work, which some other OMF missionaries do,' Pastor Chang continued. 'You would have to do that all in the evenings, after the workers get off work.'

'Well, I – I was thinking about starting work among shop-workers,' Elisabeth offered. 'It seems that there are a lot of shop-workers around this area, and – ah – that they are unreached.'

'Good idea!' he said, peppering her with suggestions. 'Maybe we could start a Sunday service at 8 a.m. to fit their work schedules ... Your co-workers will have to come out of your own group ... You'll have to disciple and train them from the beginning, when they first accept Christ.'

Elisabeth bubbled with excitement. She was thankful for the pastor's support, and thankful for the freedom he gave her in trying new things. Most of all, she was thankful for the simple fact that she now had something meaningful to do.

April 1989

'I don't really like English classes, and I don't know anything about the Bible, but we could have a birthday party!' exclaimed Elisabeth's friend, a young shop-worker. Elisabeth's ears perked up at the suggestion – she was always eager to experiment with different ways of reaching people.

During her first ten months in Panchiao, she had tried to invite shop-workers to church in several different ways. At first she encouraged them to attend the church's new 8 a.m. service, but most shop-workers worked late into the evenings and weren't interested in waking up early to worship a God they knew little about. Then she started a morning English class for shop-workers, but she discovered that most shop-workers did not have the time or interest to diligently learn English. The birthday party idea, though – that was something truly new.

The ten or so shop-workers who showed up to the party didn't seem to mind that the 'birthday' celebration was not for anybody in particular. They also didn't seem to mind that the party took place late at night after work.

'Let's do this more often!' one shop-worker smiled.

As Elisabeth laughed and ate a piece of cake, she realized that the shop-workers preferred this kind of informal gathering over formal meetings and classes. This way, they could get to know Christians without feeling pressured to commit to anything.

Although designing the gatherings effectively proved to

be important, the essence of what Elisabeth did lay in her one-on-one relationships with shop-workers. People came to her birthday gathering because, for the past ten months, she had spent most of her afternoons distributing evangelistic magazines in department stores. She tried to go regularly to each store, chatting with those who were willing. Eventually, the employees started to recognize her, and she started passing out invitations to church activities.

Even though Elisabeth spent so much time doing these 'visitations' or *tang-fang*, she was almost always beset by dread, fatigue and nervousness as she prepared to walk into a department store. But as soon as a shop-worker started talking to her, she would forget her fears.

Many shop-workers spent their long shifts standing behind their counters, waiting for customers. Those who sold higher-end clothing would sometimes pass a whole day without serving a single customer. Chats with Elisabeth naturally broke up the boredom. Sometimes, after only one or two conversations, shop-workers would start to divulge deeply personal matters, as if Elisabeth's presence magically turned their counters into confessionals. Since sharing such matters among certain friends could cause one to 'lose face', talking to an innocent-looking foreigner was sometimes less risky.

Elisabeth gave time to shop-workers as freely as she gave out gospel material, yet she always wished that she could do more. Surrounding the church was a host of clubs, movie 'theatres' that often served as adolescent make-out joints, and clandestine brothels. Several major temples loomed nearby, and fortune-tellers lined a number of streets. Around them gathered flocks of young women. Elisabeth wished that she could set up a table on one of these streets and urge the women to talk to her instead.

'Sister Wei,' Pastor Chang would laugh. 'Sometimes you're more Taiwanese than Taiwanese people!' Indeed, even though the city she lived in was becoming outwardly cosmopolitan, Elisabeth sensed that the hearts of its people – especially the less-educated people – would not be so quick to change. For their sake, she tried her best to be Taiwanese.

What Elisabeth lacked in charisma and language ability she made up for in focus. The shop-workers she got to know were not her ministry targets. Rather, they were her friends. Because she had few outside friends, loneliness visited her frequently during the next few years. During church retreats and outings she often sat alone – the only representative of a shop-workers' 'fellowship' that was still little more than a nebulous concept.

For her first six months in Panchiao, Elisabeth spent an hour each morning asking for God's guidance in prayer. It was then that he often reminded her, 'I tell you the truth, unless a kernel of wheat falls to the ground and dies, it remains only a single seed. But if it dies, it produces many seeds.'

July 1991

The verdant meadows and sloping hills of Aach, Germany, were still fresh in Elisabeth's mind as she scanned the congested pavement in front of her new Panchiao apartment. She had just returned from a year back home in Germany and was eager to start her second four-year term in Taiwan. But she was not so thrilled about her apartment.

'Do I really need to live here?' Elisabeth thought as she wondered how she would ever manage to manoeuvre past the motor-scooters, food-stalls and fortune-tellers that cluttered the pavement near the church. She took a deep breath and immediately crinkled her nose, which had received an unwanted whiff of the city's worst air. She also noticed a considerable amount of noise pollution: the clang of instruments from nearby temples, the beeps of slot machines and video games, the murmurs of a hundred conversations.

But then she looked up. Many of the dilapidated apartment buildings that surrounded hers had darkened windows.

'I wonder what happens up there,' she asked herself, though she already half-knew the answer: Prostitution. Gambling. And other illicit behaviour. 'Yes, this is where God wants me to live.'

Her convictions, however, could not protect her from the noise that often invaded the apartment at night. Sometimes it became so unbearable that Elisabeth paced through her apartment, looking for a way to escape the din. Loud, hypnotic Chinese melodies bellowed from the nearest temple at least three times a week and on those nights, the pop music of an adjacent clothing store thumped even louder, as if competing with the temple's tunes. Elisabeth looked at her watch: ten o'clock, which meant that the music would continue to play for another hour.

She headed for her bedroom. Even though she disliked its lack of windows during the day, this very trait made the room attractive when she wanted some quiet at night. When she entered the room, a rat pattered across the floor. In the coming years, she would become an expert rat-killer, exterminating more than fifty of them.

When Pastor Chang and his wife met with Elisabeth to discuss her next term, she discovered that things had gone along steadily in her absence. Before she had left, a Tuesday night Bible study for shop-workers had sprung up naturally after the 'birthday party', and while Elisabeth was away another OMF missionary continued to lead it. A handful of people attended regularly. Like most of the other activities that the shop-workers' fellowship would eventually hold, the Bible study took place after 10 p.m., when most shop-workers would have already finished their work shifts. In other news, a new OMF couple from Switzerland, Marc and Katrina Schachtler, had started to come to the church and were working enthusiastically among factory workers.

'By the way,' said Pastor Chang, 'we really love you. And we're glad you're back.'

August 1992

It all began while a short-term missions team was visiting from Germany. To accommodate the team members, Elisabeth slept in her living-room, which also served as a place where the short-termers' newly washed clothing could hang to dry. During that time, a new Christian in Elisabeth's ministry showed up at her door.

Because Elisabeth believed strongly in equipping and delegating, she saw the young woman often and had already started training her – as well as several other new believers – as a leader. A weekly 'co-workers' meeting' would eventually emerge. Since shop-workers generally had little power and authority in Taiwanese society, an invitation to join the 'co-workers' meeting' would be considered a privilege.

This time, though, it was Elisabeth's new co-worker who came to her with an invitation – a proposal of sorts.

'May I come here and live with you?'

A few hours later, the young woman reappeared at Elisabeth's doorstep with all her belongings. The two of them slept in the living-room that night, surrounded by lines of damp clothing.

Elisabeth discovered that one of the best ways to minister to the broken, problem-plagued shop-workers she knew was to embrace them in a tight-knit, closely monitored Christian community. If they lived close by, Elisabeth could evangelize or disciple them easily, giving them the one-on-one attention that so many of them craved.

From then on, Elisabeth encouraged shop-workers to live with her, and her apartment became the first of many 'shop-worker dorms' that she would start. Her vision to start the dorms was inspired by Isaiah 58:7-8, for she hoped 'to provide the poor wanderer with shelter ... and not to turn away from your own flesh and blood. Then your light will break forth like the dawn, and your healing will quickly appear; then your righteousness will go before you, and the glory of the Lord will be your rear guard.'

Though regular meetings and Bible studies – foundational to most traditional Taiwanese churches – were the feet that moved Elisabeth's ministry forward, the dorms were at its heart. Many of the shop-workers who passed through the dorms would cook, eat, pray and cry together. Many, for the first time in their lives, would feel that they belonged to a family.

May 1993

Elisabeth cringed as she gazed at the walls of the apartment, blackened by incense smoke. Even though it had formerly been used as a house temple, she reluctantly agreed to rent it.

After the walls were repainted, however, the apartment underwent a transformation. There, Elisabeth hosted Bible studies and prayer meetings, many of which were accompanied by home-cooked meals or snacks. Even after these meetings officially concluded, she would let people into her room one at a time for prayer and counselling. As one person sat in Elisabeth's bedroom, bawling over her life's troubles, other people would linger in the living-room, waiting unofficially for their turn.

Elisabeth still visited department stores several times a

week, and whenever she met a new seeker, she would start to visit or call the person regularly and give occasional gifts, Taiwanese-style. She often looked for new ways to incorporate these seekers into her budding fellowship. Her annual Christmas party attracted more than 100 shop-workers, including more than 20 serious seekers each year. Extensively planned day-trips were also effective in bonding believers and non-believers together in the name of good fun.

Elisabeth was most definitely lost as she drove her scooter back and forth at two in the morning. She had just driven a shop-worker home after a Bible study, as she often did for women who would not otherwise come to such a late meeting. Exhausted, she pulled up next to a dodgy-looking man who was ambling down the street.

'Excuse me – ah – how do I get back to the Panchiao train station?' she asked, praying that the man would just tell her the directions and let her go.

When she finally arrived home, she was exhausted, though that was nothing unusual. She had begun to feel like a leaky, over-used pair of shoes. In one moment, she would be a Bible study leader and in others, a hostess, counsellor, tour guide, mother, evangelist, cook, or confidante ... She rarely slept more than five hours a night.

She began to take brief naps in the church sanctuary, one of the few places where she could do so undisturbed. Still, her body puttered to a stop about once every three weeks, when, for more than thirty hours straight, she would plunge into an impenetrable sleep.

Altogether, the shop-workers' fellowship had about twenty steady members who, like Elisabeth herself, were active in evangelizing and serving. Some of the co-workers even sacrificed their weekly day off to help Elisabeth visit department stores. Elisabeth was astounded at what the

Lord had done. But she was also exhausted and ready to move on. Feeling confident in the group's future, she hoped that God would lead her elsewhere.

But he didn't. And in the next eleven years, she would discover why.

Notes

1. Love feast – lunch following a church's Sunday service. It is a common practice in Taiwanese churches.

Chapter 11

The spiritual din had deafened Mei's senses for three whole years. The oppression had reduced her to a mass of lifeless pulp. Like a bicyclist pedalling away from a tornado, Mei simply could not escape from the voices.

Mei's thirty-third year of life – like many of her previous ones – began with apparent hopelessness. But it ended with an unforeseen blessing that would give her a second chance at life:

Silence.

The beginning of freedom came, ironically, in the form of a voice. At the time, Mei lived in a room that belonged to a small temple. She had come to the temple at the invitation of a friend who was concerned about her unstable lifestyle. Mei had hoped that the temple room would give her a place to relax and clear her head.

But then came the voice.

'Go to church,' it said, softly. Mei considered the suggestion, which seemed to her rather arbitrary.

'Church? A Christian church? That can't be right,' she thought. The only church she had ever really had contact with was her mother's True Jesus Church – an experience she preferred to forget.

'Go to church,' the voice insisted.

Then Mei remembered the ruddy-faced teenage boy who had rescued her in Ali Mountain after her unforgettable evening with the spirits.

'I'm a Christian,' he had said to her when he found her. 'You really need to believe in Christianity.' Mei felt that the last thing she needed was a religion; in fact, she almost despised religion.

The friend who had brought her to the temple dormitory, however, had more interest in the spiritual. In addition to having connections with the dormitory, he also knew some Baptists.

'We're praying for you,' one of them had told him. 'We hope that you will accept Christ some day. Will you come to church with us?'

Mei's friend had accepted the invitation, but Mei had staunchly declined. After hearing the voice, however, she reluctantly decided to give church a try. She rarely had the courage to disobey a voice.

*   *   *

The two foreigners spoke alluringly, rousing the crowd of hundreds that had packed onto the athletic field. The music swelled. The crowd swayed. The foreigners said something about the lame and the sick, and at their cue, more than ten people were escorted to the front. Mei watched as one of the foreigners started to pray over a crippled man who was seated in a chair. The foreigner seemed to exert a great deal of energy in the prayer, and eventually the man stood up and walked around.

'He must've been pretending to be lame,' Mei automatically figured.

After the rally, the pastor of her friend's Baptist church approached her.

'Were you touched by the rallies, Mei?' he asked.

'Not at all,' Mei answered. Actually, the whole scene seemed so premeditated, so detached from reality, that it was hard for her to imagine how she could have been remotely 'touched'. But the pastor was undeterred.

'*Shangdi hui jianxuan ni*. God will choose you some day,' he said. The very mention of the Christian God made Mei feel uncomfortable. She much preferred the more general term *shen*, which the Taiwanese use to describe many different gods.

'We Christians use both terms,' the pastor explained. 'They're the same thing to us ... Anyway, let me introduce you to a group in Taipei. It's called Garden of Hope. They can help you there. Continuing to live here isn't going to do you any good.'

Mei grudgingly knew that the pastor was right. She didn't have a job, so she mostly passed the days by listening to the spirits. Although she never explicitly told the pastor about them, she had a feeling that he knew.

Garden of Hope was established in 1988 to assist victims of sexual abuse, family violence and Taiwan's sex industry. Like Mei, many of the women and girls that the organization served had been subjected to more than one form of abuse. Mei agreed to live in a dormitory sponsored by Garden of Hope because doing so guaranteed her free room and board.

Since most of Mei's belongings had been lost in her spirit-led wanderings, she came to Garden of Hope with nothing but a simple suitcase. As soon as she walked into the building, she was filled with a sense of loathing.

She was used to living alone, but now had to share a living space with seven other teenage girls. And in a sense, the dormitory's strict regulations brought back irritating memories of her childhood – she was only allowed to eat and watch television at certain times of day, and smoking, drinking and drugs were strictly prohibited.

Two adults were in charge of the facility. One of them, Ms Lin, was an aboriginal like Mei and, even though she appeared to be only in her mid-twenties, she had already graduated from a seminary. Mei admired Ms Lin's singing talent and her dedication to the dormitory, where she also lived. She appreciated Ms Lin's warmth, maturity and gentleness; unlike most of the other people Mei had lived with in the past, Ms Lin was not prone to wildly throwing a temper.

The dormitory community operated like a large family, and all its members were expected to eat together and take turns cooking. Some days, Ms Lin led the girls in a time of prayer, which was usually followed by half an hour of sharing. During these times, Mei began to see that, despite the generation gap between her and the girls, they had much – perhaps too much – in common.

One eight-year-old girl seemed perpetually afraid. She had been repeatedly raped by her father. 'I know how you feel,' Mei thought as the girl, who loved to give hugs, embraced her with both her arms and legs, as if climbing a tree. 'When I was little I was hurt in the same way, but not that bad. It only happened to me once.'

Another girl often monopolized their sharing time with complaints about her mother, who had sold her into prostitution.

'I'd rather not have a mother at all!' she said often.

'Not all mothers are that way,' Mei offered tentatively.

'But my mother's that way!'

Mei remembered how she used to despise her own mother, especially when she beat her or wouldn't make her new clothes. 'Maybe the real problem was that I couldn't be satisfied,' Mei wondered, 'because at least Ma didn't sell me like this girl's mother. I should have been grateful.'

In general, Mei kept such thoughts about the past to herself, though she occasionally shared some things with Ms Lin. After listening empathetically, Ms Lin would always offer to pray for her.

'Nah, don't pray! Why do you bother to pray?' Mei exclaimed.

'We pray to let God know our hurts,' Ms Lin replied.

'Well, that's useless. And unnecessary. Can he really hear our prayers? I've never even seen Shen. How can Shen hear our prayers if he doesn't exist?'

Even though God had become a regular topic of conversation, Mei still refused to evoke his more specific name, Shangdi.

'But he DOES exist,' Ms Lin said firmly, patiently.

Mei further tested Ms Lin's patience by refusing to get out of bed on Sunday mornings.

'Get up! Get up!'

Mei pried her eyes open halfway at the sound of Ms Lin's cheery voice coming from the living-room.

'It's time to go to church!'

'Wait a moment,' Mei replied groggily. 'Aiya, why should I go? I really, REALLY don't want to go to church!'

'OK! I'm waiting for you!' Groans echoed from some of the other rooms. Apparently, Mei wasn't the only one who was reluctant to go. 'I'll just wait here for you all,' continued Ms Lin good-naturedly. Mei forced herself into a vertical position and got dressed. She fumed all the way to church, and she fumed all the way back, as if a proverbial black cloud had hovered above her the whole time, untouched by the church service.

Mei's relative proximity to the Lord did have a major benefit, though she didn't think much of it at the time. After she moved into the Garden of Hope dormitory, the spirits haunted her less frequently – she heard them little and saw them even less. On one occasion, she did glimpse a streak of white creeping into her room. It reminded her of something she had seen at Ali Mountain. Then Mei remembered something else, something that she had recently learned.

'In the name of Jesus Christ, get out!' she said. The apparition immediately disappeared, and Mei could hear footsteps trailing off into the distance. A little while later, she heard them approach again, but they stopped when they reached her door, as if they were waiting there. Waiting for her to come out.

Hoping to veer away from the soiled career path of her past, Mei enrolled in a free government-sponsored class that taught her how to provide care-giving assistance to the elderly. She worked hard at it, paying special attention to talks about the thoughts and feelings of the elderly. Mei had spent so much of her life fighting for her own survival that she never got the chance to see how much she genuinely enjoyed helping other people. Before long, her diligence earned her a licence that would enable her to work in a nursing home or hospital.

Mei's first job as a care-giver was with an old man who lived near her dormitory. The man had received Christ at a young age and now suffered from an advanced state of cancer. Knowing that the man loved the Lord, Mei sometimes played Christian CDs for him. The music was so effective at lifting his spirits that he would wave his arms around in a physically inhibited but spiritually liberated dance.

Because of his illness, the man was unable to go to church unless someone pushed him along in a wheelchair. He begged Mei to take him to the church she was forced to attend, but she refused because of the tremendous amount of effort it would require.

'How can a person have such deep faith in God?' she thought. 'I couldn't do it. And even if I wanted to become a Christian, I couldn't ever give up drugs and all the other stuff.'

Learning about the Bible did help Mei realize that drugs, alcohol and smoking were not good for her body.

She miraculously began to develop a slight distaste for the smell of smoke and the taste of alcohol. The change was not a transformation, however, and her craving for drugs remained unhindered. After a while, she started to smoke outside the dormitory and sneak alcohol into her room. When this proved to be too indiscreet, she went out with a friend and shared drinks at a local noodle shop. Afterwards, she would pretend to be sober as she returned to the dorm, showered quickly, and feigned sleep.

It was at times like this when the spirits paid more frequent visits.

'Ah, don't stay here anymore.'

'Move out!'

Mei started to feel unquenchably restless. Even though her new job was rewarding, it paid only 30,000 Taiwanese dollars a month – a miniscule amount compared to what she used to make. She missed the easy job, the easy money. She missed the sensation of being loved by a man. And, most of all, she missed the drugs.

'Please ... don't go,' Ms Lin pleaded when Mei announced her departure. 'Stay here, and God will bless you.'

'No,' Mei replied coldly. 'I have no desire to stay.'

'When will these spirits ever leave me alone?' Mei thought, annoyed at their rampant re-entry into her life. Yet she figured that it was a small price to pay for freedom, for the chance to work, have sex, and do drugs just as she pleased.

After working in a massage parlour for less than two months, the freedom became dampened by a sense of emptiness and guilt. She began to realize that her friends at Garden of Hope were right – drugs, cigarettes and alcohol were slowly destroying her body.

Mei decided that in order to assuage her conscience, what she really needed was a drastic change of scene. So she left the massage parlour and started to do two jobs at two different hospitals. She worked days and nights, which kept her from doing drugs and drinking too often. But about a month later, she had an unexpected encounter that would number her days as a care-giver. She met a man named Big Chang.

A part-time construction worker in his thirties, Big Chang first came to the hospital to care for his ailing father. After he met Mei, though, he had a new reason to frequent the hospital. Unlike many men she knew, he was mild-mannered and controlled his drinking. He even talked about how, from a young age, he agonized over the way his father beat his mother.

'My poor mother ...' he reminisced. 'I don't want to beat my wife like that ...' It was a promise that sounded almost too good to be true, considering the behaviour of Mei's two ex-husbands.

As the two started dating, Big Chang told Mei of his grand dreams to get married and settle down.

'I want to marry you,' he said to her on numerous occasions. Still apprehensive about the possibility of marrying yet again, Mei tried to discourage him by bringing up unsavoury bits of her past.

'Does all that matter to you?' she asked.

'No,' he replied. 'I won't let that bother me.'

Mei took a cursory look at her situation. 'I'm sick of working such long hours to make a living. I'm so tired,' she thought. 'Maybe the spirits will leave me alone if I have a man.'

She quickly became so eager to get married, so naive about the future, that Big Chang's willingness to overlook her past scars was good enough to elicit the response that Mei had given twice before.

'Oooh ... OK. I'll marry you.'

Yufen Wang

Yufen stared at the scars on her legs, the dimple-like crevices that remained where nails had once been. She detested them.

'I used to have such beautiful legs, and now ...' she thought wistfully as a doctor examined them.

Noticing her displeasure, the doctor remarked, 'If you were to choose between having beautiful legs and not being able to walk, or having legs like these that can still walk, which would you choose?'

Yufen did not have to ponder the question for long. The frustration of being helplessly bed-ridden had left her with wounds just as fresh as the ones on her legs. Yufen resolved that she would try her best to ignore the side-glances, the gazes of pity that her deformed legs tended to evoke.

About two years after the accident, Yufen grew tired of living on the brink of financial worry. The unstable income generated by her husband's intermittent business ventures simply could not give her the security she felt she needed. She decided to look for a job.

In order to minimize the stress of re-entering the workforce, Yufen chose a job that would give her confidence – a job that would utilize the skills she had already mastered as a stationery store clerk. She found employment at a supermarket below the classy Far Eastern Department Store and, after a few months of this, started working in the department store itself.

During Yufen's first few days at work, she felt like a child heading off to kindergarten for the first time. The work environment seemed like another world, complete with sparkling white floors, bright lights, and the crisp scent of perfume. She was surrounded by brand names like Chanel, Gucci and Louis Vuitton, some of which she had never actually seen before. She usually looked for bargains when buying clothes for herself, but the items she sold at work sometimes cost several thousand dollars apiece.

At the beginning, Yufen carefully observed her sophisticated co-workers from a distance, noting the way they interacted with the customers and each other. When business was slow, they gravitated together to chat, and eventually Yufen found herself among them.

'What happened to your legs?' one of them asked on a day when Yufen dared to wear a skirt.

'Car accident,' she answered curtly.

Although most of their conversations remained superficial, Yufen enjoyed them, for they gave her a mental break from her frustrations at home. She also enjoyed learning from her co-workers. She noticed that, even in difficult situations, some of the other women were able to remain gentle and calm.

'Hmm ... interesting how there's more than one way to react to the same problem,' Yufen thought, imagining herself at home, angrily flinging a pile of clothes across the room. 'No wonder some people get scared of me when I throw my temper. No wonder some people can't stand to be around me.'

One day in 1995, Yufen was busy tidying her clothing racks when she saw a foreigner walk by, accompanied by a young Taiwanese woman. The foreigner, who had cropped brown hair and carried a tote bag, strolled from counter to counter. Her hand came in and out of the bag so often that she looked like a farmer sowing seeds.

'What's this person doing?' she thought to herself. 'A foreigner willing to come to this country must be here to do good things, so she's probably OK.'

The brown-haired woman reached Yufen's counter. She smiled brightly and handed Yufen a small magazine.

'Hello! This is for you,' she said sweetly, in accented Chinese.

'Thank you!' Yufen said, flipping through the magazine with obvious interest. 'Where are you from?'

'I'm from Germany.'

'Oh? What's that like?'

As forty-year-old Elisabeth Weinmann talked about her family in Germany, Yufen appeared fascinated.

'What are you doing here?' Yufen asked.

'Church work. In fact, we have a group for shop-workers nearby. Would you like to come?' Yufen felt a twinge of annoyance at the mention of church.

'No, thanks. Thanks for the magazine,' she said, ending the conversation.

After walking away Elisabeth observed the woman she had just spoken to. She sensed that the woman was hard-working and strong-willed – probably the result of a difficult family background. From Elisabeth's six years of experience in the ministry, she had discovered that this was the case for most shop-workers.

After Elisabeth left, Yufen started reading the articles and testimonies in the magazine. She found them just about as interesting as the other reading material she kept below her counter: self-help books, novels like Sha-fu (a story about an uneducated woman who stabbed her abusive husband to death), and, of course, Buddhist literature.

A few weeks after their first encounter, Elisabeth went to see Yufen again.

'Did you like the magazine last time?' she asked as she handed Yufen another.

'Yes, I did! Thanks for bringing it,' Yufen answered. They chatted for a few minutes, and Yufen mentioned her intense interest in Buddhist ideology. Elisabeth was delighted by Yufen's apparent openness to spirtual things.

'Would you like to come to church?' she asked again.

'No, thanks,' Yufen repeated, this time really annoyed. She never liked the feeling of being pressured to do something.

The next time Elisabeth came into the department store, Yufen managed to spot her from a distance.

'Hey, can you cover for me?' she said to her friend at a neighbouring counter. 'I'm going to the bathroom. When that woman comes, tell her I'm not here.'

Although Elisabeth was slightly disappointed by Yufen's absence, she was not deterred. She left a magazine on Yufen's counter and walked on. A few weeks later, she came again. Yufen's instincts told her that something was just not right. 'This woman doesn't really know me, so what does she want from me? Why does she keep on looking for me?'

'Hey, can you cover for me?' she said to her friend, shuffling away quickly. 'I'm going to take a break at the stairwell. When that woman comes again, tell her I'm not here.'

Elisabeth gradually realized that Yufen's absences were intentional. She noticed that whenever she came by to distribute magazines, Yufen pretended to be busy with other things. Sometimes, if she had nothing else to do, she would dive into a banal conversation with a co-worker and pretend that Elisabeth didn't even exist.

Elisabeth continued to give Yufen a magazine every month. A faithful optimist, she felt that Yufen's sudden change of heart was the result of spiritual warfare, and that even though the Buddhist side of her was winning now, it would not claim the victory forever.

Yufen hated coming home from work. All too often, the first thing she saw upon entering her apartment was the unpleasant sight of her husband, passed out on the living-room couch. It was a sight that kept their son Bao from ever inviting a friend to his house for more than twenty years.

While Yufen shook her head, Kai let out a snort, then licked his lips and mumbled something in the language of cheap beer. He rolled over slightly, tumbling onto the floor. To Yufen's ears, the thud of his body as it hit the floor had the same effect as the sound of a cannonball being loaded into place. In a surge of anger, she stormed over and started to kick him.

'You drunken, irresponsible ...' she yelled, finishing the sentence with a generous helping of curses. She kicked him more.

'Uuuh, nniii ...' he muttered, too drunk to defend himself. Yufen didn't care. She knew what he wanted to say, what he had already said countless times before: 'How can you do this to me? How can you say those things? When you were crippled, I carried you up and down on my back. Look at the way I took care of you.'

One day, when Kai was about forty years old, he was drunkenly tidying up a desk in the living-room when he found a familiar-looking roll of red paper. With fumbling hands he managed to unroll it, and discovered that it was a three-foot-long fortune that had been given to him in his younger years. It detailed the outcomes of every stage in his life. As his eyes followed the elegant strokes of the fortune-teller's calligraphy brush, he discovered that much of the classical Chinese script was either illegible or indecipherable. One part of the fortune, however, was remarkably clear. The part that described his current life.

'Your liver and kidneys will not work well,' it read, followed by three key phrases: '*Qi-bu-xian* – bad wife. *Zi-bu-xiao* – unfilial son. *Nu-bu-ling* – unintelligent daughter.'

Kai started to sob.

He and his wife were like two people drowning in the

sea, fatally grabbing onto each other in a counter-productive attempt to save themselves. Yufen often worried about money, so Kai would take out loans to support the family, which led to mounting debt and damaged credit. People wondered how a man from such a prominent, politically active family could face such financial difficulties, and the loss of 'face' became a wound that only alcohol seemed to salve.

Yufen's moods often revolved around how much alcohol her husband managed to drink in one evening, and if she felt particularly upset, she would start throwing things across the room. Since Kai hated nothing more than direct confrontation, he would flee the house and drink with friends instead – and the cycle would continue.

Sometimes Yufen would also leave the apartment for a few days in order to escape. Other times she would try to ignore her husband. But most of the time, she would seek solitude, letting the dark cloud that loomed over her life burst into a thunderstorm of tears.

Ling Hu

Ling's three children darted into a back alley, eyeing their surroundings suspiciously. Homeless men lay like dark, lifeless masses on the street, and dilapidated buildings seemed to hover menacingly over them. Matai shivered, but knew that it would all be over soon. Soon, he would be in his mother's arms.

The days following Ling and Yan's separation had taken on a soap opera-like quality. At first, Yan diligently tried to convince his wife to return home. When she refused to listen to him, he tried using mediators – his brother, and even Ling's sister, who was providing Ling with a temporary refuge.

'Oh, look at this pathetic old man, looking for his wife!'

mocked her sister as Yan stood at the foot of the stairs, waiting for Ling.

Around the same time, Ling's children would stop by the He-Song Soda Company after school to see their estranged mother. But when Ling showed no sign of changing her mind about the separation, Yan prohibited them from seeing or calling her. Then it was Ling's turn to beg at his door.

'Please! Let me see the children!' she pleaded, her eyes moist with tears. Since her husband had changed the lock, she waited for him to open the door. He refused. She began to lose patience.

'Are you kidding me?' she yelled. 'You've been telling everybody that you'd welcome me back anytime, but you won't open the door?!'

Once, Ling even called the police in an attempt to make Yan let her see her three children. But since Ling had not yet filed for a divorce, the case was considered a domestic dispute; the police could do nothing but show up at Yan's door and advise him in the matter, while the children peered on. But even this triggered Yan's fury, and he started arguing with Ling right in front of the policeman. His children were horrified.

'Can't you two just stop arguing!' his daughter Peijen bawled as she ran with her brother to their bedroom. As the two children cried, their father walked in.

'I'm sorry that you had to see that, but I'm doing this for your own good,' he said. 'Your mother is a bad woman.'

It became clear that if the children wanted to continue seeing their mother, they would have to sneak out of the house. Though they had to travel by dark and deserted streets in order to escape unnoticed, their joyous reunions were well worth the effort.

Little did they know that the trials were only beginning.

'Daddy, can we go to the night market pleeeaase?' they begged one evening. He consented, and they hurried to the night market, eager for another clandestine reunion with their mother.

After their meeting in the middle of a bustling night market crowd, they headed off to the apartment of Ling's sister, where they spent the next few hours together. When the evening came to an inevitable close, Ling walked her children back to the night market. It was a happy moment, having the children by her side as she pushed her bicycle along the road.

Suddenly, she saw his eyes. The eyes of her husband, aflame with anger.

He grabbed her bicycle, and as it crashed to the ground, the crowd parted like the Red Sea. Onlookers gaped in horror. Yan raised his fist.

In a flash, someone stepped forward, towering over Ling like a wall of defence. It was her oldest daughter Jun.

Yan paused.

'GO HOME ... NOW!' he roared. His children reluctantly followed as he walked away, flinging a string of loud curses at his wife.

'How did I get myself into this mess?' Ling thought as she walked guiltily in the opposite direction. 'Why am I such an unreasonable person, always looking for a fight? Why did I marry a man with no sense?'

Ling had gone to the temple in hopes of finding peace by resting in the security of the god's special favour. Instead, she left feeling like a spurned lover.

'You don't belong here,' the spirit medium had said when she had offered to serve at the temple. 'You can come back, but you can't serve here, because you don't belong.'

'What?!' Ling thought, shocked. 'Where do I belong, then? Have I worshipped so many gods that I don't belong anywhere?' Even when many of Ling's co-workers and friends had grown weary of listening to her recurring complaints, the gods had continued to be dependable companions – yet now, even they seemed to deny her.

On the rebound, Ling rediscovered a sect that had already begun to seduce her in junior high: Yi Guan Dao.

The topic came up when Ling was chatting with a former classmate who, like her, was victim to a bad marriage. At the very mention of Yi Guan Dao, Ling's ears perked up. As the classmate started to extol the glories of her Yi Guan Dao shrine, Ling couldn't help but proudly interject:

'Actually, I'm already a believer.'

'Oh! Do you want to come to some classes at my shrine?'

Ling enthusiastically agreed, and as she listened to the teachings of the shrine's senior members, religious memories from childhood started to flow into her mind. Now that she was older, she enjoyed a deeper appreciation of the classes, which focused on Confucian topics like filial piety. She also enjoyed reading Yi Guan Dao literature and understanding its worship rituals more deeply.

'Each god warrants a different worship ritual,' the teacher explained in one class. 'This must be done very carefully, because a person's life is based on how that person worships. Offering worship to a god can bring you peace and change the course of your life.' Ling's eyes widened with hope.

The worshippers knelt on mats placed in rows. One worship leader called out the name of a god, and another leader counted out the number of bows that the god required, based on its presumed importance.[1] The worshippers then bowed together, bringing their hands and heads to the ground in quick succession while reciting Confucian-like chants. A goddess like Guan Yin received more than ten bows. Jesus received only two or three. The whole process took about half an hour, and Ling loved all of it.

Since Ling had already been inducted as a member of Yi

Guang Dao in junior high, she was expected to attend these worship sessions regularly.

The shrine was a fairly new one, so its leaders solicited help from anyone who was willing. Ling was an obvious candidate. Thanks to her unhampered religious zeal, they contacted her whenever they needed help for initiation ceremonies or festivals. Sometimes she babysat. Sometimes she helped prepare food. All Yi Guan Dao members were encouraged to share their faith, but Ling was exceedingly proactive, inviting friends to the shrine at every opportunity. She also managed to sneak her children along, and even had them inducted as members. Before long, Ling's 'good deeds' earned her a position as a leader. She was bestowed with the sacred duty of collecting worshippers' fruit offerings and placing them on the altar.

Although the rituals and requirements of Yi Guan Dao were rather stringent, its members were allowed to be involved with other temples. Ling's attachment to one such temple began at lunchtime over a bowl of noodles.

'So how are things going with your husband?' asked the noodle shop's owner, a long-time acquaintance. 'How is your relationship lately?'

'The same,' Ling replied.

'What is?' a voice chimed in.

Ling turned and recognized the woman as a neighbour whom she saw on occasion. The restaurant owner briefly explained Ling's situation. The neighbour paused, then turned to Ling.

'Miss, can I tell you something? I have always sensed that you have had a guardian spirit or ghost behind you. This spirit doesn't want you to have a good relationship with your husband. Just come to our temple and do some meditation. Then your pain will go away.'

Willing to try virtually anything, Ling agreed. When she arrived at the temple, she was impressed by the enormity of the two-storey building, which contained a spacious worship area. Through the dim haze of burning incense, Ling could see enormous idols looming over the worshippers.

'The god of this temple must be powerful,' Ling presumed, awe-struck at the gloriousness of the temple. After the neighbour had given her a brief tour, Ling offered incense to each of the many gods worshipped there. At the highest point in the temple was the altar for the temple's main god, 'The God of Northern Heaven', After Ling paid special respects to this god, she was escorted to a worship space filled with chairs. She sat.

'Empty yourself,' said her neighbour. 'Connect to the god and allow it to come into your body. If it is willing to enter, you may be able to perform healings some day.'

Ling closed her eyes and began to meditate.

Almost instantly, a wave of energy surged through her body. She rose to her feet and started dancing gracefully, as if an invisible puppeteer had taken control of her body. Then came a voice.

'I am a thousand hands,' said an onlooker, referring to the nickname for Guan Yin, the goddess who had possessed Ling before. The onlooker had apparently manifested the tongue of Guan Yin, while Ling manifested the body.

The dance became frenetic and took Ling around the room in wide circles. Her feet hopped about and her arms looped uncontrollably in the air. Never before had she been possessed by such a feeling of abandon.

Minutes passed, and Ling's body gradually began to feel weary.

'Stop,' she told herself, unable to speak.

She kept dancing.

'Stop.'

More dancing.

'STOP!'

Finally, she did. Those present gaped in amazement.

'You have a deep ability to let a god come into your body,' said one worshipper. 'In the eyes of our god, your spirit is immature, like that of a little child, so the thousand-handed Guan Yin is protecting you. Your spirit belongs to her.'

Ling's neighbour urged her to return to the temple so that she could improve her mediumistic abilities. Ling returned twice. Each time she first worshipped all the gods in the temple, and each time her trances became increasingly intense. She enjoyed going, particularly because the other people at the temple were so willing to help her learn.

During Ling's third visit, she commenced as before, with a dance. Then her limbs started to jerk about uncontrollably. Her movements became frenzied and frightening, as if she had transformed into a horrible creature from a science-fiction movie. She leaped and ran around the room, faster and faster. After more than ten minutes, she could hardly breathe. All she wanted to do was sit down and rest. But she couldn't.

Then she started to spin.

'Stop.'

She spun faster.

'Stop!'

And faster and faster. Like a carousel gone haywire. She didn't feel dizzy, but her face grew hot, and her heart pounded like that of a galloping horse. Exhausted and afraid, she sensed that other people had started to gather around. Voices called out.

'Be careful, you're still in training ...'

'It's going too fast for you!'

'Slow down! Slow down!'

'Spirit of Guan Yin, don't be anxious!'

Ling continued to spin.

Panic. Fearful faces. Several people stepped forward, trying to avoid her flailing arms. Finally, someone grabbed her, pinned her down, subdued her small frame to a stop.

When Ling regained control of her body, she was petrified.

'This god really DOES love you,' a nearby devotee said, trying to sound convincing. 'Don't be scared. Things were just moving too quickly. You're still like a child. If you come here often, you can grow spiritually.'

The arguments were futile. Ling had already vowed never to return.

Ling was tired of going to work every day and bumping into her husband, the man who would not allow her to see her own children. She left the He-Song Soda Company permanently and found a position at an insurance company. Soon after, she decided to try something completely different. Something that would utilize her interest in fashion. This was how she went from being an accounts clerk to a saleswoman at Vivi, a mini-department store.

Elisabeth Weinmann had already been distributing magazines at Vivi every month for about six years before Ling strolled in for her first day at work. Two of the salesladies there had become Christians through Elisabeth's ministry.

As Elisabeth squeezed through a crowd of customers, weaving through more than twenty sales counters that were jammed close together, she tried to give magazines to sales clerks who did not appear busy. By the time she left the store, she had not noticed a perilously unhappy saleswoman named Ling Hu, and Ling Hu had not noticed her.

Notes

1. Joseph Bosco, *Yiguan Dao: Heterodoxy and Popular Religion*, In Murray A. Rubinstein, ed., The Other Taiwan, 1945 to the Present, pp. 423-444. Armonk, NY: M.E. Sharpe, Inc. p. 435.

Chapter 12

'Are you married? Do you have kids?' the woman asked sweetly.

Ling Hu looked up, excited that a co-worker had finally decided to take interest in her. 'Maybe she knows that something is wrong with me, even though I look fine on the outside,' she speculated. Ling moved her mouth rapidly when answering the question, trying to only include the necessary details – though she did not have a gift for being succinct.

'Mmm ... I see ...' the woman nodded empathetically. '... Can I ask, do you go to church?'

That was how Ling's first friendship at Vivi blossomed. Since her new friend only worked part-time, she would invite Ling over to her apartment several times a week so that they could chat longer. Kind, gentle and only a few years older than Ling, the co-worker eagerly listened to her story and quickly earned Ling's trust.

'You know,' she said to Ling one day, 'it's good to know Jesus.'

'I know,' Ling replied. 'For three years I went to a Christian high school, so I already know who Jesus is. But my parents *bai-bai* – worship idols. So after graduation, I never went to church again.'

* * *

Elisabeth Weinmann was enjoying the food at her church's 'love feast' when a woman slipped a piece of paper into her hand.

'You probably don't know me, but my name is Mrs Yee,' said the woman, slowly, compellingly. 'I do some part-time work in this department store, and I really think the workers there need the Lord. They have so many problems.'

'Mmm-hmm ...' Elisabeth nodded, in avid agreement. Mrs Yee continued.

'I started to introduce your shop-workers' fellowship to them, and one woman seems to be rather interested. Our store is called Vivi. She really wants to meet you. Please pay her a visit soon.'

Elisabeth nodded again, and looked down at the piece of paper. On it was a phone number and a name: Ling Hu.

Despite Mrs Yee's vehemence, Elisabeth was so busy running her ministry that she didn't have time to visit Ling right away. When she finally showed up at Vivi, Ling wasn't there; she had taken the day off. Disappointed, Elisabeth admonished herself for not coming earlier.

The following week, Elisabeth went to Vivi again. Then she saw: In the middle of a crowded aisle of counters stood a petite, gregarious woman. Elisabeth walked up to the woman and smiled.

'Hi, I'm Sister Wei, and I'm from Germany. Your friend Mrs Yee goes to our church. I'm in charge of a group for shop-workers.'

Ling's face lit up.

'Oh yes, I went to a Christian high school and joined Christian activities, and I really liked it,' she said quickly, as if someone was timing their conversation.

'Oh really?' Elisabeth asked. 'Then what happened after you graduated?'

'Then I didn't go to church, and then I got married, and had three children.'

'Oh, I see. How long have you worked here?'

'Well, I used to work in an office and for the past six months I've been a sales-woman here.'

'I wonder how I've never seen her before,' Elisabeth thought to herself. She handed Ling a tract called The Gospel Bridge that explained the gospel with Bible verses and colourful pictures. Then she started to mention her Tuesday night Bible studies.

'Oh, I know about that already,' Ling interjected. 'I really want to come. I'll be there!'

By the end of the conversation, both women felt energized. Ling appreciated Elisabeth's kindness and sincerity, and Elisabeth was pleasantly surprised by Ling's instantaneous enthusiasm. Yet Elisabeth had been in contact with enough shop-workers to know that behind Ling's forced smile was something else entirely.

Indeed, Ling had met Elisabeth right at the peak of her emotional turmoil. Uncertain of what lay ahead, she felt as if she was trying to swim through the bottleneck of a river churning with restlessness and sorrow.

On the Tuesday evening following their first encounter, Elisabeth waited expectantly for Ling in the church courtyard. In the next thirty minutes, Elisabeth greeted some fifty shop-workers who were heading to their small groups. The shop-workers' fellowship had grown exponentially in recent years. Each of its six Tuesday night small groups represented a different department store and was led by a person who worked in that department store. The small-group leaders had many responsibilities. In addition to regularly distributing evangelistic magazines throughout their department stores, many of which were several storeys tall, they also paid frequent visits to the members of their small groups and attended weekly co-workers' meetings. Sometimes, they crammed all of these tasks into one day a week – their only day off.

Even with all this help, Elisabeth found herself teaching, serving, evangelizing and counselling at an almost inhuman pace. As long as there were still hundreds of idol-worshipping shop-workers within one square kilometre of the church, she would not let herself waste any time.

As the small-group meetings commenced, the halls of the church resounded with chatter and singing. Elisabeth peered around, looking for Ling one last time. The fact that Elisabeth had faced similar disappointments innumerable times before didn't lessen the sting of the setback. Yet as she entered the church and shuffled towards a small group, she refused to give up hope. She knew that God was still in control.

In the following weeks, Elisabeth continued to visit Ling in her department store.

'Hello Sister Wei!' Ling said enthusiastically, and with a wide smile.

'Hi, Ling! How are you?' said Elisabeth, pulling some snacks and tracts out of her tote bag.

'Very good, very good. Hello there!' Ling turned to a co-worker who was approaching her counter. The phone rang. 'Wait, can you hold on, please?' She picked it up. 'Hello? Yes, this is ... Hello! Please take your time and look around,' she said, turning to a customer who had started to browse her racks.

Since Ling was clearly preoccupied, Elisabeth decided to step away for a moment and simply observe her from a distance, as she often did with the people she ministered to. For the next few minutes, Ling cheerfully and efficiently rushed around her messy counter, which was cluttered with paper. But as soon as she had taken care of business, her content expression dulled into a tired, lifeless gaze.

'I bet she hasn't had an easy life ...' Elisabeth guessed. 'I wonder what's troubling her ... I wonder what's in her heart ...'

A few weeks after their first meeting, Elisabeth was greeting shop-workers in the church courtyard as usual when she spotted Ling.

'I'm so glad that you could come today!' she exclaimed. 'They're already waiting for you. Would you like to go inside?'

'OK,' Ling replied with a smile. As she chatted, Elisabeth escorted her to a newly formed small group. As soon as Ling walked into the room, several women greeted her warmly, eager to celebrate the arrival of their fledgling group's first seeker.

Ling appreciated the acceptance she felt in this new group, especially since the wound from being cut off from her own family was still so fresh. As she listened to the other group members share about their experiences with God, fond memories from her days in the high school fellowship started to resurface.

Food was an essential part of almost every event that Elisabeth hosted, so the shop-workers munched on snacks and sipped tea as they read the Bible together. Elisabeth noticed that even though Ling said little, the newcomer was proactive in making sure everyone had their fill of food and drink. After the meeting ended, she even stayed behind to help Elisabeth clean up.

Ling was obviously passionate about getting involved in church, but Elisabeth could tell that her interests were divided. Even though Ling zealously invited her co-workers to attend small-group meetings, she rarely managed to show up at the meetings on time – if at all. Some days she was busy running errands. Other days, she was busy sleeping. Even though the church was located only ten minutes away from where she lived, for some inexplicable reason the distance was, at times, psychologically impassable. In Ling's mind, Jesus was 'just another god' in her pantheon of heavenly helpers. The fact that her mother, who was still devoted to her household gods, did not approve of Ling's church involvement only exacerbated the situation.

When Ling did attend small-group meetings, her face usually bore a distant, vacant look when she wasn't saying anything. Elisabeth sensed that something was smothering Ling's naturally animated personality, and she yearned to find out what. She frequently visited Ling's counter. There, she listened to Ling talk about her devotion to the gods and her dependence on temples.

When Elisabeth felt that a mutual sense of trust had developed between them, she asked the question that had been bothering her all along: 'So ... are you and your husband still together?'

In response, Ling was surprisingly forthcoming, willing to share the depths of her frustration with someone she was just getting to know.

'... My biggest sorrow is that I can't see my children,' she continued. 'I'm worried about him beating them – especially my son – and taking their money away. I just want to be with them.'

Elisabeth furrowed her bushy eyebrows and nodded slowly.

'I hope that someday we can talk about these things more,' she said sweetly, with genuine compassion. 'I really hope we can talk again.'

Ling did start to talk to Elisabeth. But she also talked with fortune-tellers, for she felt that she needed all the help shw could get with her mounting family problems.

'You have been through much, so be patient,' one fortune-teller said cryptically. It was hard advice to follow, for the conflict between Ling and her husband had already dragged on long enough. Since no one solution seemed to solve her problems, Ling went interchangeably to temples, church and her Yi Guan Dao shrine, where she still served.

Ling shared her worries with temple workers and the gods, but she felt confused and troubled, as if two spirits were warring inside of her, stretching her in torturously opposite directions. But then she remembered:

'God is the only true God,' her small-group leader had emphasized in one Bible study. 'You can always rely on him, always pray to him. You can even ask him to help you dedicate your life to him, and him alone.'

Finally, Ling decided that it was time. It was time to stop seeing her religious life as a series of consecutive affairs with different gods. It was time to start settling down.

'If you are the one true God ...' she prayed, '... if I am your child, then help me come to church regularly. Help me meet with you. If you are real, then I'll leave all these idols behind.'

Like a prisoner released from the captivity of a ball and chain, Ling immediately felt that going to church became easier. Urgent errands no longer surfaced just as Ling prepared to go to Bible study, she no longer felt overcome by fatigue or lethargy when thinking about church, and her phone no longer rang incessantly with invitations to temples. Furthermore, as she browsed through her younger brother's bookshelf one day she was pleasantly surprised to find a Bible there. Upon further inspection, she also found a thoroughly highlighted copy of the classic devotional *Streams in the Desert* by Mrs Charles E. Cowman, an American missionary who had served in China and Japan during the first two decades of the twentieth century.

'Where did you get this from?' Ling asked excitedly.

'A college classmate gave it to me,' he answered, giving it to Ling.

'You know, I go to church now,' she confessed.

'*Hen hao*, very good.'

'Do you want to come to church with me sometime?'

'No ... Mum wouldn't be happy about that ... But we should pray for our family.'

Ling was thrilled to have found a spiritual ally within her own family – a luxury many Taiwanese Christians do not have. After she sneaked home from Bible study every week, she would go to her brother's room and talk to him about what she had learned that evening while the rest of her family slept.

'God, you really do answer our prayers. You really are the most powerful God,' she began to pray.

Though Ling believed this in her head, her heart still longed to worship at temples. Whenever she felt frustrated about her inability to see her children, her instinctive reaction was to turn to the gods, instead of God, for help. After all, it had been a lifelong habit, which almost everyone around her was involved in. When one of her co-workers started boasting about a temple, saying that worshipping there was a panacea for all her personal troubles, Ling decided to give it a try. She went once. Then she went again. And again.

'I've taken time off work,' Ling said to her co-worker one day. 'Can we go to the temple together?'

'Er ... you don't have to go,' came the unexpected reply.

'Why? Are you going to go?'

'Yes.'

'So why can't I come?' Ling started to feel uneasy.

'Our god doesn't want you to come, so you can't.'

'But why?'

'You have worshipped too many different gods, so our god won't let you go.'

Ling was horrified. The fear that was festering inside

her had finally been verbalized; her worship had finally gone too far. But her co-worker was not finished.

'Also, the gods have communicated with each other, and your God won't let you go.'

In an instant, Ling's spirits were lifted.

'Well, that means that my God must be bigger than your god and has authority over your god, so your god is too small for me anyway,' she said defiantly. 'I don't even want to go with you any more.'

Renewed vigour poured into Ling as she continued to attend church and her small group. She was always eager to talk about developments in her spiritual life. Yet trying to read the Bible one-on-one with her was like a game of cat-and-mouse.

For the Christians in Elisabeth's ministry, *pei-du*, or leading non-Christian friends through one-on-one evangelistic Bible studies, was evangelism at its best. It was something that Elisabeth had always emphasized over typical acts of Christian service, like ushering or singing in a choir. And for the past few months, several Christians had wanted to *pei-du* with Ling, since she was such an enthusiastic seeker. Elisabeth had wanted to give these Christians the chance, but Ling's inconsistency had tried the patience of each one of them.

The third attempt was by an experienced church leader. One evening, Elisabeth received a harried phone call from the woman.

'How could Ling just not show up?!' the woman complained. 'Last time she was so late that we only had a few minutes before she had to go to work! And this time, I called her right before and she said that she would come. How could she not come? If I go out for nothing again … Well, I just can't take it any longer!'

'I understand,' Elisabeth said, trying to sound

encouraging. 'If you want me to do it next week, I can.' So after skipping through the hands of three Bible study leaders in two months, Ling found herself in the tender embrace of Sister Wei.

Since the two were no longer constrained by the rigidity of Ling's work environment and the constant possibility of interruption by customers, they were able to deeply discuss the issues that mattered most to Ling. Through Elisabeth's patience and willingness to listen, Ling discovered an aspect of God that fulfilled one of her greatest needs – her need to be heard. As they prayed together, Ling realized that only God could take away the burdens in her heart. Only he could clear away the worries and accusations that cluttered her mind.

After completing a handful of Bible studies with Ling, Elisabeth felt that it was time to take the next step. She pulled out the first tract she had ever handed to Ling, the Gospel Bridge, and started to explain it. The next time they met, she explained it again.

'Where do you think you are in your spiritual walk?' she asked, pointing to a diagram in the booklet. 'Are you on the side of heaven, heading towards the light, or are you still on the side of darkness?'

Ling thought for a moment. Then she pointed to the cross, which served as a bridge between the two.

'I'm at the beginning of the journey, climbing up onto the cross,' she said.

Elisabeth beamed, her eyes moistening. A few minutes later, Ling prayed a prayer of confession and accepted Jesus into her life.

Indeed, the journey had just begun.

'What? How did you get baptized?' replied Lillian, shocked.

Since Mei now realized that the spirits that tormented her were from Satan, she desired to cut them off through baptism. Long ago, her mother had warned her that one woman in her True Jesus Church had failed to fully wet her head in baptism. As a result, Satan still had a relationship with the woman. So when Mei went to the bathroom and put her head under the faucet, she let the water pour generously over her.

'Jesus, I believe in you!' she proclaimed. 'In the name of Mei Chen, I baptize myself. Amen.'

'Oh!' Lillian exclaimed, somewhat amused. 'That doesn't count! You need to do it publicly! You need to have witnesses.'

Lillian knew that she needed to encourage Mei to go to church. She gave Mei information about several churches near Mei's home, and out of these Mei chose one to attend. Although she thoroughly enjoyed the feeling of being cared for by the members of the church, the church had one drawback: its members were primarily *wai-sheng-ren*, or people who had emigrated from mainland China along with their political leader Chiang Kai-shek[1]. Mei's husband despised *wai-sheng-ren* and strictly prohibited her from going to Sunday services there.

Mei's father-in-law also opposed her church attendance, but for different reasons. He still hoped that Mei would dutifully *bai-bai* – worship Big Chang's ancestors. Sometimes he would even guard the door to the house on Sunday mornings, piercing her with judgmental glares if she dared to go out.

* * *

To Yufen Wang, ancestor worship was nothing more than an insignificant habit that could be easily removed from the exterior of her life. What affected her much more deeply was the Buddhist worldview, which was intricately entwined with her thoughts and motivations. Yufen felt that it would be impossible to distance herself from Buddhism. Its philosophies, like those of Confucius, Mengzi, Laozi and others, influenced almost every aspect of Taiwanese culture and history.

The omnipresence of Buddhism muddled Yufen's thoughts whenever Elisabeth or anybody else tried to tell her about God: wasn't Christianity just a Western form of Buddhism?

'Aren't all religions pretty much the same?' she asked Elisabeth.

'No, they're very different ...' Elisabeth said as she tried her best to offer an explanation. '... So you see, you can't believe in both Buddhism and Christianity. Do you want to believe in Jesus or Buddha?'

Yufen answered with silence. 'How could God think that he's the only one who's good, and that all the other religions are not good?' she thought to herself. Elisabeth's question made her uncomfortable, for she never liked the feeling of being pressured to do anything, from helping her husband with his problems to making a decision about Christ. This she had made clear to Elisabeth before.

'I know one day I'll get baptized,' she had said bluntly. 'I know that this is the only way that my life can get better. But I'm telling you, don't rush me or give me any pressure. I still have too many doubts, too many questions. I need lots of time.'

Even though Elisabeth still presented Yufen with direct challenges from time to time, Yufen was so sure of Elisabeth's love for her that she tolerated them. From the beginning, Yufen knew that Elisabeth welcomed visitors into her apartment at virtually any hour; since Yufen worked close by, she often took advantage of Elisabeth's unconditional offer. After work, she would often share her struggles with Elisabeth for hours, venting her hates and hurts, her sorrows and fears. Her complaints, especially those about her husband, often repeated themselves like a broken, cacophonous music box. Yet Elisabeth listened patiently. She suspected that Yufen merely wanted someone who would love and listen, not give advice. She also suspected that Yufen's mind was like a soaked rag; old thought patterns would need to be squeezed out first before it could fully absorb biblical truth.

Indeed, Yufen often asked herself, 'Through Buddhism, I learned how to be joyful and avoid suffering, how to find meaning in life. What's so wrong with that? Do I really need to desert what has been so familiar to me for an unfamiliar God?' Buddhism had accompanied her through decades of chaos, and she was terrified of what would happen if she chased it away.

Months passed. Even her son Bao sensed that something was moving within his mother's soul, but she refused to fully acknowledge it herself. Her husband's chronic career switches, among other things, made her fear change. Drastic changes, like those of a religious nature, seemed simply insurmountable.

* * *

Despite Mei's apparent religious fervour, something kept her from really processing through what it meant to be a Christian; her lips expressed understanding of Lillian's teachings, but her heart remained preoccupied with a problem that, to her, still dwarfed the problem of sin. After knowing Lillian for about nine months, she decided to break the intolerable silence.

'My husband does something to my daughters ...' she began. As she described the situation in detail, Lillian could hardly believe Mei's words.

'If only Ting-ting was being molested, I could believe that ... but Little Hui too?! She's so ... little!' For a moment Lillian doubted the veracity of Mei's story – she thought, perhaps, that Mei was simply being delusional. 'But Mei took so long to tell me this ... and it seems that she struggled a lot before deciding to say it ... and she really loves her family so much ...'

Mei went on to say that her father-in-law knew about the problem too, but kept quiet in order to save face. She felt that she had no allies, no way out of the situation.

'Will you talk to my husband about it?' Mei asked in desperation.

'Mei, I can't do that. I can be a good friend to him, but I can't convince him to stop ... We're dealing with a major psychological problem here ... The outcome of all this will ultimately depend on you, and whether you're willing to leave him ... In the meantime, you need to watch over your children carefully but try to act normal, so that your husband doesn't know that we're really trying to do something about it.' Lillian knew that the consequences of offending Big Chang could be dire – he might beat Mei violently and prevent her from ever seeing Christians again.

Cautiously, secretly, Lillian helped Mei take her children to the hospital. The doctor there confirmed Mei's story. The girls had been injured by objects that had been forced into them. Although the doctor was not allowed to initiate any legal action, he was incensed.

'This situation needs to be resolved quickly!' he warned.

But further legal inquiries revealed that a resolution would come neither quickly nor easily. A trip to Taipei County's Bureau of Social Affairs taught them that, if Mei tried to run away, the government could only guarantee physical protection in a safe house for two weeks. Since Big Chang had connections with some major gangs, Mei could easily be attacked and forced to return home after those two weeks. It was very common for men like Big Chang to mobilize small armies of supporters by simply telling other men that their wives were crazy.

Lillian also discovered that, if Mei wanted to prove the abuse and gain permanent custody of the children, she would need more extensive proof and witness testimony – a near impossibility, since the children were still too young to speak cogently and consistently. At that time, courts did not tend to rule in women's favour. Even the social workers whom Lillian contacted lacked sympathy.

'If you want to leave, then leave. If you don't want to leave, then don't,' Mei was often told.

A psychologist who specialized in sexual abuse proved to be more helpful.

'Let's get the husband in here and see if he's willing to talk,' the psychologist said. After being coached in how to broach the subject, Mei approached her husband.

'We went to the doctor and the doctor said that the children's thing ... is torn,' she said gently to him.

'What?! It's YOU who started it. You did it! You have a mental problem or something. It's you who has the problem!'

'You're right,' Mei replied, trying to stay calm. 'It's my problem and I need to see a doctor. Will you go with me to see a doctor about it?'

The strategy worked, and Big Chang agreed. But the victory did not last long. Although the psychologist tried to direct his initial questions at Mei, the true intention of the interview soon became obvious. When they started discussing the abuse of the children, Mei's husband said curtly:

'You just teach her to be good, OK?'

It was the last time that Big Chang would go with Mei to

the psychologist. When they returned home, he was livid. And ready to strike.

From then on, Big Chang stayed home more frequently, carefully monitoring Mei's activities. When he saw Lillian, he often shot her spiteful looks.

'You'd better teach her! This is all your fault!' he snapped at her.

Mei and Big Chang started silently battling for time with the girls, and whenever Mei managed to gain the upper hand, her husband's temper would explode; his behaviour had become an insatiable addiction. Since all four family members slept in the same room, Big Chang even tried to take advantage of his daughters at night after Mei fell asleep. At first Mei tried to stay awake all night, but her eyelids would inevitably clamp shut, then fly open again at the sound of a daughter's cry.

Mei felt trapped, as if she had no choice but to endure the abuse. She was too afraid to speak up, too afraid to fight back, too afraid to run away. Lillian had already made all the necessary arrangements for Mei's escape, but in the end, Mei was too frightened to follow through. She was convinced that even if she left, the courts would give her husband custody of the children, and she would be forced to grovel back home.

Lillian knew that this was a legitimate fear, but also began to harbour different fears of her own. 'What if this man starts to abuse other children someday? Or what if the community finds out what's been going on?' she wondered.

Lillian's concern heightened when Ting-ting stood in front of her jubilantly, flipping up her skirt like she had done on the day they met.

'Daddy touch me! Daddy touch me!' Ting-ting exclaimed proudly as her skirt billowed in the air. Lillian turned to Mei.

'Someday, when your kids start going to kindergarten or elementary school, they're going to start telling people about this. And one day someone is going to come after your husband.' Lillian knew that if Mei wanted to keep her family alive, and if she wanted to make any further progress in her own spiritual life, change was necessary. Drastic change.

OMF missionary Katrina Schachtler had started her work in Taiwan at the Panchiao Gospel Lutheran Church, while Elisabeth Weinmann was on her first Home Assignment. For the past five and a half years, she and her husband Marc had reached out to factory workers in Panchiao and Tantze, and they were ready for a change.

Lillian first met Katrina at the wedding banquet of a mutual friend. After realizing that they had similar burdens for Taiwan's working class, they immediately bonded and eventually started doing visitations in hospitals and homes together. Lillian was impressed by Katrina's compassion and ability to make sound judgments. She also admired OMF for putting so much effort into reaching out to working-class Taiwanese – a target group more spiritually needy but more difficult to reach than the more educated Taiwanese.

'Our group hasn't ever really dealt with resolving a problem like Mei's, and anyway OMF can deal with things better in the long term ...' Lillian thought to herself. After reading the Bible with Mei for one and a half years, Lillian felt that it was time to do something she had never done before – let someone else take over. 'If a foreigner takes care of Mei, maybe her husband will feel less suspicious, less pressured,' she reasoned. In fact, there was a good possibility that the man would even enjoy telling his friends that his wife had befriended a foreigner. Hopefully, Lillian reasoned, the ego boost would blind him to the fact that the foreigner was there to help his wife get away from him.

Lillian sat Katrina down and told her Mei's story.

'Oh my! If this happened overseas, it would be considered a very serious matter!' exclaimed Katrina.

Lillian went on to explain the obstacles they had faced so far, and the obstacles that inevitably lay ahead.

'The government will only protect and support her for three months,' she warned, 'and after this time passes, many women resort to selling themselves in order to support their families. So we have one shot to get her out. One shot.'

'Well,' Katrina said, 'there's this other OMF missionary ...'

Mei had been more than hesitant when she heard that her future would lie in the hands of a complete stranger, a foreigner. But now that Katrina Schachtler sat alongside Lillian in her living-room, she felt more curious than anxious. Katrina was one of the tallest, whitest female creatures she had ever seen. She had a full head of curly brown hair, and when she spoke, the sound that came out was as pleasant as birdsong. Mei's mind bubbled with questions, one of which curled her lips into a smile:

'I wonder how this person came to know Jesus.'

If Mei's relationship with Lillian Tsai was a ripple that pushed her towards God, then her relationship with Katrina Schachtler was a tidal wave that propelled her towards full life in Christ.

Once Mei started to emerge from her shell of cautious reticence, she told Katrina about her childhood, and how being raped by her older brother plummeted her into a lifetime of feeling worthless. She talked about her work as a prostitute. She talked about inviting the spirits into her life, and how they had directed her thoughts and actions.

Katrina found that she could easily sympathize with all that Mei shared, as she had completed a course on sexual abuse run by a missionary at a counselling centre in Taichung.

'Oh, so when this happened to you, did you feel this way ...' Katrina would ask, helping Mei to identify her feelings. For one of the first times in her life, Mei began to feel truly understood.

'Jesus can heal you,' Katrina assured Mei, praying for her and showering her with encouragement. As Katrina allowed herself to deeply feel Mei's hurts, she began to see Mei as a dear friend; it was as if their lives had been inexorably joined by the secrets that Mei had begun to reveal. Katrina even invited Mei to live with her, though the plan turned out to be logistically impossible.

Through their times together, Katrina came to realize that Mei was not yet strong enough to fully overcome her hurts through in-depth counselling. Her unhealthy home life was still an overwhelming distraction that blocked the path to healing. And more important, she had only a shallow relationship with the ultimate Healer. Her understanding of sin was particularly incomplete, for whenever the topic came up, she would utter:

'But look at my husband. He's worse than me. He's sinned more than I have.'

As Katrina led Mei through the Bible, she started with the basics: explaining who Jesus was. They read through Jesus' miracles, some of which Mei still found difficult to believe.

Although Mei was not yet ready to believe every word of the Bible, she continued to be drawn to the nature of God, which became more and more palpable as she observed Katrina's enthusiasm, patience and love. The True Jesus church nestled in Ali Mountain had introduced her to a God who was strict and easily angered. Now she understood God's power and love, as well as his justice. With all her heart, she wanted to love him back.

Mei started reading the Bible on her own. She also tried hard to go to church every week, even when her father-in-law frowned upon it. Whenever he was home, Mei and Katrina met in a nearby McDonalds to avoid unnecessary conflicts.

Such precautions were generally unnecessary with Big Chang, who was quite courteous to Katrina when he happened to be home. He even opened up to her on occasion, blaming his need for alcohol on his father, who used to beat him severely. He adamantly denied doing anything wrong to his daughters or to his wife. Katrina listened attentively and sympathetically, though she remained on the alert. On the one hand, Big Chang seemed as soft and harmless as a teddy bear; on the other, she knew that he could be as violent and dangerous as a real one.

Meanwhile, Mei's frustration with her husband continued to mount. To keep Mei from disclosing their family 'situation', he prohibited her from seeing friends often, or from going to public places with lots of people – which, for any Taiwanese city-dweller, would make leaving the house nearly impossible.

Mei unveiled her troubles to Katrina bit by bit, and even confessed that she had been tempted to just end it all.

'But the lives of children are not ours to take away,' Katrina said tenderly. 'Only God has the authority to do this.'

'Hmm ... that's true,' agreed Mei. This was typical of the sponge-like openness with which she generally regarded Katrina's teaching and advice.

It was not easy for Mei to continually trust the Lord, especially as the family's financial situation worsened.

After spending most of his money on gambling and alcohol, her husband gave her only 500 Taiwanese dollars a month for herself and the children. Mei even resorted to wearing her husband's clothes when hers wore thin. Sometimes, her father-in-law pitied her and secretly gave her some cash.

'Use this to buy some food,' he said furtively, 'and don't tell your husband about it.'

Around the time when Mei first met Katrina, she came up with an idea. She removed the iron door from the front of her house and, in the suffocating Taipei heat, started to sell ice at the doorway.

'Ice for sale! Ice for sale!' her two- and three-year-old daughters would call out as they stood at the door with their mother. Since the road in front of their house was a bustling thoroughfare, the venture proved to be profitable. Invigorated by the possibility of having more money to spend, Mei also tried selling tea-leaves from her brother's farm in Ali Mountain.

Running the business was not easy, however. If Mei's husband happened to see the same customer twice in one day, he would remark:

'Why does that person keep on coming back to buy ice?'

'Because ... he likes to eat ice?'

'Hmmph! You're probably sleeping together!'

Eventually Mei's 'shop' caught the eye of a businessman who offered to let her use one of his electronic slot machines. Placed in front of the 'shop', the machine immediately produced easy cash – sometimes as much as several thousand dollars a day.

But the temptation was more than Mei's husband could bear. He stopped working and spent his days 'guarding' the machine, though he actually spent much of the time using it himself. Finally, Mei's father-in-law decided to intervene.

'Take this thing out of here!' he said to Mei.

'But why?' she replied innocently.

'If you leave it here, your husband won't work. He'll get lazy. He loves to drink. He loves to gamble. And now he doesn't even want to work. I'm getting old, and I can't keep on supporting you all.'

In the end, Mei closed the 'shop' entirely. This brought her back to her original problem.

'I'm so bad at managing money,' she lamented to Katrina. 'I've never been good at it, even when I was living by myself.'

Katrina knew that $500 a month (about $17 US) would be scarcely adequate for even the most frugal mother, but tried to help anyway by giving Mei shopping tips. It was one of the first times that someone had really taken the time to teach Mei how to manage her money.

'Oh, it's so wonderful!' Mei remarked a couple of weeks later. 'I have enough money now. I'm so grateful.'

The euphoria did not last long. Even when Mei tried her hardest to save money, she could do nothing about the fact that her husband sometimes gave her money late or not at all. The financial pressure was crushing.

* * *

'I think you should move out of the house for a little while,' Elisabeth said to Yufen Wang, 'because it really looks like you're going to explode from all this pressure.'

Each time Yufen had gone to Elisabeth's apartment to vent, her frustrations had become more apparent, her admissions more profound. And now, it was obvious that the psychological pressure caused by her husband's alcoholism was reaching a hazardous level. Elisabeth continued:

'I can prepare a room for you here in the dorms so that you can have a break from your situation at home. OK?'

Yufen considered the proposal. Her husband Kai was unemployed and continued to shirk his family duties by drinking every day. No matter how hard she fussed and fought, nothing seemed to improve. Perhaps her absence would force Kai to take responsibility for his nineteen-year-old daughter, who still lived at home.

On the day of the move, Elisabeth prepared Yufen's room in the typical way – with fruit, flowers, and a large-print Bible that would be easy on Yufen's ailing eyes. Unlike most newcomers, Yufen refused Elisabeth's offer to help her move her things. She insisted on doing things herself.

Yufen arrived at the dorm with only a fraction of her possessions. She looked forward to living a simple and quiet life in the dorm, without having to worry about her husband storming in drunk.

She quickly discovered that her new living situation came with problems of its own. Her two new room-mates, considerably younger than her, often left the apartment in what she considered to be a state of unacceptable disarray.

'They make themselves look all good and pretty on the outside, and then their homes are such a mess!' she observed.

When Yufen demanded more help with the housework, hot tantrums often ensued. Since all three women came from broken, tempestuous family backgrounds, they hardly knew how to relate to each other in a healthy way. Elisabeth often intervened by mediating late-night discussions about their volatile state of affairs.

Also, Yufen's temporary absence did not make her husband's problems magically disappear, as she had hoped it would. The first time Kai successfully paid the rent for their apartment would also be the last. Furthermore, Yufen discovered that he neglected to pay their utility bills.

'I don't care and I'm not going home,' Yufen wanted to

say to him. 'See what you can do about that!' But she couldn't feign nonchalance for long – especially after her daughter was forced to literally live in the dark. From then on, Yufen started going home one or two days a week to take care of household matters, and when she stayed at the dorm, she occasionally called her daughter.

'How's the situation at home? Did your dad come home?'

'No,' came the usual answer.

Sometimes such troubles left Yufen too tired and lazy to do anything but stare at the television and lose herself in the comfort of food. But for the most part, living in the dorm gave her enough relative respite to start thinking seriously about the Lord.

Most days after work, Yufen returned to the dorm and turned on some soft orchestral music. She sat down and rubbed her legs. Paying the painful price for a full day of standing, they reminded her that they had not yet fully recovered from the accident.

Letting herself unwind to the melodic serenade of her CD player, Yufen started to read the Bible. She read slowly, drinking every word deeply. Though her mind easily absorbed the concepts of the Bible, her heart was more obstinate. She was committed to her church activities – and often arrived before her leaders did – but she could not yet profess unswerving faith in God.

Elisabeth went to the dorm often, and as Yufen sat comfortably on her bed, they chatted quietly, like old friends. Their talks no longer centred around Yufen's cyclic family problems; Elisabeth discovered that Yufen not only enjoyed sharing what she was learning from the Bible, but she could also movingly express how she saw God working in her life. It was as if her stubborn, cold exterior was melting, and a warm, tender and joyful heart was starting to peek out.

Of course, pain and frustration still welled up

sometimes. Many of these times, Yufen would come home and find a bouquet of flowers waiting for her. Tears would drip down her face as she read the brief note that accompanied them: 'Love, Sister Wei.'

One day, not long after Yufen had a session with her Christian counsellor at MacKay Memorial Hospital, she was relaxing in the dorm on one of her few days off. After tidying up a little, she turned on some music and sat down to rest. She contentedly propped up her sore feet and stuffed a juicy piece of pineapple into her mouth.

Without warning, she started to weep.

She wailed with her mouth wide open, revealing the half-chewed pineapple still inside. She wailed so loudly that she had to stumble to the windows and close them, so as not to alarm the neighbours. For the next thirty minutes, miseries and memories flowed out of her through a torrent of tears.

Just as she began to regain her composure, the phone rang. It was Elisabeth, who hadn't heard from Yufen for a few days and wanted to see how her counselling session had gone.

'Yufen, how are you?' Elisabeth asked sweetly.

'I ... just cried miserably,' Yufen replied, erupting into tears again. For a few minutes, Elisabeth listened silently to Yufen's sobs. Finally, Yufen resumed: 'I realized that I'm so lonely. So empty. All the burdens suddenly became so real and strong ...'

Elisabeth listened empathetically, thanking the Lord for using her to comfort Yufen at just the right time.

'This is good,' Elisabeth said. 'You wash your body every day, and sometimes you need to take your heart out and wash it too.'

Even though Yufen was generally an emotional person, she had never before experienced such an uncontrollable feeling – like something outside of herself was penetrating her heart. It wasn't until later that she found words for the feeling: the Holy Spirit.

One September day, Elisabeth suddenly thought of Yufen and went to the dorm. The conversation began unremarkably; Yufen talked about her family, her loneliness, then started to cry.

'But,' she said, drying her tears, 'in the dorm I can read the Bible and meet the Lord.'

Elisabeth looked into her eyes. She knew it was time.

'Will you put your whole trust in the Lord? Are you willing to get baptized?'

Yufen gravely considered the question. Indeed, she wanted to know God more deeply and to know how to rest in him.

Together, they prayed about it. Elisabeth rarely pushed people to get baptized quickly – lest the person rescind the decision later, as often was the case. But this time she felt the need to be firm. To her it was clear that Yufen was just afraid of verbalizing an eternal commitment to God. She had found it difficult to trust people, and even more difficult to trust the Lord. So Elisabeth asked again.

'Can we prepare to have you baptized at the end of October? I really think you should do it.'

A pause.

'OK. If you think I'm ready to do it, I'll get baptized.'

Even after the baptism, Yufen did not feel fully secure in her faith. Some parts of Buddhist thinking were still lodged in her mind, and she found it impossible to trust in the Lord completely for a reason she could not pinpoint.

In the next six months, she moved back home and came to the sober realization that their family could no longer afford to live there. She prayed over the decision and found a nice, significantly cheaper apartment fit for two: Yufen and her daughter. Yufen informed Kai about her intentions, but he refused to acknowledge that his wife wanted a separation.

On their last day together, Yufen immersed herself in last-minute packing, frustrated by her husband's lack of cooperation.

'The movers will be here soon,' she said, turning to her son and daughter. When she turned back around, her husband was gone.

Once all their belongings had been moved into the new apartment, Yufen began the equally tedious task of unpacking. She thought little about Kai, figuring that he would spend the night at his brother's apartment, as he often did after a drinking binge. But at around eleven o'clock that night, Kai appeared at their door. He was covered in mud, blood and the smell of alcohol.

As he passed out on their wicker couch, Yufen continued to unpack, ignoring him.

'Right in the middle of this hectic move, and he has to go and get drunk. Instead of helping, he brings more chaos!'

Yufen left her husband on the couch and went to bed. In the middle of the night, she woke up to go to the bathroom. And gasped. The toilet was full of dark, red blood.

Shocked, she sent Kai to the hospital. She eventually discovered that he had been taken home that evening by a sugar-cane seller who had seen his body in a ditch. Kai had staggered towards the ditch in order to relieve himself but had toppled over in the process, badly injuring himself. Thus began Yufen Wang and Kai Lee's period of separation.

After the move was complete, Yufen and her son went back to their old apartment one last time. The apartment was barren, save the family's now-empty ancestor shelf, which had been neglected ever since Yufen started going to church.

In front of the ancestor shelf was the crumpled figure of

Kai. He had wrapped himself in curtains and passed out while facing the ancestor shelf, as if performing some sort of religious rite that could bring his family back.

For the last time, the apartment echoed with sobs.

* * *

The summer holidays had come, and Katrina brought her two children, Matthias and Tabea, to the McDonalds where she and Mei read the Bible together. As the two children played with Mei's daughters, Mei admired their pleasant behaviour and thought about how rowdy her own children could be when she and Katrina were trying to read the Bible in her home. She hoped to imitate Katrina's patient parenting style: the way she was not too strict, but not too lenient.

Mei came to realize that she appreciated Katrina not only for what she had to teach, but also for the kind of person she was. Her care for Mei was genuine, and she did not invest in Mei's life simply to see Mei 'progress' spiritually. It was through Katrina that Mei began to really notice the difference between believers and non-believers.

Gift-giving was customary in Taiwan, but was almost always tinted with an ulterior motive – the expectation that one would eventually receive something in return. Katrina, in contrast, was unconditionally generous. She often came to Mei's home bearing small toys or second-hand clothes.

In accepting these gifts, Mei never felt obliged to wonder, 'What does this person want from me?' Through Katrina's generosity, Mei began to understand the nature of God's grace. Sometimes Mei cried until daybreak, confessing her sins to God. She realized that without God's mercy, she would have agonized over her mistakes for the rest of her life.

What she began to experience was very different from the beliefs she had known all her life. The gods of Taiwan had conditions. If they blessed you, joss money had to be burned and offerings had to be purchased in order to pay them back for their favour.

Even though Mei had never been as devoted to idols as Ling had, she and her husband – like most working-class Taiwanese – were used to welcoming them into their lives whenever an appropriate occasion arose.

One day Mei wearily confessed to Katrina, 'Recently things have got really bad at home. I feel this tightness in my chest, and we have a lot of fights in the house. My kids keep on crying and fighting with each other.'

'Well, let's see ...' Katrina said, starting to ask Mei some questions that would help her identify the source of the problem. In the process, Mei mentioned that her husband had recently purchased an idol from a temple. Formed in the shape of two copulating pigs, it was said to make the men who worshipped it more virile.

'Ohhh ...' Mei said. 'Maybe it has something to do with this idol.'

The two women then prayed fervently, commanding the idol's spirit to leave Mei's house. At the end of the prayer, Mei opened her eyes, visibly relieved.

'That's much better. I immediately felt ... a release,' she said.

Mei confronted her husband about the idol and with astonishing willingness, he returned the idol to the temple. He even got his money back.

Katrina's husband Marc Schachtler rode a taxi to the 3,000-member Bread of Life Christian Church, an independent, charismatic church that had grown unusually quickly compared to most other Taiwanese churches. On the way, Marc did what most missionaries would do: He invited the taxi driver to church.

'Me?' the man said, astonished. 'I could never go to that church. I'm not good enough. I'm not a white-collar person.'

Fortunately, Mei Chen, unlike most working-class people in Taiwan, had the opportunity to understand the gospel before such a preconception could deter her. Her contact with Bread of Life began through an acquaintance of Lillian Tsai, and she was invited to a Bread of Life small group in the summer of 1999.

Nothing spectacular occurred at the small group. Nothing, that is, until the small group leader abruptly invited Mei to be baptized.

'Next month we have a baptism service,' said the leader. 'It's special because we don't do it every month. If you want to be baptized, you can do it then.'

Mei pondered the possibility. Several people urged her to do it. Finally, she agreed.

The decision didn't come without regret. The baptism service was to take place in the afternoon, and that morning she began to worry that her husband wouldn't let her out of the house.

'I've already agreed to get baptized. I can't just not show up.' But she thought about how her father-in-law had repeatedly growled at her, 'Don't take the kids there ... don't lead them in that direction ...' She also thought about how her husband had beaten her, shouting, 'What kind of church are you going to?!' when she refused to offer incense at their family altar.

Fortunately, Big Chang worked that afternoon, and Mei was able to peaceably leave the house with her children. Since she had never attended a Bread of Life service before, she was surprised to see so many people there. The church members were lively and supportive as the handful of people being baptized that afternoon were led into the baptismal one by one.

As Mei stood in the water, her heart was at peace.

'So this is what's it's like to feel holy,' she thought.

After the service, Mei rushed home, politely pushing past crowds of people who tried to congratulate her. As she walked out of Bread of Life's doors, she couldn't help but imagine what her husband would do to her if he happened to return home before she did.

Notes

1. Chiang Kai-shek – leader of China's Nationalist Kuomingtang Party. He fled to Taiwan after being overthrown by the Communist Party. After taking over Taiwan's government and imposing martial laws across the island, he continued to claim authority as the official ruler of China.

Part 5

New Roots

Make sure there is no man or woman, clan or tribe among you today whose heart turns away from the Lord our God to go and worship the gods of those nations; make sure there is no root among you that produces such bitter poison.   Deuteronomy 29:18

I will sprinkle clean water on you, and you will be clean; I will cleanse you from all your impurities and from all your idols. I will give you a new heart and put a new spirit in you; I will remove from you your heart of stone and give you a heart of flesh.   Ezekiel 36:25–26

Chapter 15

When poison ivy grows wild for many years, its gnarly roots can start to look like monstrous caterpillars several inches in diameter, choking virtually everything within their reach.[1] But as undesirable as the ivy may be, few people are eager to eradicate it themselves. When touched, its sap causes excruciating rashes. When burned and inhaled, it can even lead to death.[2]

So it was with the poisonously sinful habits and thought patterns of Ling Hu, Yufen Wang and Mei Chen – since they had spent most of their lives ignorant of God's truth, the vines that entangled them would not simply let go.

The reason poison ivy is so difficult to remove is that its roots – a long, dense maze of reddish fibres – penetrate deeply into the earth. Unless every single part of the poisonous root is removed from the ground, the ivy is likely to re-sprout in the most inconvenient places.[3] And at the most inopportune times.

To Mei's relief, Big Chang was not home when she returned from the Bread of Life Christian Church as a baptized believer. Although she would never again attend a church service there, she went back to the Bread of Life small group a few times. During one of their prayer meetings, Katrina agreed to go along.

As Mei, Katrina, and two other women prayed, Mei began to feel overwhelmingly dizzy.

'There are demons ...' she proclaimed, swaying involuntarily. Suddenly, the other women knew what they were dealing with. Fervently, they prayed that Mei would be cut off from her past sins and would no longer be bound by the spirits.

Mei felt torn, as if the spirits were wrestling to stay inside her body. The fight was long and hard, but the women kept praying, passionately ordering the demons to leave Mei's body. Finally, the prayers quieted.

'It's gone,' Mei said.

Although the spirits paid her brief, occasional visits after that, they were much less consuming. And whenever Mei sensed their presence, she would worship the Lord in song and prayer. The more she got to know Jesus, the more joy started to seep into her heart. Once cold and impenetrable, it was becoming a heart of flesh. For the first time in her life, Mei had hope. She had someone to lean on. She had love.

Mei, who had always been well aware of her own shortcomings, now understood her profound need for God's forgiveness. But she found it excruciatingly difficult to forgive others – others who, in her lifetime of sorrow, had abused her in almost every imaginable way. To forgive them seemed as counter-intuitive as intentionally embarking on another chilling hike through Ali Mountain.

'How can I forgive my husband when he keeps on hitting me and hurting the children?' she thought, diving into an even thicker sludge of anger. 'I just don't have the strength.' Nor did Mei have the strength to leave him.

'This is very, very harmful to your daughters,' Katrina had warned sombrely, 'and unless the Lord does a miracle in his life these problems usually get worse rather than better.'

Mei had hoped that Katrina would be wrong. She hoped that taking the girls to sleep in a separate bedroom with her would lessen Big Chang's chances of hurting them. The solution seemed to work for a time. But then her husband's carnal desires became so overpowering that he devoured every possible opportunity to be alone with his two- and three-year-old daughters: when Mei was busy cooking, when she turned her head away for just a few minutes ...

Whenever his desires went frustratingly unfulfilled, his temper would erupt. Once when he came home drunk, he brought with him an expression so foreboding that his daughters ran and hid under a table. Mei bravely tried to talk with him. But instead of calming him, her words infuriated him, and he beat her with a chair, then threatened her with a knife. On another occasion, when a normal-sized kitchen knife did not seem threatening enough, he used a gardening sickle to frighten her.

Sometimes when Big Chang came home drunk and bruised from a fight, Mei followed the example of her daughters – she ran to the bedroom and locked the door.

'Open the door! OPEN THE DOOR!' her husband roared, pounding on the door. He stormed out of the house. Just as Mei was about to feel relieved, the bedroom window shattered. After several more bare-fisted punches, Big Chang pulled his body through the glass. Then he swung at his wife.

'Dear Lord, if all he did was beat me, then I would just stay. But what he does to the kids ... When can I take my children out of this place? When can I leave? I just can't live like this any more. I really, really can't.'

Mei had already cried through the night several evenings in a row, and her body was growing weak from the realization that, after all that she had been through, her innocent daughters were being siphoned into a similar cycle of abuse.

She wanted to run away. But so crippling was the fear of

her husband and the unknown that Mei could not even get near the door to her house.

'If you run away, I know that in two or three days, you'll be back,' her husband threatened. 'And if you come back, I'll humiliate you. I'll hit you. I'll beat you even worse than now.'

'Either that, or I'll just die on the streets,' Mei thought.

To ensure a successful escape, Mei clearly needed someone to pave the way for her. Katrina generally opposed divorce, but after much prayer, she decided to help Mei escape. Lillian helped make legal enquiries and, after weaving through a mass of red tape, decided to take Mei's case to the Taipei County Bureau of Social Affairs. She made sure that Mei could undoubtedly prove her husband's crime, and that all of the evidence was still valid.

Katrina advised Mei to entrust her most important belongings to a woman in her small group – little by little, week by week, so that her husband wouldn't notice that she was packing up to leave. Like a prisoner trying to dig an escape passage with a plastic fork, Mei had to make every move slowly and secretly.

Katrina knew that the government would only offer Mei physical protection for three months, after which she would be forced to live on her own. Fortunately, she also knew of someone who could help: Elisabeth Weinmann.

Elisabeth felt that it was time to open a dorm for single mothers, but she lacked one thing. She needed a capable dorm leader.

When she asked Ling Hu to move in and take charge of the dorm, Ling hesitated but eventually agreed. Elisabeth was overjoyed. She had feared that Ling was becoming spiritually stagnant, especially since she had little quiet time at home to read her Bible. As was the case in most

Taiwanese homes, the blaring television often competed for Ling's attention.

As Elisabeth prepared Ling's room for her arrival, she affectionately gazed at its furnishings. 'I hope she can really read her Bible while sitting on this chair,' she thought. 'I hope that this desk will give her the space to really prepare her Bible studies.'

When Ling moved into the dorm in February 1999, she immediately felt liberated from the pressure of living with her parents, of being constantly reminded about her mounting debts. Like Yufen, she began to read her Bible more in the quietness of the dorm.

Because Ling now lived only two floors above Elisabeth's apartment, she started visiting Elisabeth in the mornings before work. In what would become an almost daily ritual, they spent an hour praying together for the growing shop-workers' fellowship, as well as for Ling's personal problems. Often, Ling would pray on and on unless Elisabeth interjected.

'I also want to pray. Can you let me pray too?' Elisabeth said, half-jokingly. In the history of her ministry, she had never met anyone with such a deep love for prayer.

Equally strong was Ling's desire for close fellowship, though Elisabeth sadly noticed that even Ling's own small-group members did not fully accept her. So whenever Ling came to her apartment, Elisabeth reminded herself to be patient – even when listening to Ling was as monotonous as watching tumbleweed skip across a desert plain.

Elisabeth wished that she could help Ling solve her money problems, get her children back, and cleanse her mind of all Buddhist thoughts so that she could focus on her relationship with God and her role as a small-group leader. Yet she knew that only God could make Ling change, and that he would do it in his timing. Meanwhile, Elisabeth simply loved.

The single mothers' dorm turned out to be as transient as a halfway house, with people constantly moving in and out of its four rooms. On average, the dorm housed six to seven people, including several children.

Amid the chaos, Ling's steady temperament proved to be a great asset. Her first three room-mates were women she had already ministered to personally. One of them, a pregnant mother named Feng, was particularly desperate for a place to stay. She had just escaped from a husband who drank, beat her, and accumulated substantial debts through gambling.

One day, in the middle of a co-workers' meeting in Elisabeth's apartment, a shout bellowed from the staircase. Someone rushed out to take a look.

'Feng's husband is here!'

Quickly, Elisabeth instructed Ling to go to the man. Experienced in keeping a straight face in the flames of conflict, she managed to extinguish the man's anger and convince him to leave.

Even though Ling was capable of assisting the other women in the single mothers' dorm, she seemed to be powerless when it came to her own problems.

'Do you think I should take my husband to court to fight for custody?' she repeatedly asked Elisabeth, who unfailingly responded with a cautious 'Yes.'

Yet Elisabeth's encouragement never brought Ling any closer to initiating any legal action. She had finally freed herself from the incessant quarrels that characterized her marriage, and she was not eager to engage in further dispute. Instead, she continued to devise secretive ways of maintaining contact with her children. Sometimes, Elisabeth even served as her go-between. Elisabeth would call the children at home, and if Yan answered, she would immediately hang up. If he didn't, she would ask:

'Is your father at home? Can you talk with your mother right now?'

Elisabeth also invited the children to her apartment and let them come to fellowship outings for free. But these limited interactions were not ideal, so Ling continued to pray for a solution.

Deep in her heart, Ling still adhered to the traditional notion that divine favour could be earned, as in temples. She believed that if she read the Bible, prayed often, and served as a small-group leader, God would surely give her the children and eradicate her debt problem.

Ling's debts were so substantial and her credit record so tainted that banks refused to continue lending her money. In order to keep up with her galloping debt payments – 40,000 Taiwanese dollars per month for her family's biao-hui alone – she raced to borrow money from anyone who still trusted her. She borrowed from one of the single mums in her care and failed to pay it back. She was so desperate that she even made enquiries about 'underground banks' run by gangsters.

The final straw came when Elisabeth prepared to embark on a half-year trip home to Germany. Before she left, Yufen came up with the idea of collecting a special small-group offering for Elisabeth's ageing mother. Enthusiastic about the idea, the small group collected $6,000 and entrusted it to Ling, their leader. But instead of giving it to Elisabeth, she used it to pay off part of her most urgent debt.

While Elisabeth was still in Germany, she felt suddenly and inexplicably compelled to call Ling. When Ling picked up the phone, she started to cry.

'I just don't want to go to small group ...' she wailed. 'I just want to give up ... I don't want to do ministry any more. I don't want to be a small-group leader any more ...'

Ling cried about the rumours that assailed her, both at work and at church. She was so burdened by the judgmental stares that she even missed a small-group meeting that she was meant to lead.

One final problem topped Ling's heap of grievances. In January, both she and Yufen had started working together at SOGO, one of the largest department store chains in Taiwan. They became close friends. But because they had very different ideas about how things should be done at work, their relationship had begun to sour.

In the heat of their disagreements, Yufen started to admire the way Ling remained calm and refrained from reacting too quickly or intensely. And as she and Ling reconciled, she asked God for help in controlling her own emotions.

'Mum, you really have an explosive temper!' her son Bao had once said to her. Yufen thought about Matthew 5:16: 'In the same way, let your light shine before men, that they may see your good deeds and praise your Father in heaven.'

'I'm not a light to my family,' she thought. 'I'm more like a raging fire!'

The more Yufen got involved in church, the more she saw how bad tempers – especially those of top church leaders – impaired many ministries. She thought about how, during her earlier days in the church, she had even seen a seminary student strike a child in anger. 'I don't want to be associated with rotten people like that!' she had thought at the time.

Yufen had also noticed that Elisabeth's co-workers' meetings were riddled with an unpredictable concoction of moods. Since many of the co-workers came from broken family backgrounds, they were often used to expressing discontent by shouting, for this is what they had been taught at home.

Once, when Elisabeth asked a certain member of the

fellowship to lead music at one of their outings, a particular co-worker adamantly objected.

'I don't think this is a good way to do it,' she asserted.

'Well I think she can do it, even though she's not a small-group leader yet,' said another co-worker.

'I really don't think this is the best way!' The first co-worker stood up, suddenly furious. 'So I won't join this outing! I won't do anything!!' she shouted, storming out of Elisabeth's apartment.

Elisabeth had grown weary of such childish emotional outbursts, that sometimes occurred as often as every week.

'Well, I'd better go home to Germany, then,' she thought on occasion. But then she reminded herself: 'This is just something I need to go through. I must not let the enemy get a foothold by accepting any sin or weakness in my own walk.'

So even when 'offended' co-workers ignored Elisabeth's phone calls, she refused to give up. Emotional outbursts occurred frequently among Taiwanese Christians, she reasoned, because of the spiritual darkness that clouded the whole nation. In her mind, the spiritual attacks that frequented her co-workers indicated that the enemy felt threatened by them.

Even though some of the co-workers seemed impervious to Elisabeth's humble attempts to appease them when they were angry, most were profoundly affected by her actions in the long run.

Yufen, for example, tried her best to follow Elisabeth's example. Once when she still lived in the dorm, her roommate came home shouting curses after being stood up by a friend. Then this professing Christian started turning over furniture and throwing chairs around.

'This isn't the kind of behaviour a church sister should have!' Yufen exclaimed, infuriated. They fought, and in the end Yufen abruptly left the apartment. Eventually though, Yufen felt convicted to go back and apologize.

'Sorry. I shouldn't have lost my temper,' she confessed.

Yufen began to recognize that the problems in her own life were caused or exacerbated by her temper. She began to see that what mattered most in her life wasn't the misfortune that framed her life, but rather the picture she chose to paint within it.

The picture of Mei's life was bleak. A beast attacked her from behind, and a precipice waited for her in front. She had heard that beyond the edge lay a deep pool of water that would break her fall. But she wouldn't be able to see it until she jumped.

'Don't worry, Elisabeth has a place where you and your two children can live,' Katrina assured her. 'If you leave now, things will be OK. The kids are still small. There will be people who will help you take care of them.'

'Really? But could a place like that really exist?' Mei wondered sceptically, and for good reason: secluded and without any first-hand access to information, she knew very little about the options that lay ahead; she was even prohibited from taking the children to a nearby park to play. And she remained convinced that, if she tried to take her problem to the authorities, they would ultimately rule in her husband's favour and send her home.

One day, without thinking much of it, Mei ambled to a nearby betel-nut stand to chat with a friend who worked there. She took her two children with her, as was typical for a working-class woman who wanted to pay a casual visit to a friend. The mood was light as others sat around them, joking over beers and cigarettes.

Then Mei looked up. Her husband charged at her.

'You can't come out here by yourself! You can't bring the children over here until I give you permission!'

Silence. By the smell of his breath, it was clear that he was drunk. He picked up someone's beer bottle and smashed it. Mei quickly took her children by the hand and got up to go home.

Mei walked ahead, trying to avoid her husband's hateful gaze. She held Little Hui tightly in her arms. Suddenly, Big Chang shoved Ting-ting to the ground, and the girl fell face-first onto the pavement. Though her head was grazed, she bravely stood up and continued walking. Another shove sent Mei and Little Hui to the ground.

'This can't go on ...' Mei thought.

Big Chang hurled the dustbin lid at Mei's face. Her nose bled profusely, but he was not finished yet. This time, he seemed ready to kill. His brother and sister tried to restrain him and protect Mei, but he overpowered them both. His father ran to the phone and called the police.

Big Chang grabbed his wife and reached for a screwdriver.

'I'M GOING TO PUT THIS THROUGH YOUR NECK!'

At the time, the police were rarely called upon to resolve domestic disputes, which were usually regarded as private affairs beyond the scope of their legal authority. Even though Mei's father-in-law had long been aware of his son's elicit behaviour, he had refrained from calling for help until now.

'I'M GOING TO PUT THIS THROUGH YOUR NECK!'

Fortunately, the police arrived before Big Chang could carry out his threat. After assessing the situation, the officer calmly took Mei outside.

'You need to move out ... Collect all the things that you need and either pack them in a small bag or give them to a friend ...' he said, telling her to report to the police station after three days.

Mei gathered her national identity card, her health insurance card, some clothes and books, and sent them to Ali Mountain – all the while telling her daughters nothing, fearing that they would accidentally inform their father about her plans.

Then came the big day. To her dismay, Big Chang refused to go to work, as if he knew what she was about to do. Mei was wondering what to do next when the phone rang. It was his boss, ordering him to report to work immediately.

As soon as Big Chang left the house, Mei frantically stuffed clothes into a bag. She tore up and threw away all documents and phone numbers that could help Big Chang find her. Carrying just enough money for one taxi ride, she hailed a cab. Her children, anxious and confused, pulled back.

'Mum, where are we going?'

'I don't wanna! I don't wanna!'

But after years of praying and waiting, Mei had finally made up her mind. She cajoled her two daughters into the taxi and, once they were all safely inside, told the driver to take them to the police.

About three years had passed since Mei Chen had called the Helping Hands hotline in suicidal desperation. After reporting to the police station, she was escorted to a government safe house, where she would be required to stay for at least two weeks. Nobody was allowed to contact her there. But Mei could make outgoing calls, and she told Katrina about all that had happened, starting with her husband's threat.

Meanwhile, Big Chang also busied himself with phone calls. He had dug through the dustbin and had found the phone numbers that Mei had tried to destroy. After piecing together the bits of paper, he called Lillian Tsai.

'Do you know where my wife went?' he asked calmly. Lillian was both shocked by and afraid to hear his voice.

'How did he get my number?' she wondered. 'Uh-oh, he knows where our office is ...'

Cautiously, Lillian tried to assure him that she still saw him as a friend; she remembered how Mei had said several times that she hoped her husband would always remain open to accepting Christ, whatever the outcome of their marriage. But Big Chang continued to press the issue.

'Do you know where my wife is? I really want her to come back.'

'Well, I haven't been to your house for a long time, right?' said Lillian.

'Yeah. But could you think of where she might be?'

'Well I already let Katrina handle everything, and she's the one who's been helping your wife, teaching her how to raise children and do the housework better, right?'

'Right.'

'So I really don't know where your wife is.' Indeed, the whereabouts of the government safe house was a well-kept secret.

Afraid that Big Chang had not been satisfied with her answer, Lillian mentally prepared herself for a confrontation with him at her office. But such planning was unnecessary, because Big Chang had already managed to track down a more viable source.

'Please give me my wife's phone number,' he said to Katrina over the phone. Although he was polite to her as usual, she detected something different in his voice. A certain sadness.

'I'm sorry but I can't give it to you because I don't have it. I'm not allowed to contact Mei at all,' Katrina replied cordially.

His first call would not be the last. Sometimes when he called Katrina, he let his voice rise in a crescendo of anger; most of the time, though, he sounded vacantly desperate.

'It was all her fault. I saved her from prostitution ... She was a bad woman ... I never abused my daughters. She made it all up. It was all part of her fantasy ... I'm really not a bad guy at all ... Please give me her number ... All I want is my wife back. I'm sad that she's gone, and I really want her to come back ... Please, just give me her phone number!'

So incessant were the calls that Katrina expected Big Chang or one of his cronies to show up at her doorstep one day. Fortunately, that day never came.

A dark, desperate ambience filled the basement of the government safe house. Some women spontaneously burst into sobs. Others gloomily nursed bruises that covered their entire bodies. But Mei felt relieved, almost joyful. 'Running away wasn't that hard after all,' she thought. 'Why did I think it would be so hard?'

She thought about her last pregnancy and how Big Chang had ordered her to get an abortion when he found out it was another girl. When she refused, he threatened, then beat her. In the end he hit her womb so hard that she started to bleed.

'I might as well get an abortion. Who knows what Big Chang will do anyway ... ?' she thought mournfully. Then she started to pray: 'God, please take the spirit of my baby to heaven ...'

In retrospect, Mei realized that if she had given birth to the baby, she would not have been able to run away so soon. For this she was grateful, as the safe house was a much-needed respite from her agonies.

The safe house's broken residents usually ate meals cooked by volunteers, though Mei sometimes helped out so that she could earn $100 per meal. As she cooked, her two daughters sat quietly on a sofa while other children darted around them.

When Mei fled, Elisabeth happened to be in Germany, and the church pastor insisted on waiting for Elisabeth's

374 Dead Women Walking

return before allowing Mei into the dorm. So during Mei's extended stay at the safe house, she observed an almost constant flow of residents to and from the twenty or so bunk beds. One of them was a beautiful but sombre young girl who caught Mei's eye.

'It's so hot. Why are you still wearing long pants?' Mei asked her, handing her a dress she had found in a pile of donated clothing. 'Here, try this on.'

'I don't want to wear a dress,' the girl replied. 'People will take advantage of me if I wear a dress.' She went on to explain how she used to enjoy dressing up – until her mother started associating with men who repeatedly raped her.

On a seemingly normal Sunday in July – the one day in the week when Mei was allowed to venture outside the safe house – she took her children to church, as usual. She dared not let them venture out of her sight in order to attend Sunday school, so they sat through the worship service together and then immediately returned home.

When they got back, Mei called Katrina. To her surprise, there was news: Elisabeth had returned from Germany. Mei eagerly wrote down Elisabeth's phone number and dialled.

When Mei and her two daughters stepped out of the taxi, they looked like lost refugees. Elisabeth immediately noticed the tentativeness in Mei's voice, as if one wrong word would relegate her to life on the streets.

'Thank you, Sister Wei. Thank you, thank you,' Mei repeated profusely, making no effort to hide her vulnerability. When she attempted a smile it seemed unnatural, like that of a cheap plastic doll. Even her children were eerily quiet, Elisabeth observed.

'I want to love these children and give them everything I have,' Elisabeth thought to herself. 'I want them to know that life is not so bitter, that there are joyful things in this world, and that it's OK for them to just be themselves.'

She paused and took another look at Mei. Somehow, though few words had been exchanged between them, she felt that the helpless woman who stood before her would end up being a dear friend.

As soon as Elisabeth had escorted the family to the fifth-floor apartment, Mei felt uneasy, as if something inside of her was telling her to turn around and run. Her anxious thoughts were interrupted as Elisabeth invited her to come over for dinner later that evening. Over their meal Elisabeth asked Mei about her background and her relationship with Katrina.

Mei quickly discovered that Elisabeth genuinely loved to listen. Within their first few conversations, Mei vividly talked about her third marriage. Then, as if peeling an onion, layer by layer, she began to share tear-stricken stories from the past, from her former work as a prostitute to her abused childhood to the vices of her youth.

Even though Katrina had helped Mei get a restraining order on Big Chang, the fears she experienced after leaving her second husband crept back into her life: What if he spotted her on the street? What if he found and kidnapped the children?

Mei had mistakenly left the proof of her care-giving certification in her husband's home, so she was unable to get a job right away. This made her ineligible for national health insurance, which she needed since Little Hui suffered from a heart condition.

'I don't have any money to pay, but can you please give me insurance?' she begged the clerk at the government office. 'See, the situation is ...'

'We can't do that. Go back to your husband and get him to pay it for you,' the clerk answered curtly. In silent fury, Mei stormed off.

With nowhere else to turn, Mei often found herself ringing the doorbell to Elisabeth's apartment.

'Do you have time for me?' she asked meekly, like a daughter yearning for her mother's affection and trust.

'Yes, yes, of course!' Elisabeth replied.

Then came the typical barrage of questions:

'Do you think I should buy this notebook for the children, or should I wait? Which kindergarten do you think is better? Can I borrow some money to get a jacket for my daughter? Do I have permission to buy a pair of shoes?'

Since Mei had virtually no money, she often borrowed from Elisabeth. She learned to manage her spending and always returned the money as soon as possible. Yet sometimes she felt so frustrated with her financial predicament that she locked herself in the bathroom and sobbed before the Lord. 'God, I really can't pay for this. Please help me.'

Elisabeth prayed with Mei every day, but occasionally Mei felt so impatient that she found it difficult to join in. 'I still don't know how I'm going to survive, and you want to pray? What I really want is help with our money problems. Prayer, prayer – what use is it?'

In these most difficult times, Mei didn't want to attend fellowship activities either – though this was technically a requirement for people living in the dorms.

'I don't like their style,' she rationalized. As usual, Elisabeth did not give up.

'Come to our meeting tonight, OK?' she reminded Mei every week.

'I can't ... Well, we'll see,' came the half-hearted reply.

'You really need to come to our activities,' Elisabeth insisted, pointing out that the meetings took place merely two floors below Mei's apartment.

'But I'm afraid that if I leave the children alone up here, they'll be scared and cry.' This, actually, was true. Since the meetings were designed for shop-workers, they often ended after midnight, so her daughters were both unwilling to go and unwilling to be left behind.

Despite Mei's dogmatic refusal to go to church, Elisabeth's care for her did not waver. 'Whenever you need something to eat, you can just look in my refrigerator and take whatever you need,' Elisabeth said to her. The government gave Mei rations of rice and noodles, but apart from that, she and her children often had nothing else to eat.

Another time, just when her children's whopping $30,000 kindergarten fees were due, the pastor's wife from her former church in Chungho contacted her.

'Do you have enough to live by?' she asked. 'I have some money here for you that was taken as a love offering.'

Despite Mei's financial woes, she initially found it difficult to break certain habits. Sometimes she took the children to karaoke evenings that lasted until one or two in the morning. But as soon as Elisabeth discovered that Mei had gone out, she would call Mei like a concerned mother.

'Mei, where did you take kids?' she asked sweetly, lovingly.

'Uh, karaoke.'

'Mei, you can't do that. It's not good for your health.' Her gentle voice was so difficult to disobey.

'That Sister Wei,' she thought. 'She must be so close to God. Otherwise, how could any person love me so much?' 'Sorry, I have to go home,' Mei dutifully said to her friends.

The generosity and kindness of the Christians who surrounded Mei were slowly, almost imperceptibly cracking through her hard protective shell. One of these Christians was her room-mate, Ling Hu.

The first time Mei met Ling, she was automatically taken by Ling's ebullient friendliness. Whenever Ling got home from work, usually after ten, she always invited Mei to pray, chat and read the Bible with her. Her enthusiastic offers were difficult to refuse, especially since Mei deeply, quietly longed to be accepted – a dream so grand that it seemed impossible to her at the time. Impossible, for she could hardly accept herself.

Mei swept the floor fastidiously, determined to do a good job since, for the time being, Elisabeth was allowing her free rent in exchange for her janitorial services. As she thrashed the broom around, her youngest daughter shot her a concerned look.

'Mama, can you help us find a new Daddy?' said Little Hui. Mei froze.

'What did you say?'

'A new Daddy can help you make money and sweep the floor.'

On hearing this Mei's oldest daughter brimmed with anger. She was already beginning to have a new-found understanding of the past.

'Why do you want a new Daddy?!' Ting-ting exploded. 'If we have a new Daddy, he will make fun of you and get mad at you and hit you!'

Even though Little Hui never again dared to bring up such a suggestion, her sentiments had correctly encapsulated Mei's own worries about the future: How would she manage to raise her daughters alone? How long would she survive without the love of a man?

Gradually Mei found solace as she got involved in a love relationship that, for the first time, was not destined for destruction. Since she was still unemployed, she had a lot of time to read the Bible, pray and get to know the Lord who had pursued her for so long. In reading Streams in the Desert, the same devotional book that had played an important role in Ling's spiritual life, Mei began to feel stripped of her worries. Reborn, even. She thanked God for bringing her to a refuge where she was not ostracized as a single mother, and she asked him to guide her next steps.

Notes

1. www.forestry.msu.edu/extension/ExtDocs/posioniv.htm
2. www.en.wikipedia.org/wiki/Poison_ivy
3. www.forestry.msu.edu/extension/ExtDocs/posioniv.htm

Chapter 16

August 2000

The ride was abnormally quiet as Ling Hu perched on the back of Elisabeth's motorbike. Usually, she chatted non-stop on the way to their department store visitations, but this time she said nothing as the scooter puttered along.

Her mind was on many things: her children, her debts, her shame ... Though her hands went through the motions of passing out magazines, just as before, she had no heart left to give to the people she met. Though she had once been proactive in getting to know the shop-workers they encountered, she now served as little more than Elisabeth's shadow.

Still, she insisted on taking every Thursday off work to help Elisabeth.

'Lord, I want to serve you for the rest of my days and share the gospel with non-believers, just as Paul shared the gospel with the Gentiles,' she had prayed early on in her Christian walk. And even when her own spiritual life was muddied by depression, she at least continued to swim forward through the muck.

She also continued to lead a small group. Though the content of her Bible studies still had much room for improvement, the small group itself teemed with life.

Never before had Elisabeth seen a group that cared so genuinely, prayed so vibrantly, and gave so generously. Their meetings often lasted until one or two in the morning.

Ling constantly encouraged the group members to challenge themselves, grow and serve. She had inherited from Elisabeth a knack for framing suggestions so sweetly and beautifully that it was difficult to say no. Ling was particularly keen about financial giving, which had played a large role in her religious life before becoming a Christian. But her ideas were not always appreciated by her small-group members, especially after they discovered that she had pocketed their offering once.

Ling was also passionate about prayer – though it was hard for her to keep it in proper perspective. 'If I pray hard enough for someone, then God will love that person more,' she reasoned. Also, she subconsciously felt that her prayers deserved to be answered.

'How come your sales have been so good if you don't *baibai* any more?' her co-workers had asked when Ling first started going to church.

'Well, because Jesus is blessing me even more,' she replied, reminiscent of the way she used to extol other gods. In those days Ling was proud of herself for being successful at work – the result, she figured, of being obedient to God.

But eventually Ling realized that God did not always answer her prayers in the ways that she would have hoped. The people she prayed for did not immediately accept Christ, and her debts did not magically disappear. Something seemed terribly amiss, though the answer was not far from her grasp.

A Bible story that had affected her profoundly was the healing of a blind man after Jesus was asked if he or his parents were to blame for his blindness. Something inside of Ling had shifted as she read Jesus' answer in John 9:3:

' "Neither this man nor his parents sinned," said Jesus, "but this happened so that the work of God might be displayed in his life." '

For forty years, Ling had believed that her troubles were the result of sins committed in past lives, and she had given herself to religion in order to prevent further suffering in subsequent lives; there was no room for more sins, more mistakes. After so many years of idol worship and false belief, it was difficult for her to fully accept the sovereignty of God, and the ramifications of salvation based on faith, not works.

Elisabeth tackled the challenge by encouraging Ling to read her Bible. She saw Ling's heart as an old, large house in a state of extreme disrepair. A house that could only be renovated by the Word of God.

'Poor Ling ... When will she get complete peace and a joyful heart? How long will her journey be before she gets free from all this?'

Though the house had already been given over to a new owner, much work had yet to be done: cleaning out rubbish, tearing down walls, repairing pipes, replacing furniture ...

'Well, at least it's getting cleaned up,' Elisabeth thought, filled with hope.

Matai tried not to think about what his father did with all his free time, but he couldn't help but notice that the man had a lot of it.

'Dad, where does all your money go?' he asked once.

'How am I supposed to know? It's just the way things are,' Yan replied. Matai was suspicious. When a credit card company called and informed him that his father owed them several thousand dollars, he incredulously conveyed the message.

'So, wow. What are you going to do, Dad?'

'Oh it doesn't matter,' his father replied with cool nonchalance. 'I'll pay it eventually.'

To help out, she followed in her mother's footsteps and got a part-time job at a department store. There she earned as much as $1,000 a day but hardly had time to spend it before it was confiscated by her father.

Even when his children worked, Yan found ways to complain about them.

'Your mum didn't teach you well,' he said to them. 'You don't know how to help me out with the cooking, washing, or whatever. She was a bad wife ... That woman is the one who's causing all this trouble in our lives.'

Sometimes Yan blew up without explanation. He was particularly harsh with Matai, and when he got really angry he grabbed Matai by the ears and lifted him off the floor.

One day, Jun, Peijen and Matai told their father that they wanted to go out to eat, but on the way the two girls stopped by a comic-book store. While Matai waited for his sisters outside, he spotted his father driving towards him on his motorbike.

'What are you doing here?' Yan asked sternly.

'They wanted to look at some comic books,' Matai replied nervously.

After escorting his children home, Yan lashed out at Matai.

'Why did you tell me you wanted to go out to eat, and then went to the comic-book store instead?!' Yan grabbed a long pole that was used to dry clothes and aimed it at his trembling son.

As the blows fell upon Matai's small frame, the boy cried out, 'It wasn't me who wanted to look! It was them! Why are you hitting me and not them?'

'Because you're a man! And you need to be trained to be responsible!'

Every day, Yan gave Matai nerve-racking quizzes in

maths – a subject that Matai detested. Each time he answered incorrectly, his father punished him with a slap. Matai grew so afraid of offending or displeasing his father that whenever he talked, he did so in a timid whisper.

News of the beatings pained Ling just as much as it pained the children. But as her prayers for her children seemed to go unanswered, she became aware of her tendency to be self-reliant and proud. In her utter helplessness, she began to have faith in God's sovereignty, no matter what the outcome. Greatly encouraged by the Bible's promise, 'Come to me, all you who are weary and burdened, and I will give you rest,' she prayed:

'Father, you know that my deepest desire is to have my children back. Please help me. More important, may I always trust in you. May your will be done.'

October 2000

It started out as another secret rendezvous with their mother. The children went shopping, then stopped by their mother's dorm on their way home.

'Where did you guys go?' their father inquired suspiciously when they came back.

'We went shopping,' one of them answered. Yan was not satisfied. He continued interrogating them until the truth finally came out:

'We went to Mum's,' Matai confessed.

'You liar! Don't you lie to me!' their father screamed. He started to viciously pound his son as if he were going to kill him.

'Stop hitting him!'

'Please stop!'

It was no use.

After Yan finally left for work that night, the children

started to talk. The more they talked, the more upset they became.

'What did we do wrong?'

'Nothing. Whether we see Mum is our own business.'

'Yeah!'

A pause. A sniffle.

'Let's go home, OK?' Matai offered meekly, his body still throbbing from the blows. His sister Jun hugged him, then picked up the phone.

When Ling came to Elisabeth's door in the middle of the night, she was shaking.

'Jun called to say that Yan beat them. They want to come home ...' she said, her voice quavering. 'I've had enough. I'm just going to take the children with me, no matter what happens ... Will you go with me? I've already called the police.'

Elisabeth sat Ling down and prayed with her. She later realized that something inside of Ling snapped that evening.

Her pride.

She had sunk into deep desperation that made her fully comprehend how powerless she was, how badly she needed God, and how worthy he was of her total trust. As she let go of her pride, she felt ready to follow instead of lead.

By the time Elisabeth and Ling arrived at Yan's house, they had already secured the assistance of Ling's younger brother and two policemen. While the three men accompanied Ling upstairs, Elisabeth stayed downstairs and prayed.

'Lord, please make Yan willing to give up the children without violence ... Please protect them ... Please make him not aggressive tonight ...'

Time crept past. Both the anticipation and the lateness

of the hour wore at Elisabeth's tired nerves. Finally, she heard footsteps at the top of the stairs.

When Ling finally trudged down, she was not alone. Three years after walking out of her husband's life, her children were allowed, at last, to walk with her.

* * *

Elisabeth knew that it was only a matter of time before Yufen was ready to become a small-group leader. Unfortunately, Yufen could not have disagreed more.

'If you tell me to be a small-group leader, I'll immediately stop coming to church,' she had said with her usual dramatic flair. Because her familial obligations drained most of her energy, she had hoped that church would remain a place where she could be free of any responsibility. In reality, though, her innate diligence prevented her from being just a spectator in anything.

For six months, Elisabeth refrained from mentioning leadership again. She simply left room for Yufen to serve others in subtle ways, like driving them home after a small-group meeting. She did such tasks with great willingness, which further confirmed Elisabeth's suspicions that she would make a good co-worker. In spite of Yufen's objections, Elisabeth felt that an official leadership role would be good for Yufen, just as it had been with Ling. Then, instead of focusing all her energy on the problems in her own insular world, Yufen would have to look outward – a process of stretching that would inevitably be coupled with spiritual growth.

When a new small group sprang up in the SOGO department store where Yufen worked, she naturally got involved. In January 2001, Elisabeth asked Yufen to lead the group.

'I don't want to lead,' Yufen answered, but with less certainty than before. Elisabeth knew that her objections meant little now. Yufen was already the ad hoc leader of the fledgling group, and merely lacked the title.

When Yufen started helping Elisabeth and Ling distribute magazines at the SOGO, she went through the prototypical fears of rejection. But after her third visitation, God helped her overcome them, to the point where she was even willing to go on her own.

As Elisabeth showered her two new middle-aged co-workers with attention, she received an unexpectedly vehement reaction from others.

'You have never loved me,' one of her long-time co-workers said. 'It's all just for show. You don't have to say anything, I just know that you love her more. You do everything for her. You're only nice to me because I do all the things you want me to do.'

'That's not true ...' Elisabeth said quietly. Though she occasionally defended herself sternly so that the accuser would snap out of her foul mood, she usually turned the other cheek and replied with flowers or home-baked cakes – even grander displays of her love.

Still, two or three co-workers refused to accept Ling and Yufen, who had accepted Christ so recently, and much later in life than many of the other shop-workers. The co-workers' snide comments drove Elisabeth to tears and even ate away at her drive to continue ministry. She tried to tell herself that their attitudes simply demonstrated their vital need to maintain a sense of belonging within the fellowship – the only family many of them had. But the heartaches remained. They served as poignant reminders that, like Yufen, Ling and all the others, Elisabeth was only human.

* * *

In January 2001, Yufen's husband tried once again to open a business. His beef-noodle shop, like all his other entrepreneurial exploits, began well; business was so good that he and his partner hired help, a widow less educated and slightly younger than Yufen. Then in February, he hired one of Yufen's church friends who needed a job. Her name was Mei Chen.

While Kai happily ran his business, Yufen was happy too. She even went to the noodle shop regularly to chat with him. One night after a fellowship meeting, she decided to drive by the shop to see if Kai was around. It was already 1:30 a.m., but Kai worked so hard at the shop that he slept there sometimes, in a small attic he had built for that purpose.

When Yufen arrived, she saw her husband's motorbike parked in front. The door was closed and the shop was dark, except for a dim light that shone from the attic. When she entered the shop, she walked towards the steps leading to the attic and looked down.

On the ground were two pairs of house slippers. One for a man, and the other for a woman. A chill surged through her. She pictured the attic, and how her husband had designed it with a ceiling so low that it was impossible to stand up inside. All it was really good for was serving tea and sleeping ...

Yufen rang the doorbell. She waited and waited. Nobody opened the door.

'What were you doing up in the attic?' she asked Kai when she went to the shop the next day.

'Nothing,' he replied.

'With two pairs of slippers at the door, what else could you be doing?'

'We were drinking tea ... Why is this any of your business? I'll do whatever I please.'

Though Yufen had heard these same words in relation to his drinking, they had a raw, abrasive effect on her this time. She felt as if her life was slowly seeping out of the wounds that they had caused. Her thoughts sprinted around in circles.

'That widow ... that woman is so uneducated, illiterate and simple ... what could he possibly want from her ... ? Wait, am I so different from that woman, just being used by him? It's obvious that he doesn't love her and is just using her, just using his charm to get her to work hard since the two of us can't work together any more ... Am I that stupid, that I used to worship him, when all he wanted was ...'

She marched up to the woman, who was busy preparing food.

'What did you do last night?' she demanded, trying to act calm.

'Nothing,' the woman replied.

'What were you doing up there with the light so dim? If you were just making tea, you could have done that downstairs. Upstairs is for sleeping.'

From then on, Yufen stopped by the shop every day to monitor her husband's activities. The suspicions became so consuming that she began to feel physically ill. Meanwhile, Kai continued to deny her accusations.

'Ask Mei about it. She knows nothing happened,' he asserted. 'You're just trying to mess up my business, just like you did all those other times. Everything was going great, and then you had to come and mess it up.'

In the midst of the chaos, Elisabeth had an opinion of her own. She suspected that Kai might have been too drunk to fully reject the woman's advances, but that they had not gone so far as to sleep together. Elisabeth felt certain that if anything immoral had happened at all, the relationship was a superficial one that posed no major threat to Yufen's marriage.

But Yufen's anger was already like a bowling ball knocking down anything in its way. On the third day after the incident, Yufen sneaked to the shop in the morning, guessing that Kai was too cunning to attempt anything further at night. Again, the attic door was closed. Again, the slippers were on the floor.

Ready for a showdown, Yufen called Kai's mother, aunt and sister, inviting them to come over and witness the alleged affair with their own eyes. As she waited for them to arrive, she guarded the door. The attic door remained closed.

Ever since Yufen's baptism, she had gradually learned to guard her temper. But as she stared at the door of the noodle shop, she suddenly felt like a starving lion only inches away from prey. She just couldn't wait.

She picked up a large piece of wood and smashed a window. Kai and his widowed employee rushed down from the attic, startled by the noise.

Yufen clubbed everything in sight – windows, chairs, dishes. She had been violently angry many times in her life, but this topped them all. She glared at the woman. Then she swung at her.

Numb to the woman's shrieks, Yufen thrashed her wildly. The woman raised her arms to defend herself from the stick's erratic blows, but Yufen didn't care.

Time passed in a blur. Unable to sleep that night, Yufen drove around and around.

'I'll never forgive myself for being with a man as dirty as him. For even having children with a man like him. There's nothing good about this man. He met none of my expectations, and broke all trust. I will never be able to forgive him.'

At around three in the morning, she went to Elisabeth and wept. 'How could this happen?' she wailed repeatedly as Elisabeth cried with her.

Yufen also broke the news to her twenty-one-year-old son Bao. The following day, he went with her to confront Kai in front of the noodle shop.

'Are you drunk again?!' Yufen fired.

'No,' Kai replied, obviously lying.

'I saw you sleeping with her on the second floor! I saw you ...'

Bao's entire life had been inundated with fights like this.

'I told you, we didn't do anything!'

During each fight, Bao had said and done nothing, miserably treading water while his parents crashed at each other.

'Bao, who would you choose if we got a divorce?'

Suddenly, Bao was knocked down by a torrent of emotion that had swirled inside of him all those years.

'I WOULDN'T GO WITH EITHER ONE OF YOU! I HOPE THAT BOTH OF YOU JUST DIE!'

Elisabeth gloomily accompanied Yufen to the courthouse, where she would have to wade through a mound of paperwork. Her victim had decided to sue. When Yufen tried to explain the incident to the judge, she was reminded that she could not physically prove that the woman had slept with her husband. In the end, Yufen voluntarily paid $100,000 to compensate for the woman's injuries. She then slapped her husband with divorce papers, which he refused to sign.

Elisabeth soon realized that any attempts to calm Yufen's fury only made her more furious. 'Should I push her or let her realize for herself what she has to do?' she pondered. Choosing the latter, she called Yufen regularly –

not to sermonize, but to listen. She encouraged Yufen not to think too much, not to make things even more complicated than they already were. But she knew that, ultimately, only the Holy Spirit could help. As Yufen's depression dragged on and their conversations became predictably repetitive, Elisabeth continued to listen. She loved Yufen so much that she was filled with pity rather than impatience.

Eventually Yufen realized that her desires were insatiably paradoxical: For a long time, she had claimed that she didn't want Kai any more, yet the thought of him sleeping with another woman still tortured her. The alleged affair made Yufen aware of her unhealthy dependence on her husband. Even though she read her Bible fervently, spent four nights a week with the shop-workers' fellowship, and selflessly cared for the women she had started to lead, her dependence on her husband – and all the disappointments that came with it – had levelled her spiritual life to a plateau. Her husband had been her idol, the centre of almost all her thoughts and actions. Isaiah 54 spoke to her vividly:

'For your Maker is your husband – the Lord Almighty is his name – the Holy One of Israel is your Redeemer; he is called the God of all the earth. The Lord will call you back as if you were a wife deserted and distressed in spirit – a wife who married young, only to be rejected ... Though the mountains be shaken and the hills be removed, yet my unfailing love for you will not be shaken nor my covenant of peace be removed,' says the Lord, who has compassion on you.

In the aftermath of Yufen's grief, she finally discovered the major root of many of her problems. In pulling out the root, she let go of her husband. And reached towards God.

Chapter 17

For years, several of Kai Lin's friends had advised him to get a divorce, but he had been determined to stay in his marriage, as unhappy as it was. For years, his wife had accused him of not loving her, of not caring for the family, but he had kept telling himself that she was simply impossible to please. Like many Taiwanese men with similar frustrations, he reacted to the almost constant criticism by running away from Yufen and using alcohol to soothe the sting of her words.

But this last accusation was something else altogether. Before long, what was left of his former ambitions had dissipated. Closing the noodle shop, he drowned himself in the warm comfort of alcohol.

* * *

Elisabeth first met Kai Lin in 1998, about half a year after his wife had started coming to the shop-workers' fellowship.

'Oh, she's probably here to preach to me,' he thought casually when she showed up at his home. An expert at social graces, he set aside his apprehensions and politely offered tea to her. Yufen brought out some fruit for them to eat, and as she interacted with her husband, Elisabeth immediately noticed that their relationship was a chilly one – though Kai tried to pretend that nothing was wrong.

He kindly thanked Elisabeth for taking care of his wife and daughter.

'People who come here from Germany are all so smart!' he said, lavishing both her and her country with praise. They spoke briefly about Christianity, and Elisabeth handed him an evangelistic magazine. Then she left.

'He won't be able to believe in Jesus,' Yufen informed Elisabeth after the meeting. Like most Taiwanese men, Kai had a serious obligation to worship his ancestors. He also believed personally in fortune-telling and considered himself a Buddhist. He felt that his wife's new-found interest in Christianity was nothing more than a joke.

'What's this believing in Jesus business about?' he said to her once. 'You're still not nice to me, so what good does it do?'

Yet Elisabeth tried to maintain contact with Kai. And she visited him after the noodle-shop trauma, when severe binge drinking landed him in the hospital.

'Brother Lin, is your health improving?' she asked respectfully as he lay in bed. That someone from the church truly cared for him warmed his heart, and he listened eagerly to Elisabeth's words.

During her visits, she went through two lessons of a seeker's Bible study with him. Kai was so momentarily enthusiastic that he even agreed to invite Jesus into his heart. But as he repeated a prayer of decision line by line, Elisabeth knew that, though his mouth had moved, his heart had not.

After Kai was discharged from the hospital, he moved to a mountainside house in Tucheng, where it was hoped that he would be rehabilitated. Owned by distant family members, the house was more than forty years old and in filthy condition. But after Kai moved in, he managed to keep the place remarkably clean – especially considering the fact that he tried to raise chickens in one of the rooms.

Even though Yufen could not yet forgive her husband for the alleged affair, she still brought food to his new home. Unable to face the man alone, she always enlisted the help of her good friend Ling. Not only were the two women growing together in the Lord and serving in the fellowship side-by-side, but they could also empathize with each other; both of them had suffered dearly in their marriages.

Yufen knew that the way she had dealt with her husband in the past did not please the Lord. She yearned to be tender and gentle, no matter how frustrated she felt, and for this reason she admired Ling, who was more well-tempered. Whenever Yufen caught her husband drinking during her visits to the mountains, her anger would rise. But before it had the chance to overflow onto old wounds, Ling would babble brightly in an attempt to lighten the mood. With help that only the Holy Spirit could give, Yufen patiently kept her mouth shut.

Yufen and Ling weren't the only ones who visited Kai. Bao tried to drop off food and money about twice a month, though he could hardly stand to be around his father for more than two hours at a time. Watching the man stumble around drunkenly evoked too much disappointment, too much shame.

Although living on his own forced him to be responsible, Kai often used what little money he had to buy alcohol instead of food. To Bao's disgust, Kai was even willing to eat spoiled food so that he could save money to buy drinks. Once a connoisseur of fine wine priced at 1,000 Taiwanese dollars a bottle, Kai now downed foul-tasting $30 rice wine just to satisfy his cravings.

'Do you have to treat yourself like this?' Bao asked his father once. Kai merely smiled in reply.

Kai clearly enjoyed the freedom of not having to work,

pay rent, and live under the critical eyes of his wife. But Bao knew from his face that he was far from satisfied. Kai was so determined to protect his own dignity that he even invited homeless men into his house for drinks so that he could say he was still capable of entertaining guests.

One Sunday afternoon, his daughter Little Ping, now in her mid-twenties, took Elisabeth to the mountains to visit him. Their tiny, low-riding car jolted nauseatingly the whole way up, and eventually got stuck in the road. As Elisabeth and Little Ping contemplated their next move, Kai bounded down the mountain and proudly helped them free their vehicle. He was obviously delighted to see them.

Thus began Elisabeth's weekly ritual of visiting Kai. But the person who ended up having the most influence on Kai was one of her new co-workers, an extraordinary young man named A-fang Tan.

* * *

A-fang Tan was born in 1978 to a father who was a construction worker and a mother who ran a tiny general store. Though his parents, like many working-class Taiwanese, did not put much emphasis on education, he was a good student – that is, until a unexpected series of events bombarded his world.

For as long as A-fang could remember, his mother had a vicious temper that often led to serious quarrels with his father. But it wasn't until she started having an affair with another man that A-fang's parents got a divorce. So when A-fang was in kindergarten, his older sister Hua was sent to live with an aunt, while A-fang and his younger brother remained with their mother and the new man in her life.

The man turned out to be an expert at inspiring fear. Treating the two boys like second-class citizens, he established a stringent set of rules for them. They couldn't touch anything in the living room, including the sofa. If they forgot to brush their teeth, he forced them to do it with a rough piece of metal until their mouths were full of blood. If they didn't make their beds properly, he forced them, in the almost suffocating summer heat, to sleep with blankets over their heads. Meanwhile, A-fang's mother did little to protect her boys from the frequent and brutal punishments; after all, she too was subject to beatings.

A-fang's stepfather also controlled the family finances, and he was so tight-fisted that A-fang often ate nothing but a bit of rice and an egg for lunch. Sometimes he and his brother even stole school food to satisfy their hunger pangs.

Before long, A-fang's mother and stepfather decided to emigrate to Canada – without their children. A-fang's father refused to take the boys back, so the children were exchanged back and forth like an unwanted purchase.

Eventually they were left in a vacant Panchiao apartment to fend for themselves. Their older sister joined them, and since the three children had no idea how to take care of each other, they fought and hit each other constantly. Their father did little more than send them money regularly; their lives were completely unsupervised. It was as if A-fang had been released from a strait-jacket and tossed into the open sea.

By junior high, A-fang had grown tired of simply submitting to the callous circumstances in his seemingly meaningless life. Since nobody cared to look at his report card, he stopped studying. Determined to be perceived as powerful instead of pitiful, he started bullying the other students in his class.

'What are you looking at?!' he blurted fiercely, kicking the chair of a student who had only glanced at him. No response. Even his teacher seemed to fear him. Since there was nobody at home who could be contacted about A-fang's behaviour problems, he remained as formidable as a live machine-gun.

Outside of school A-fang got to know some drug dealers and occasionally purchased their wares. He was also recruited to help out with temple processions – activities that were known to involve *bu liang shao nian*, or juvenile delinquents. Many of these boys would drink, smoke and discuss their gang connections as they waited for the processions to begin. When the signal came, they would then heave massive idol costumes onto their shoulders and saunter down the streets, adding bounce to their steps so that the idols would appear more 'alive'. Sometimes A-fang and his friends marched for three days, as onlookers worshipped along the side of the road.

A-fang was not altogether pleased with the new direction his life was taking, but he felt it was the only way to preserve his fragile sense of dignity. Abandoned by his parents and scorned by his extended family, he had little else to hold on to.

'Look at how bad those kids are ...' his relatives remarked about him and his siblings. 'They're little thieves!'

A-fang was sick of being looked down upon. He was sick of constantly fighting with his siblings. So after Junior high, he quit school and left the city – without even leaving a phone number behind.

The dark-coloured luxury vehicle forebodingly approached the small-town karaoke bar where A-fang worked. A group of drunk young people was mingling around outside, and one of them haphazardly shouted at the car. Its doors opened, and several men stepped out. A gunshot.

A-fang's eyes widened as he saw – for the first time ever – bona fide gangsters get really angry. The gangster had only fired the gun into the air, but his intent was clear. The leader of the group outside darted into the karaoke bar and asked for a knife.

'No, you can't borrow it!' the waiters objected, determined to stay out of the conflict. When the young man went outside again, one of the gangsters grabbed him and pummelled him. Nobody dared to help – even the local police seemed hesitant to intervene.

'Oh, these young people are so unimportant,' a policeman said respectfully to the gangsters upon his arrival. 'Just leave them alone. Forget about it.'

The incident left A-fang awestruck.

'So this is what it means to have real power,' he thought.

Eventually, A-fang had his own chance to exhibit power. When the son of a gangster tried to bully a friend of his, A-fang started to punch him. A crowd gathered as the fists continued to fly, and others even joined in.

Thanks to A-fang, the boy was hospitalized for a month. But he hardly cared, since he earned $2,000 to $3,000 a night at the karaoke bar. In fact, he was so relaxed about spending that he didn't bother to wash his dirty clothes, opting to buy new ones instead.

Even though his aggression had managed to send someone to the hospital, A-fang considered himself fairly innocent compared to other men he knew – men who were addicted to drugs or had gone to prison. Since A-fang had either been neglected or abused throughout his childhood, men such as these served as his only role models. From them he learned the meaning of such sayings as: 'Men are like blood brothers. Women are like clothes – you can always switch them.'

The cause of the fight was uncertain, though the result was obviously dire. Chaos had broken out in the karaoke bar as two groups of customers started fighting against each other. The confusion pitted friend against friend, and even A-fang's co-workers were getting involved.

One person who found himself in the middle of the fight was a friend of A-fang, a tall, strong boy who had often protected him in the past. In the hysteria, someone slit his throat with a knife. Then someone else grabbed a heavy iron chain and approached a man who had collapsed to the floor. A-fang tried to intervene, but someone held him back.

'Don't do anything! Just stay here!'

A-fang watched in horror as the chain looped in the air and struck the body. Blood spewed out of the man's mouth. The chain struck again with a crack, the sound of breaking bone. Then the attacker left.

It was then that A-fang decided he was ready to go home. He had had enough of the never-ending violence that would give him nightmares for years to come.

Only one thing kept him from immediately heading back north. The father of his then girlfriend was released from prison and asked A-fang to help him run a night-market booth. The man had been a long-time gangster and drug dealer but wanted to start anew.

The determination didn't last long. Suspicious-looking men lurked around the night market searching for him, and he spent a good part of each evening injecting himself with heroin. A-fang watched in dismay as the man crawled back to his former way of life.

Meanwhile, something life-changing was happening to A-fang, though he did not realize it at the time. He was being prayed for.

Hua, his older sister, had got baptized at Panchiao Gospel Lutheran Church, which had been introduced to her by one of her teachers. She passionately urged her small group to pray continuously for her missing brother.

After two years of not communicating with his family, A-fang suddenly decided to go back to Panchiao. Overjoyed by his return, Hua started telling him about the Lord.

'That's a religion for good people,' A-fang thought disgustedly. 'Yeah right, like God can save me.'

Despite her conversion, Hua still had a child-like temper that easily led to heated arguments. So before long, A-fang decided to leave his siblings and share an apartment with friends instead. He lived and worked in Hsimen-ting, a bustling part of Taipei, and became involved with a number of women.

But Hua refused to lose her brother again. She tracked him down and took some church members with her to visit him. Not surprisingly, he rudely brushed off her evangelistic entourage and forced them out of his apartment with a barrage of cruel comments. Their constant mention of love, grace and other abstract concepts annoyed him, giving him the impression that Christianity was a weak, almost feminine religion. Furthermore, church seemed like a whitewashed, refined place unsuitable for people like him – people who smoked, drank and swore. The last thing he wanted was to enter a strange, upper-class culture that would make him feel vulnerable and dumb.

But Hua did not give up. She and the other church members continued to visit A-fang, and though their words did not impress him, their resolve did. He especially appreciated the perseverance of his sister, who continued to care for him despite his unyielding protestations.

A breaking-point finally came when an agonizing break-up with one of his girlfriends thrust him into the poisonous embrace of depression. He had lived for nothing but his own happiness, yet he was still unhappy. His life was as free as a raft floating in the open sea, but its choppy waves had begun to make him sick. Insomnia, which had bothered him on and off since junior high, now beleaguered him. He went without sleep for days at a time, and when he did manage to drift off, nightmares would torment him. In his physical and emotional weakness, he reached for his sister. Ever since his return to Taipei, she had been irritatingly cheerful most of the time; he yearned for just an ounce of her joy.

'Why are you so happy?' A-fang asked her one day. 'We have no family. Our parents gave us nothing. They left us.'

Hua hesitated.

'Because Jesus loves me,' she answered, preparing herself for yet another rebuff from her hard-hearted brother. She paused. 'Let me pray for you. Then we can see what happens.'

'Is this real?' wondered A-fang, choked by desperation. 'Can these prayers give me answers? 'I've tried everything else so I might as well try this...'

'OK' he said. 'You can do it.' Ecstatic, Hua began to pray.

'Dear Lord, we pray that you will give A-fang good sleep ... We pray that you will give him peace ...'

Immediately, A-fang was filled with an unfamiliar sensation: stillness. His heart slowed and his mind cleared.

'I want to go to sleep,' he declared when Hua finished praying. He went to bed, and for the first time for as long as he could remember, he enjoyed the freedom of serene, dreamless sleep.

Two years after Hua's answered prayer had inspired A-fang to start going to church, he decided to get baptized. He even went back to school, specializing in fine arts. He became an active member of the church youth group and lived in the church as its informal 'security guard'. Yet other parts of his life were more resistant to change. His menacing reputation had preceded his arrival at church, and he took advantage of this by bullying other youths in the church and leading them to play hooky at youth camps.

Sometimes his unruly, dominating behaviour even made the youth leader cry.

A turning-point came when he graduated from high school and started his mandatory military service. Out of the hundreds of men he met in the military, only one other was a Christian. All of them spent time with prostitutes during their terms. Faced with a multitude of temptations, A-fang had nothing but the Word of God to rely on. He prayed and read his Bible every night. His faith soon became obvious to his comrades, especially since he sang praises to God during certain military exercises.

'Ha! You say you're a Christian ... You're a fake!' accused one comrade.

As A-fang got involved in seemingly inevitable conflicts with other men, he became aware of the pride that saturated his spiritual life and the faults that hindered his Christian witness. Right before he was scheduled to be discharged from the military, he was caught spending the night outside the compound and was sent to the military jail. With nothing else to do there but sit, he started repenting of all the past sins that came to his mind, bathing in God's forgiveness. So during his last five days in the military – as he sat silently in a jail cell – his heart soared.

When A-fang Tan returned to the Panchiao Gospel Lutheran Church, he felt lost. He could no longer attend the youth group, since he had already graduated. Yet he knew he needed fellowship.

One day, the husband of A-fang's former youth leader approached him.

'I think you would really fit best into Sister Wei's shopworkers' fellowship,' he remarked.

By this time, A-fang had started working as a cook at a Japanese restaurant, and his boss was a member of the shop-workers' fellowship. One day, Elisabeth came to the restaurant for a visit. She noticed immediately that, although A-fang was usually friendly and pleasant, his moods tended to swing at the slightest provocation.

But she also sensed within A-fang a deep desire to change and learn. And as he started attending the shop-workers' fellowship, it was as if his spiritual life was placed in an incubator at the perfect temperature. He quickly discovered that most of the other shop-workers came from backgrounds as broken as his own, and for one of the first times in his life, he did not feel alone.

Through praying with A-fang, Elisabeth discovered that his life was plagued with many problems common to Taiwanese working-class men. As stories from the past bubbled out of A-fang's mouth, it became apparent that – deep inside of him – hate still simmered. His past hurts wounded him deeply, leaving him utterly insecure, and he attempted to fill the void by claiming power over others. Because he didn't have a healthy self-esteem, he was prone to lash out whenever he felt attacked. Also, ever since A-fang's mother had abandoned him, his life had lacked discipline; he smoked often. For all these reasons, A-fang battled against many temptations during his first two years as a Christian.

As he grew spiritually, A-fang also longed to do more than just attend fellowship meetings. When the shop-workers' annual Moon Festival party approached, he helped out by carrying a hefty bag of charcoal up six flights of stairs. And this was only the beginning. In the coming years, A-fang would assist Elisabeth in many menial, but important ways: buying food for outings or special events, preparing meals, cleaning up late at night after meetings, preparing apartments to be used as dorms, moving shop-workers in and out of the dorms. Before A-fang had volunteered himself as Elisabeth's helper, these many obligations had often left Elisabeth feeling drained and despairing.

When Elisabeth and Ling Hu started a small group in Taipei, A-fang helped them drive people home after the late-night meetings. Gradually, he shared with Elisabeth some of his deepest hurts as he steered through traffic. Elisabeth came to appreciate him and his gifts more and more, despite the fact that she sometimes fell victim to his temper.

'Can I pray for you?' she would ask at times like these, her eyes brimming.

As they prayed together, A-fang began to repent. He had never before met a person so full of grace, patience and encouragement. Elisabeth's attitude and behaviour helped him see his own sins even more clearly. And something miraculous occurred. His temper began to dwindle.

A-fang's idea had seemed brilliant: a lunchbox delivery service for shop-workers. And at the beginning, he ran his new business enthusiastically, whipping up meals in the kitchen of the men's dorm where he lived. But, like many working-class men, he got easily discouraged when he could not achieve the high goals he set for himself. So about six-months after starting his business venture he decided to give it up.

Fortunately, A-fang refused to give up when it came to ministry. As a man, he filled a desperate need that most Taiwanese churches have: he ministered to other men, penetrating their thick, protective shells in order to lead them to Christ. Such ministry was often frustrating and difficult as many obstacles stood in their way: their bondage to bad habits, their exhausting work schedules, their filial responsibilities to worship their ancestors, their general hardness of heart. Yet A-fang persevered and was willing to invest deeply in their lives. He didn't just teach the Bible to the men he cared for; he lived with them too.

As a result, he naturally emerged as the spiritual leader of the men's dorm.

A-fang also worked extensively with the youth of the fellowship – many of whom were the children of shop-workers – and helped about ten of them accept Christ. He accompanied Elisabeth on visitations to department stores and hospitals.

At one of these hospitals, he met a desperate but stubborn-hearted man whose body had already begun to limp towards death – a man named Kai Lin.

When Kai moved to the mountains, A-fang started to read the Bible with him. It was as if a window in Kai's heart had started to creak open. At first, Kai even tried to pray and read the Bible on his own. But as he had done with so many things in his life, he eventually gave up.

* * *

Bao gaped disgustedly at his father's right hand, a swollen mass of flesh that took on almost cartoon-like proportions. Apparently, Kai had broken his hand a few days earlier, though he had remained too drunk to notice.

It wasn't to be the only time that Kai's isolation would jeopardize his health. One day as Kai was drinking, he started to feel unusually dizzy. His blood-sugar level soared and he could feel himself losing consciousness – with nobody around to help him. Kai knew that the end was near. He panicked.

'Lord ... give me the strength ... I need to ... get down to the road.'

Miraculously, Kai took one step. Then another. He hobbled all the way to the main road, a considerable distance away. From there, he got a ride to a hospital. When Elisabeth and A-fang went to visit him there, he eagerly told them about his experience.

'God really gave me the strength to walk down there,' he said.

Kai's heart was opening gradually to the gospel, but he was not yet ready to give his entire life to the Lord. Even though doctors told him that continuing to drink would surely kill him, alcohol remained his master.

As Kai's health deteriorated, he moved back to the city, where his family could care for him more easily. They rented a small private room for him, though his new home quickly turned into a den of temptation. It was surrounded by restaurants where alcohol was readily available, and his old friends continued to invite him out for drinks. He often had to borrow money from them as his drink tabs accumulated.

One day when Elisabeth decided to visit Kai unannounced, she found him sitting quietly at a little table in front of his building. Bottles of beer and wine littered the table, and even though he was distressingly aware of Elisabeth's presence, his tongue lolled around, unable to form coherent sentences. Elisabeth looked at him sadly and thought about how much A-fang had invested in him.

'Even though Kai has really experienced the Lord, he has just given up,' she sighed.

Kai's entire body shook as he carried a bouquet of flowers down the aisle at his mother's funeral. His mother was the only woman in his life who had adored him unconditionally until the very end, and her death drove Kai into such a deep state of despair that he could hardly walk.

So profound was Kai's grief that he lost the desire to do anything but drink. Amid throngs of other mourners, he downed one drink after another, oblivious to everything, even his own bowel movements. He simply sat in the funeral parlour and relieved himself in his pants.

When Elisabeth came back from her trip home in July 2004, Yufen immediately informed her that Kai was in the hospital again – but that this time, his days were numbered.

Upon arriving at the hospital, Elisabeth discovered that this was no exaggeration. Barely conscious, Kai was unable to recognize Elisabeth, even though she was one of the few foreigners he knew. It would not be long before he slipped into a coma, the doctors said. They hoped that by operating on him soon, they would be able to save him.

As Yufen looked at her husband's sallow body, she knew that it was time.

'Let go, and let me do the work,' she felt the Lord telling her. Though her husband was no longer the centre of her life, there was still a part of her that hoped to help him, to control him. Yufen looked at Kai again. Forgiveness no longer felt like an unimaginably distant concept as she gazed at him with new feeling – a feeling of sisterly love.

Elisabeth and Yufen prayed fervently for Kai's recovery. They prayed that Kai would finally be able to accept Jesus into his heart. They knew from experience the implications of their request. The spiritual journeys of Yufen, Ling and Mei had been long and arduous, with many twists and turns along the way. What they were asking for was a miracle.

That night, Kai was drifting off to sleep when he felt a touch against his hand. Unable to open his eyes or speak, he suddenly realized that the touch was not that of a human being.

'Lord, is it you? Are you here to see me?'

Kai started to pray.

So rapid was Kai's recovery that even the doctors were astounded. When Elisabeth and A-fang paid Kai a visit the following day, he was already well enough to speak clearly.

'I spoke with God last night and already settled things,' he said matter-of-factly. 'I've done too many things wrong. I've already confessed my sins to Jesus. I've asked him to help me get better ... I want to believe in him and give my life to him.'

The second time that Kai prayed through a prayer of decision, Elisabeth was overjoyed. This time, she knew he meant it.

Chapter 18

Something was wrong with Mei Chen, though the reason was not outwardly apparent. The shopworkers' fellowship provided her with a steady support network during her difficult period of transition. Money was no longer a major concern, for she had secured a job as a care-giver at a Catholic nursing home. After a two-year legal battle, she had finally gained permanent custody of her two daughters. And her spiritual growth had been remarkable. If her time with Katrina was like a tidal wave that propelled her towards spiritual maturity, her time with Elisabeth was like a tsunami. With childlike faith, she soaked up the Bible's teachings and applied them to her daily life. She was a humble and eager learner, and very naturally put other people's interests over her own. She even started a small group for single mothers. Early on, Elisabeth knew that Mei possessed great potential for making a difference in the lives of broken people like herself.

Despite all this, Mei felt depressed. She found praying and reading her Bible agonizingly difficult, and her heart felt stormy even though there were no clouds in sight. Finally, she went to Elisabeth and confessed her suspicions – that evil spirits were still oppressing her.

The admission surprised Elisabeth. Outwardly, Mei was blossoming spiritually, and it seemed as if they had already prayed over most of her past. But they had not prayed over all of it. In distressingly vivid detail, Mei started to confess her darkest experiences with the spirits – the witchcraft, the delirious mountain trek ... Elisabeth knew that something drastic had to be done.

'There is nothing too big for the Lord,' she assured Mei. 'We just have to pray in the name of Jesus and drive it out.'

The following Thursday, Elisabeth invited Mei to share her predicament with all the other co-workers at their weekly meeting. About ten people were present, and all of them – including Yufen, A-fang, and even Ling – were shocked by what they heard.

At around 9 p.m., the co-workers started to pray over Mei. A nauseating, turbulent sensation overcame her, as if something inside her body was being yanked out. She started to involuntarily choke up.

'No, no, no, I don't want you to pray ...' she protested, her arms and legs flailing about wildly.

They continued to pray out loud, sometimes one at a time, sometimes all at once. Mei interjected often with loud, unintelligible sounds, but the others tried their best to ignore them.

About an hour later, Elisabeth began to feel helpless. Although she had driven out spirits through prayer before, she had never witnessed such strong opposition.

'I don't know how this all will end, but we'll leave it up to Jesus,' she thought, glad that she had fasted beforehand. The prayers continued. Eventually, Elisabeth felt that it was time to address Mei.

'You need to pray for yourself,' she said. 'You need to cut off this evil spirit and announce that you want to get free ...'

Immediately, Mei felt her jaw clench.

'What's the spirit's name?' Elisabeth asked slowly, deliberately. As much as Mei tried, she could not open her mouth.

'In the name of Jesus Christ, I tell you to open your mouth!' someone cried out.

'It's the Shaman's Spirit, the Evil Spirit of the Mountain,' said Mei instantly. Then she prayed against the spirit according to Elisabeth's instructions. When she had finished praying, she grew quiet – for the first time in the past one and a half hours.

'Let's glorify the Lord together,' Elisabeth announced. As the shop-workers started to sing together, Mei – to everyone's amazement – started to join in.

'The name of Jesus is so powerful,' Elisabeth rejoiced inwardly. 'Even though we're a normal, inexperienced group of people, we only needed to use his name to drive these demons out.'

Within three days, Mei was starting to feel better. Other prayers of renunciation were still to come, though they all paled in comparison to what Mei had already endured. On one occasion, Mei told Elisabeth privately that the voices had returned, and that they would enter her head and remind her of the past whenever she tried to pray or read the Bible.

As Elisabeth prayed over Mei, her body started to protest, though the reaction was not as severe as before.

'Is there another spirit in you?' Elisabeth asked her.

'The Spirit of Debauchery,' Mei answered, wobbling the table with her hands.

As before, getting rid of Mei's unwanted guest took nothing more than prayer. Mei had worshipped many different gods in her lifetime – so many that she could hardly remember them all – and so many more prayers were required in order to send off the spiritual baggage that remained within her. Once, when she suffered from frequent, inexplicable dizziness, Elisabeth put her hand on Mei's head and prayed.

'In Jesus' name, we renounce any influence that Mei's past is still having on her,' Elisabeth declared. Peace poured into Mei as she felt the Lord sweep away the hope-less, irrational thoughts and memories that had recently cluttered her mind. Her dizziness disappeared.

As Mei came to fully depend on the Lord, she loved communing with him, whether through praying, singing along with Christian CDs, or speaking in tongues. Through seeking the Lord's help, she even conquered her fear of darkness – the fear that had started when, among the other terrors she experienced at the age of eight, she had been beaten and locked in an outhouse.

*   *   *

Mei thirsted for a monogamous love relationship with God, but one thing kept her from it. The thing that had been cheapened long ago by her lustful older brother: a desire to be loved by a man.

Around the time when Kai Lin's physical health took a turn for the worst, Mei's spiritual health also started to deteriorate. She started to date a man who often took her out for drinks, and Elisabeth feared that the situation would spiral out of control when she went back to Germany for six months. She knew that Mei still harboured feelings of inadequacy about being aboriginal, and she worried that Mei would follow these feelings until they led her away from the fellowship.

Elisabeth was right. After her departure, Mei gradually stopped coming to co-workers' meetings. Ling, Yufen and others tried to reach out to her, but she furtively eluded their care. She ran to her boyfriend instead, indulging her-self with alcohol and karaoke. Sometimes she spent as much as 2,000 Taiwanese dollars on a single bottle of wine.

As soon as Mei started revisiting old habits, temptations flooded into her life. Friends from the past reappeared, and she started to get drunk one night after another. A gay friend from work even encouraged her to look for love in unconventional places. 'Why not? I haven't been able to really find love yet ...' Mei thought as she walked into a lesbian club. Fortunately, it didn't take long for her to feel overcome and leave.

Though Mei used to carefully guard her daughters at all times, she began to lose her qualms about leaving them alone in the house as she went out with her friends. One night, her seven- and eight-year-old daughters were so bored in their mother's absence that they decided to play outside on the roof. As Little Hui ventured out onto an aluminium awning, her tiny feet suddenly slipped.

'HELP!' she cried out. In a panic, Ting-ting managed to pull her to safety.

Another time, around midnight, Ting-ting was waiting impatiently for her mother's return when she saw a familiar figure in the park below their apartment. The girl raced downstairs.

'Mummy! Mummy!' she shouted.

But to her horror, the shadowy figure was not her mother.

'Hello, little girl,' came a deep voice. Terrified, Ting-ting ran home. When Mei finally returned two hours later, her daughter's face was still wet with tears.

'Did he hurt you? Did he hurt you?!' Mei asked in a panic, expecting the worst.

'No, no ...' Ting-ting answered, though her mother did not believe her at first.

Appalled by the consequences of her behaviour, Mei was certain that, this time, she had traversed beyond the reaches of God's grace. In Elisabeth's absence, she had failed to read her Bible, go to church, and even lead the small group she was in charge of. She was convinced that her Christian life was over.

When Elisabeth received Ling's desperate phonecall, she was not entirely surprised, though it was still difficult to imagine that Mei's spiritual state had plummeted so drastically. Since it was not yet time for her to return to Taiwan, Elisabeth felt momentarily helpless.

She picked up the phone and dialled. The dejected woman who answered was clearly not the Mei whom Elisabeth had come to know.

'The Lord has given me so much – a place to stay, a place to work, a church and good fellowship, enough money – and I've disappointed him so much that I just can't come back,' mumbled Mei. 'He was willing to forgive everything, and I threw it all away.'

'You're not able to throw away God's grace,' replied Elisabeth. 'The Lord has already died for the sins you've been doing, and you can come back to his open arms any time.' Elisabeth desperately tried to re-explain salvation to Mei. But she refused to listen. So Elisabeth decided to pray aloud.

'In the name of Jesus, I pray that as soon as Mei starts to drink, she starts to feel sick,' she said. After this, Mei suffered from headaches whenever she drank, but even this could not convince her that God had not given up. So Elisabeth continued to call Mei, again and again.

A few weeks later, as Elisabeth told Mei about the permanence of God's grace yet again, something happened. Her words uprooted Mei's insecurities, her dependence on the love of men, and the spiritual poison slowly seeped out of her. She began to feel alive.

'Now pray and accept God's grace again,' Elisabeth encouraged.

'OK,' said Mei, now fully convinced that God would never forsake her. 'Lord, thank you for awakening my soul. Thank you that by your grace, I am your child. I used to lean on the world, but now I want to lean completely on you.'

Part 6

When Spirits Rise

If you spend yourselves on behalf of the hungry and satisfy the needs of the oppressed, then your light will rise in the darkness, and your night will become like the noonday. The Lord will guide you always; he will satisfy your needs in a sun-scorched land.   Isaiah 58:10–11a

Chapter 19

Summer 2004

In sixteen years of ministry, Elisabeth Weinmann had seen more than 100 shop-workers put their trust in the Lord. She had trained up thirteen of them to become small-group leaders, and about thirty shop-workers attended her weekly co-workers' meetings.

Although her ministry functioned as intensely as a military operation, Elisabeth never drew up complex strategies about how to expand the shop-workers' ministry. Instead, she formed new small groups and explored uncharted department-store territory according to the burdens that God would give her Taiwanese co-workers. If one were to ask her for a reason behind the unprecedented success of her ministry, she would point first to God, then to her co-workers, rather than herself.

For a long while, it had been obvious to Elisabeth that beyond her treasure-chest of believers in Panchiao was a trove of lost coins that had yet to be explored – a trove only a short distance away from Panchiao and almost five times as large.[1] All Elisabeth needed was a co-worker to initiate the expedition.

'You know, we should start something in Taipei,' Ling Hu said to her one day. And so the journey began.

* * *

Elisabeth knew that the shop-workers' fellowship would be in good hands if she chose to leave, thanks to her team of solid co-workers, but a larger question remained: Who among her existing co-workers would be willing to uproot themselves and move to Taipei for the sake of helping Elisabeth start a new church?

By 2004, Elisabeth had successfully identified her team: Ling Hu, Yufen Wang, Mei Chen and A-fang Tan – growing Christians who, in Elisabeth's eyes, possessed great leadership potential. After a flurry of decisions, A-fang scouted out potential apartments in Liuzhangli, a neighbourhood in the up-and-coming Da-An District of Taipei. He quickly found three: The first would become a single mothers' dorm, led by Mei; the second would be used as a men's dorm, led by A-fang; and the last would double as Elisabeth's home and a ministry centre. Mei would lead a Saturday night Bible study at the centre, Ling would lead a Wednesday night Bible study in one of Taipei's busiest shopping centres, Yufen would lead a Bible study near her home in Yungho, and A-fang would lead a men's group. He would also attend Bible College while serving at the new church full time. His role was pivotal in bringing men to the church.

The plan was already more elaborate than Elisabeth had initially imagined; to be surrounded by a team of energetic co-workers was far more comforting than starting a church alone, as she had done in 1988. But she knew that the spiritual battle would be just as intense as it had been back then, and that her four co-workers would find themselves in the centre of the fracas.

Yet there was a great deal of hope. Since Yufen Wang, Mei Chen and Ling Hu had all accepted Christ in mid-life, they had experienced the unfulfilling ways of the world and understood the futility of life without Christ. Even though all three women had much room to grow, they rested on a firm foundation that would carry them. They all had a profound awareness of their sinful natures and their desperate need for the Lord. They were committed and obedient, and hungered for the Word of God – they even enrolled in various seminary classes to enhance their understanding of it. Like all Christians, they continually struggled to become more Christ-like, but they had already submitted their lives to the authority of their Commander-in-Chief, and were ready for battle. Despite attacks from all sides, they were well aware of the commands and promises of 1 Corinthians 15:57–58:

> But thanks be to God! He gives us the victory through our Lord Jesus Christ. Therefore, my dear brothers, stand firm. Let nothing move you. Always give yourselves fully to the work of the Lord, because you know that your labour in the Lord is not in vain.

Most of Ling Hu's spiritual skirmishes would take place on the battlefield of financial integrity.

'I'm bound by money,' Ling cried to Elisabeth early in her Christian walk, as she discovered that her past involvement with the gods was not the only form of spiritual bondage that she needed to reckon with. 'Money really controls our family. Why do I always feel like I don't have enough? I am the Lord's child and I know he provides for me. Why do I always borrow more?'

Ling also discovered that she was also bound to pride, which had greatly affected her relationship with her ex-husband, who had come from a lower class than hers. When she and Elisabeth began to pray for her release from these different forms of bondage, Ling's head started to spin.

'Stop ... stop ... I can't pray any longer ...' Ling protested, overcome by nausea.

'Ling, call out to the Lord in Jesus' name!' encouraged Elisabeth.

Ling complied, and the dizziness disappeared. They continued to pray.

From then on, Ling's dependence on money, mainly due to habitual gift-giving, began to diminish. But the amount of her debt did not. In October 2003, Ling's debt problems became so grave that she was only days away from dialling the number of an illegal, underground bank.

It was then that the Lord provided an unexpected way out of the situation. Ling eventually became debt-free.

Even though Ling's efforts to serve the shop-workers' fellowship were often under-appreciated and undermined by gossip, she loved serving the Lord diligently. In Panchiao, she trained two small-group leaders and then personally led yet another group. In the new Taipei church, for which she had a deep burden, she followed the same pattern and proactively started several different small groups. In the meantime, her own understanding of the Scriptures matured.

Ling had come a long way. Her identity, which formerly revolved around idol worship and her abilities as a spirit medium, was now in Christ alone. She was wholly dedicated to serving the Lord through the fellowship. Ever since Ling had started living in the shop-workers' dorms, she had prayed regularly with Elisabeth. And after starting their new ministry in Taipei, they continued to pray together three or four times a week, sometimes joined by Yufen. Through their times together, Ling and Elisabeth became close friends who were able to communicate with each other through nothing more than a simple look.

'Elisabeth is my spiritual leader, teacher and mother,' Ling would say after their move to Taipei. 'I can tell her the deepest things in my heart – things I don't feel comfortable sharing with others, including my own mother.'

The relationship was a reciprocal one – whenever Elisabeth urgently needed prayer, she too knew whom she could call.

Mei Chen's partial relapse to her former ways had not lasted long. By the time Elisabeth returned from her six-month stay in Germany, Mei's spiritual health had been restored. In fact, the incident left her with an even deeper understanding of God's grace.

After Mei moved to Taipei, evil spirits attempted to re-enter her life on a few occasions. Each time, the Lord reminded her of past sins that she had not yet confessed, and although the process seemed never-ending, she prayed her last prayer of renunciation in the autumn of 2005. She was finally free.

Like Mary Magdalene, from whom Jesus had driven out seven demons, Mei followed and loved Jesus deeply. As Jesus claimed complete victory over her former enslavement to sin, her life bore extraordinary fruit. When she first came to the dorms, she was an anxious, unstable woman who often spoke and acted recklessly. But two years later, she had become so patient, merciful and mild-mannered that she was more admirable than many long-time Christians.

Mei's body had suffered from different kinds of abuse for so long that she was eventually diagnosed with liver disease and became too ill to work. Even when she depended on government cheques for sustenance, she tithed unfailingly. Fatigue tempted her to give up her role as a co-worker on a number of occasions, but Elisabeth encouraged her to press on. She firmly believed that Mei possessed a unique gift for empathizing with and reaching out to broken people.

In the dorms, Mei easily won the confidence of several

women who had also suffered from domestic violence, and she spent many nights chatting with them over pots of Ali Mountain tea. With servant-like humility, she worked hard to create a warm, emotionally safe environment in her dorm in order to serve the hurting, non-Christian women she lived with.

Even though Mei felt too self-conscious about her lack of education to comfortably lead Bible studies, she was a master of one-on-one evangelism. 'You need to believe in Jesus,' she said often to the elderly men and women she used to serve at work. 'Jesus is the real God, and the other gods aren't.'

'Where's Jesus?' one man responded after her continual efforts to share the gospel with him.

'He lives here.' She pointed to her heart. 'Do you want to accept him too?'

'Yes. I do.'

To Mei, reaching out to the poor, the hurting and the sick came naturally, for she was well acquainted with the feelings of all three.

'I believe that God's Word is very important,' she would say weakly in the more advanced stages of her illness. 'And I really believe that God is doing work in my life. So I want to serve him. Even if the road ahead isn't very clear, I want to just follow him. Being here with Elisabeth has been the most happy time in my life.'

'Yufen Wang, you've changed. You're different now,' said Yufen's friend as they caught up on old times.

'Really?' Yufen smiled. 'How?'

'I can't say, really. I don't know how to describe it. I just know that you're different.'

Though her friend could not pinpoint the change, Yufen could. With Jesus in her life, she had been able to conquer her formerly irrepressible temper and her abrasive, prideful way of dealing with people. She had even apologized repeatedly to her children for her past mistakes with them – a very un-Taiwanese act.

'I was really stupid,' she said to them. 'I'm sorry for hurting you so much. I hope we can start over.'

Although Yufen had entered into leadership with much reluctance, she took her new responsibilities very seriously. In addition to caring for her small-group members, Yufen led several women to Christ. One of these women was Qin, a shop-worker with a choleric personality that even frightened Yufen on occasion.

Not long after Qin had moved into one of the new shop-workers' dorms in Taipei, she stormed home at around 1:30 a.m. Her room-mate woke to the sound of shattering glass, objects being hurled around the living-room, appliances being smashed to the ground. Shocked and shaking, the room-mate locked her bedroom door.

As soon as Yufen heard about what had happened, she rushed to the dorm. Both she and Elisabeth prayed fervently and patiently over Qin until about five in the morning, when Qin finally managed to calm down.

'Poor girl. She's just like I used to be ...' Yufen thought as she swept pieces of broken glass off the floor.

'I thank the Lord for his forgiveness and for making me into a new person,' Yufen would eventually say. 'Now I understand how the hopelessness of people is the beginning of God.'

October 2004

The dark-skinned man hunched over as water was sprinkled lightly onto his head. The crowd clapped and cheered. Among them, three middle-aged Taiwanese women and a white-haired German felt particularly moved. This was, after all, the first baptism celebration of the Taipei

Shop-workers' Centre, which they had founded only a few months before.

After the baptism, one of the women went up to the man and presented him with a bouquet of flowers. As she gazed at him admiringly, she was grateful for the months that had passed since he had given up alcohol over-night – one of the many blessings God had brought into her life in recent years. She knew that it was only by God's miraculous grace that she and her husband had become Christians. They had both been prideful and obstinate, yet the Lord had called them out of darkness when they had needed him the most.

A camera was pointed at the couple, and the woman smiled dazzlingly, donning a God-given expression that had not passed across her face for many years. In that moment she looked like a young woman again, happy and in love.

Notes
1. www.english.taipei.gov.tw/dbas/index.jsp?categid=1334 (Taipei City Government, 2004); www.english.tpc.gov.tw/web66/_file/2173/cache/web/SELFPAGE/22016/null37206null_en.html (Taipei County Government, 2006).

Epilogue

How, then, can they call on the one they have not
believed in? And how can they believe in the one of
whom they have not heard? And how can they hear
without someone preaching to them? And how can
they preach unless they are sent? As it is written, 'How
beautiful are the feet of those who bring good news!'

Romans 10:14–15

The first time I wept for Taiwan was on my
way home from a church service in Kaohsiung, a city in the
southern part of the country. The speaker had just
preached on Deuteronomy 18:10–12:

Let no one be found among you who sacrifices his son
or daughter in the fire, who practises divination or sor-
cery, interprets omens, engages in witchcraft, or casts
spells, or who is a medium or spiritist or who consults
the dead. Anyone who does these things is detestable to
the LORD, and because of these detestable practices the
LORD your God will drive out those nations before you.

Following his sermon, the speaker issued an invitation: 'If
any of you have participated in these kinds of practices and
are willing to confess your sins, please come forward,' he
said. To my horror, almost every single Taiwanese person
in that room filed towards the altar.

With this image still fixed in my mind, I turned the corner into my neighbourhood. Suddenly, the Lord opened my eyes to something I hadn't seen before. I noticed that looming behind the screen doors of almost all my neighbours were ancestor shelves, topped by red lamps that made the whole street glow like the West does at Christmas-time. I drove around and around, hoping to find a sign – any sign – of a Christian presence in the neighbourhood. But I found none.

So I wept.

According to Taiwan's Ministry of the Interior, about 13.1 million Taiwanese profess to be either Taoist or Buddhist. But because idol-worshipping traditions derived from these two religions have become such an integral part of Taiwanese culture, it is more accurate to say that around 70 per cent of Taiwanese people worship idols.[1]

As Julian F. Pas of the University of Saskatchewan writes in the Journal of Chinese Religions: 'In contrast with China, where some of the surviving great temples of past dynasties have become museums and tourist attractions, Taiwan temples, buzzing with activity, are lively centres of worship and social intercourse.'[2] Temples are so central in Taiwanese society that it is common to see toddlers there, awkwardly grasping incense sticks with their tiny hands as they are taught how to worship. And even if a child isn't taken to temples often, traditional religion is likely to inundate his or her life in other ways – through school, religious television channels, pop culture and, of course, the primacy of the household ancestor shelf.

Even though new foreign missionary involvement in Taiwan has slowed to a trickle in the past decade, this is in no way an indication of a diminishing spiritual need. In fact, Taiwan has been dubbed as 'the only Han Chinese population in the world where the spiritual breakthrough has yet to come.'[3] According to official government statistics,

3.9 per cent of the 22.9 million people on this island are Christian. But various mission organizations have estimated that among Taiwan's working class, which comprises 61.7 per cent of the country's population, less than 0.5 per cent are Christian.

Working-class Taiwanese, like the three women in this book, are not necessarily poor, though they are typically less educated; so in a society where education is paramount, they are made to feel like 'nothing'. All too often, working-class men, like the husbands in this book, respond to this sense of inferiority by giving up on themselves, their work and their families. This often has disastrous consequences, especially since studies have shown that the Taiwanese tend to view aggressiveness and thoughtlessness as positive traits in men.[4] The kinds of family problems detailed in this book are distressingly typical amongst Taiwan's working class.

Another defining characteristic of working-class Taiwanese is their affinity for tradition. Traditional religions are particularly appealing to them because they offer practical ways to 'resolve' the multitude of day-to-day problems that would otherwise be beyond their control.

Working-class Taiwanese, in their lack of social status, bear an uncanny resemblance to the kinds of people Jesus had special compassion for when he was on this earth. But instead of reaching out to them, the church in Taiwan has largely avoided them.

'Our society does not have compassion for the working class, and our churches are the same ... Some white-collar people in Taiwan hear the gospel five times when working-class people don't even hear it once. It's embarrassing,' says Lincy Tu, a well-known local evangelist who has planted five working-class churches in the past ten years. 'We need to repent and reach the working class if we want to see revival in Taiwan. We need people who will invest a lot of time into this kind of work, and we need churches to send workers.'

Indeed, even though working-class Taiwanese are considered an unreached people group,[5] few missionaries and pastors are willing to focus their evangelistic efforts on them. Recently, Lincy Tu personally invited about 100 pastors to a meeting about how to effectively reach the working class. Only one pastor attended.

'We don't want to do this kind of ministry because all of our church members are well educated,' confessed one pastor who rejected Lincy's invitation. About a week later, he called her again.

'I've found that our church does have one working-class member,' he said. 'Please help us introduce her to another church.'

Even though the rejection is not always so blatant, the very ways in which most Taiwanese churches present Christianity tend to seem foreign and unwelcoming to most working-class people: Western, academic styles of teaching and preaching, text-heavy church bulletins, English Bible studies, long, abstract prayers, and other highbrow church customs make it difficult for most working-class Taiwanese people to draw a connection between Jesus and their trouble-filled lives.

'The message that Taiwanese working-class people often get from the church is, "You have to be more highly educated if you want to know who Jesus is. You have to stop being the way you are, because you just don't fit in,"' says OMF missionary Seann Gibson. 'In reality these people are open to the gospel if it's presented to them in a way that they can understand. But if church services are conducted like school – the one thing they failed at – it won't work.'

Now that OMF Taiwan has sharpened its evangelistic focus on planting churches among the unreached working class, it is actively seeking new missionaries with fresh perspectives and humble, non-judgmental attitudes towards ministry and an eagerness to learn.

'Taiwan really needs new missionaries! We especially need men who can reach out to other men,' A-fang Tan reminded me on a number of occasions. 'It's really foreign missionaries who can reach out to working-class Taiwanese.'

Ministering to Taiwanese working-class people is often challenging and frustrating – this I have learned first hand, even in the process of writing this book. But the Lord can change and is changing the hearts of working-class Taiwanese, for nothing is impossible with God (Luke 1:37). As missionaries have experienced here, even amidst the most formidable difficulties, the Lord is always faithful to his promise: 'And surely I am with you always, to the very end of the age' (Matthew 28:20).

Indeed, once I had been part of the Taipei Shop-workers' Centre long enough to earn the trust of its members, they showered me with love. The more I got to know Ling, Yufen and Mei, the more I realized that we were not as different as we had once seemed. We all shared the experience of dreams deferred. We all shared continuing struggles with sin. And we all shared an ultimate Love that drew us out of comfort zones and onto the path of obedience.

* * *

The sloping silhouette of an all-too-familiar mountain stands forebodingly in the distance as Mei Chen joins her family in a tribal song. It's the birthday of Mei's father, and virtually the whole mountain village has gathered together to celebrate.

Nestled in the acrid smoke of burning wood and cigarettes, the men joke coarsely and swig beers. One of the men leans towards Mei's two daughters.

'How beautiful you girls are!' he exclaims in jest. Little Hui's face tenses, as if the remark has triggered a deeply buried memory.

Uninterested in the alcohol that is being passed around and speedily consumed, Mei suggests that we take a hike. Well-carved trails now wind through thick forests that Mei used to explore barefoot.

Though she is not yet fifty, Mei's worn body takes each step slowly, deliberately. Meanwhile, her oldest daughter Ting-ting peppers her with questions.

'What do the shamans do? Can you still use the power of the evil spirits?' And then to me: 'Are there shamans in America?'

Considering all that she was forced to endure before the age of seven, Ting-ting is a spirited child who displays remarkable maturity for her age. Thanks to her mother's influence, her dream is to enter full-time ministry someday. Though still in elementary school, she's already managed to help lead one of her mother's friends to Christ.

A bit short of breath, Mei sits down to rest. Glancing at a nearby precipice, she is reminded of something and scoots away from the edge.

'This drop is nothing compared to that one from before,' she says.

We continue walking, and we pass a rock formation that is said to house a ghost who afflicts people with illness when it's not properly worshipped. Mei starts to get a headache.

'Let's pray,' she suggests, fully confident in the Lord's ability to deliver. After all, her whole life encapsulates the beauty of what happens when, after the ugliest twists and turns, God makes a dead woman walk.

'You are the God most worthy to be praised!' Mei prays, her voice soaring confidently above the sound of the rushing stream. 'You've conquered my past, you've conquered

432   *Dead Women Walking*

the spirits, and you've conquered Satan! Lord, we ask you to let your glory fall on this place ... for this is YOUR land.'

> The harvest is plentiful but the workers are few. Ask the Lord of the harvest, therefore, to send out workers into his harvest field.   Matthew 9:37–38

Notes

1. David Eastwood, *Buddhism in Taiwan*.
2. Julian F. Pas, 'Religious Life in Present Day Taiwan; A Field Observations Report: 1994–1995' in *Journal of Chinese Religions* (136).
3. *Operation World*, 2001.
4. The stereotype that men possess courage and energy, logic and independence, aggressiveness and thoughtlessness. When John Williams and Deborah Best examined sex stereotypes in 25 countries, they found that the male stereotype was endorsed by 90 per cent of the Taiwanese sample – the highest level of endorsement in any of the societies. Michael Harris Bond, *Beyond the Chinese Face: Insights from Psychology*, Oxford: Oxford University Press, 1991, p. 46.
5. Definition of UPG according to The Joshua Project, www.joshuaproject.net/definitions.php